'Moore's writing is lively an[...]
ward, his case studies unpred[...]
interest in architecture will fi[...]

'A subtle, often eccentric but always entertaining guide to themes that have been consistent through the ages – sex, power, finance, eternity, hope . . . A fascinating work of love, intellectual curiosity and endurance'   **Bryan Appleyard,** *Literary Review*

'Thoughtful and elegantly written, *Why We Build* will appeal to anyone with an interest in architecture . . . It benefits from a clear style and years of architectural criticism . . . the argument is forceful, but not prescriptive, the satisfying result of prolonged and sensitive observation of both buildings and human nature.'   *Spectator*

'A paean to the way we inhabit, which explains why good architecture changes constantly'   *Financial Times*

'Moore has a lot to offer those who like verbal flexibility and thought-provoking aphorisms. There is also a sense of mischief . . . if famous architects were a coconut shy, Moore would go home with the giant teddy . . . Elegant and witty, with a sometimes eighteenth-century sensuality, this is a hard-hitting book with great panache.'   *Sunday Telegraph*

'Intelligent and cultured . . . packed with passionately held ideas about the epiphanies, farces and humanity in architecture'   *Independent*

'Moore writes with economy, clarity and wit'   **Will Wiles,**
Building Design

Why We Build

Rowan Moore is the architecture critic for the *Observer* and previously for the *Evening Standard*. He is also a trained architect, and between 2002 and 2008 was the Director of the Architecture Foundation.

Rowan Moore

Why We Build

PICADOR

First published 2012 by Picador

First published in paperback 2013 by Picador
an imprint of Pan Macmillan, a division of Macmillan Publishers Limited
Pan Macmillan, 20 New Wharf Road, London N1 9RR
Basingstoke and Oxford
Associated companies throughout the world
www.panmacmillan.com

ISBN 978-0-330-53582-3

9 8 7 6 5 4 3 2 1

A CIP catalogue record for this book is available from the British Library.

Printed and bound by CPI Group (UK) Ltd, Croydon, CR0 4YY

Visit **www.picador.com** to read more about all our books
and to buy them. You will also find features, author interviews and
news of any author events, and you can sign up for e-newsletters
so that you're always first to hear about our new releases.

To L, H and S

Contents

1: *Desire shapes space,*
and space shapes desires

A helicopter flew through the desert air, evoking, as such machines do, attack: marines, Desert Storm, Francis Ford Coppola, 'The Ride of the Valkyries', the smell of napalm in the morning. Here it had a more pacific purpose. Hung from its muttering blades was a capsule of journalists, imported to admire the works of His Highness Sheikh Mohammed bin Rashid al-Maktoum.

Below were the Sheikh's achievements. There was the famous Palm Jumeirah island, where Dutch engineers had been imported to create 110 kilometres of new beach, carrying eight thousand valuable homes and over thirty hotels. Using skills earned in their country's centuries-long resistance to the sea, the Sheikh had invited them to go on the offensive, carving out of the ancestral adversary a giant inhabitable logo of trunk and fronds that would become world-famous before it was built. There were scatterings and bunchings of towers. There was the biggest shopping mall in the Middle East, and a newer one about to surpass it. There was the Burj Dubai, the tallest structure in the world and still rising, slipping on its sheath of stainless steel like a snake reversing into its skin. The flying journalists were being taken to see the site of the Harbour Tower, which would be yet bigger than the Burj Dubai, as was dutifully reported in Western newspapers in the following days.

What couldn't be seen from the helicopter was the crisis in the drains. Dubai's buildings emptied their sewage into septic tanks, whence they were taken to the Al-Aweer sewage works, on the road out towards the desert and Oman. The sewage works had not kept pace with the city's growth, and a long line of tankers, some painted with flowers by their Indian drivers, stood for hours in the heavy heat as they waited their turn to offload. (And I, though unable to take up the invitation I was offered on the helicopter ride, did get to see this turgid caravan.)

Some drivers, tired of waiting, had taken to pouring their cargo at night into the rainwater drainage system, which discharged straight into the sea. The owner of a yacht club, finding that his business was affected by the sight and smell of brown stuff on the bright white boats, took photographs of the nocturnal dumpings and gave them to the press. The authorities responded, tackling the symptoms but not the cause, by introducing severe penalties for miscreant drivers.

Both helicopter ride and sewage crisis occurred in October 2008, and the combination of celestial fantasy and chthonic reality revealed a city on a cusp. Before that month journalists and trendy architects had been lining up to feed on the flow of amazing-but-true tales of construction that the Emirate released at a steady rate, interrupted only by mutterings from the liberal press about the conditions of migrant workers. Afterwards equally juicy but less welcome headlines were generated: abandoned building projects; Donald Trump pulling out; and out-of-work expats leaving their Ferraris in the airport car park, keys in the ignition, fleeing Dubai for ever because they could not keep up the payments on the loan. Nakheel, developers of the Palm and the proposed Harbour Tower, laid off hundreds of staff.

In November a party was held to celebrate the opening of the Atlantis Hotel, at the tip of the Palm, a $1.5 billion work of tree-trunk columns and writhing chandeliers, a Blofeltian phantasmagoria of giant aquaria and rooms with views of sharks, which suffered the rare ignominy of being accused of bad taste by the British tabloid the *Sun*. The party was an epic of extravagance: Kylie was hired to sing for a large fee, other celebrities were flown in, and a firework display was mounted seven times greater than that put on for the Beijing Olympics. The event cost £13 million, or £6,500 for each of its two thousand guests. As Dubai's stock exchange had by then fallen by 70 per cent from its peak, it made too perfect an image of hubris for reporters to miss, and they did not. This was an end-of-empire party, the last excess before the fall, Romans indulging themselves with the barbarians at the gates. Soon further rumours swirled, that the Palm, and with it the Atlantis hotel resort, were, like the ancient city of the same name, sinking. All the disbelief suspended in the face of Dubai's dazzling growth (who and what are these buildings for?) returned.

Dubai lives off abstract fluctuations of money, which it strove to make concrete with construction. Here building became a fable, a source of identity, an end in itself.

The emirate's modern growth was driven by the fact that it has less oil than its neighbours, and so must base its future economy on other business, including financial services and tourism. It set out to be an Arab Singapore, a trading city-state that lives off its wits, and off an advantageous position on routes between larger countries. Its assets were its relative stability and peacefulness, its ability to position itself between the Islamic and the Western worlds, and a willingness to respond to the desires of business. It also has winter sunshine at a distance and in a time zone that are reasonably convenient for northern European tourists. Combined with security from mugging and dangerous diseases, and high-quality tax-free shopping, it could make itself a popular destination for holidays.

These assets were fragile and not unique. Other cities could do something similar. And so Dubai had to make the intangible tangible. It had to create a brand, an image of itself to convince others of its pre-eminence. The brand would be created through construction, which would be pleasing to Sheikh Mohammed: like other rulers, from Rameses II to President Nursultan Nazarbayev of Kazakhstan, he loved building things.

Mohammed was also a ruler who, as the third of four brothers, had to secure his position. Less than a century ago, in this region, multiple fratricide was a common solution to the problems arising when rulers left many sons, by more than one wife. In more civilized times, Mohammed secured his position by force of character. He became the Crown Prince and effective leader of Dubai in 1995, and the official ruler in 2006, following the death of his oldest brother, whose son had also died. He built his authority in several ways. As a graduate of the Mons Officer Cadet School in Aldershot, and as the United Arab Emirates' Defence Minister since the age of twenty-eight, he had a military reputation. When, in the 1970s, Dubai was a popular stop-off for hijacked airliners, he negotiated with hostage-takers, delaying them, defusing their threats, and getting them to fly on either to Libya, where they were set free, or Mogadishu, where they were gunned down by German commandos.

He was, with his brothers, an enthusiastic owner and breeder of racehorses, but outshone them all to become the most successful in the world. He distinguished himself as a rider, in endurance races over 120 kilometres. He was, and is, a poet in the Arab dialect of Nabati. According to his personal website, he is 'widely acknowledged as one of the finest exponents of Nabati verse . . . poetry has allowed Sheikh Mohammed to express the creative, sensitive side of his nature, which he has little chance to display in the political arena.' He has written:

'Triumphs whoever stands firm
And for his right fights.'

Also, in 'The Path of Lovers', after talking of 'eyes like the eyes
of the kohled lanner falcon',

'Oh lanner, ever assailing –
Your prey, if strikes, always slain'

He first published under pseudonyms, 'as he wanted to be sure
that people genuinely thought his poetry was good'. Now his
poems are often publicly recited, including at the richest horse race
in the world, the Dubai World Cup.

And alongside his military, equestrian and poetic prowess, he
was a businessman and a builder. The wave-shaped six-hundred-
room Jumeirah Hotel, which opened in 1997, was his development,
followed by the sail-shaped Burj Al Arab in 1999. The Maktoums'
sibling rivalry had been played out with jockeys' silks, maroon, blue,
and yellow, on the green turf of Newmarket and Epsom; now it
drove developments of mounting spectacle. The banner of this new
contest was the developer's tricolour, the blue sky, white building,
and green landscaping of sales images. After Mohammed won, he
found other rivals with whom to compete: other cities, emirates,
and nations.

So Dubai began to offer tales of building that were immediate,
well known, and accessible. Stories of the East were once arduously
quarried by explorers of the Arabian peninsula, like Richard Burton,
Freya Stark, Gertrude Bell, and Wilfred Thesiger; they learned
Arabic, adopted local customs and dress, endured hardship and
danger, and slowly won the trust of tribesmen. Modern Dubai
offered its travellers' tales readymade and available in PDF and on
YouTube. The seven-star hotel, the Palm, a bigger Palm, a yet bigger
Palm, an archipelago like the map of the world, a snowy ski slope in

the desert, Atlantis, the tallest building in the world, the even taller tower, the yet taller tower of unknown height: all near-instantly placed 'Dubai in the consciousness of the world', to quote a promotional video. Actually completing the projects was secondary, and the billions who heard of these wonders mostly wouldn't have known which were finished. The ever-changing maps of Dubai showed without distinction places hoped-for, under construction, and completed.

There was a synergy of fable, architecture, and press release. Each project was what it said it was, and looked like what it was. The Palm was a palm was a palm. Each passed the elevator test: you could explain what they were to some miraculously ignorant Rip Van Winkle between the seventy-eighth and eighty-fifth floors of an express ride. To quote the video again, Dubai was 'a destination that captures the imagination and doesn't let go'.

Dubai's manufacture of image first became famous with the completion of the Burj Al Arab, the white sail-shaped tallest hotel in the world, built on what had been sea, with its seven-star rating and restaurant reached by simulated submarine journey, on whose helipad they got Agassi and Federer to play tennis. The Burj was effective, a Statue of Liberty aimed at a more exclusive catchment than the latter's huddled masses, which like the statue featured on local licence plates and was honoured by thousands of reproductions in the city's gift shops.

Next came the Palm Jumeirah, the artificial island visible from space. The Burj Al Arab had been a maximal version of something already familiar, the show-off luxury hotel. As a device of seafront iconicity the sail motif was well worn, from the Sydney Opera House onwards, and the zeitgeist that engendered the Burj also threw up the near-contemporary but somehow less thrilling Spinnaker Tower in Portsmouth. The Palm, however, was something genuinely new, an artificial island that combined in one brilliantly simple

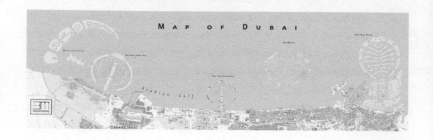

concept mighty engineering, audacious property speculation, and high graphic impact.

The Palm started construction in 2001 and was largely completed by 2008. A company, Nakheel (meaning 'Palm'), was set up to create it (slogan: 'Where Vision Inspires Humanity'). Where the Burj Al Arab had to be completed to attract attention, the Palm made itself and Dubai famous before it was built, aided by the magic of computer-generated images. As far as the rest of the world was concerned it was as if it was already there, although there was also a certain will-they-or-won't-they frisson that accompanied its unveiling.

The Palm had logic. It grew from the realization that Dubai's 70 kilometres of beach, on which development was encroaching, were insufficient for the city's ambitions as a tourist destination. Consultants were asked to devise ways of making more coastline, and came up with a circular island attached to the land by a jetty, like a lollipop. Then it was realized that still more could be made by cutting inlets into the circle. Sheikh Mohammed is credited with the idea of turning the sliced-up shape into a palm tree.

This stroke created another 110 kilometres of beach. Here, according to Nakheel, all the homes sold out within forty-eight hours of going on the market, and their price of $0.5 million went up to $8 million. The Palm inspired imitations: a 'Pearl Island' is under construction in Qatar, and there were suggestions of a phoenix-shaped archipelago off Russia's Baltic coast and a Cedar Island in Lebanon, and a rumoured maple leaf off Toronto. The figurative false island entered the world's inventory of urbanistic devices.

The essential ingredients of the Palm were audacity, graphic impact, and actual achievement. Also the nimbleness of its image combined with the might of its engineering – the fact that so much heft went into this seeming whimsy. Also that it is against nature, a quality it shares with the ski slope's idea of creating a man-made snowscape in a desert country. The very outrageousness is part of the power, and the appeal. Finally, there is the conceptual brilliance of taking sand and seawater, two valueless things of which Dubai has all too much, and making them into valuable beach. It realized a formula: sand + seawater x engineering x marketing = value.

After the Palm Jumeirah came the World, the not-yet-complete archipelago whose islands were to be sold to invited individuals at prices from four to fourteen million dollars. Also the bigger Palm Jebel Ali, where the land reclamation was completed, and the incomplete Palm Deira, which had a projected population of one million. Having taken the land into water, it was planned to take water onto land, with the 75 kilometre Arabian Canal. Nakheel started planning Waterfront, a twenty-year project to create 'the most sustainable city in the world', bigger than Manhattan, Beirut, or Hong Kong island.

Palm, World, and Burj all created ready-made headlines that advertised Dubai's ambition. They engendered glamour, which translated into higher values, which helped pay for these extravagant constructions. Alongside the fabled projects were others, promoted by advertisements that started at the airport and continued in newspapers and magazines, and on billboards along the city's multi-lane main artery, Sheikh Zayed Road. 'Index. The most iconic residential space.' 'Love story. Al Barari residences for life.' 'Stallion Properties. Born to lead. Born to excel.' 'Salvatore Ferragamo Penthouses. Bespoke penthouses for the distinguished few.' 'Kensington Krystal. The benchmark of corporate luxury.' 'Limitless. We're weaving humanity into the urban fabric.' Images of desirability, of speedboats and women, spread many storeys high across buildings.

These adverts dominated, more prominent than Calvin Klein and Coca Cola. They created a narrative of construction, supported by omnipresent cranes, dust clouds, construction vehicles, hoardings, and platoons of blue-clad immigrant building workers. Part of the point, part of the ohmigod-I-don't-believe-it power of Dubai, was that impossible things really, truly were built. It was like reality TV at an urban scale. Rising over it all as a guarantor of intent was the slender spiral of the Burj Dubai.

Part of Dubai's story was its outrageousness, and its power to subdue obstacles. It positively sought opportunities to demonstrate this power: land on water, water on land, snow in the desert, but also victories over history, decorum, propriety, and good taste. Thus the Burj Dubai, essentially a work of American corporate modernism, would sit next to the 'Old Town', a brand-new approximation of an historic Arab city that had never actually existed in Dubai, with a pasted-on look of adobe construction. Once, in the West, such a juxtaposition would have been seen as improper, or funny, or kitsch. Here developers did it because they could.

The array of towers along Sheikh Zayed Road plundered history, culture, and nature. There is one that mimics the eighteenth-century French architect Ledoux, as filtered through 1980s postmodernism. Another is a thousand-foot Venetian campanile. There are twin ersatz Chrysler Buildings, a tower so good they built it twice. There is a giant pearl and a tower allegedly inspired by a tulip. The eye-aching potential of mirror glass, in green, pink, gold, and peacock blue, was fully exploited, and blobs and balconies and bits of stuff were plastered onto buildings without regard to use; there are many thousand unpopulated balconies in Dubai. Copies of traditional wind-catching towers, originally invented in Iran as a cooling device, were glued to air-conditioned office blocks and housing developments. Shorn of their original purpose, they encapsulate Dubai's triumph of look.

Architectural forms in Dubai performed the same functions as adjectives in press releases and adverts. Futuristic, traditional, sculptural, flower-shaped, Venetian, Chrysler-shaped were like luxury,

prestigious, legendary, ultimate, dream, waterfront. They filled a space. Their meaning was unimportant, beyond being upbeat and borrowing authority from somewhere. They brought a sense of something to properties which would otherwise fear being nothing.

Palm, World, and Burj pushed emotional buzzers, more or less randomly, as did sea, beach, and sun. The sea is important to Dubai because it is expected of a tourist destination, and because it is useful as a pretext for sail-shaped hotels and artificial islands. But the placid, near-tideless waters of the Gulf and the narrow feature-less beaches are not essential to the experience of the city, not even for tourists, as hotel swimming pools are usually more enticing, even when there are not sewage spills. The sea in Dubai is experi-enced more as a sign of itself than directly and physically.

Dubai cast its mythology before it, creating a version of its future self which it hoped would become real. This was a possibly necessary condition of a city that had grown fast. It had to imagine itself and sell itself before it could exist. 'The remarkable is becom-ing the new reality', went the sales pitch. Buildings represented the purpose they might contain – if offices and homes and hotels were being built, it was easy to believe that there were the businesses and the people to occupy them.

The philosophy, expressed by the Sheikh himself, was to build first and plan later. If development caused traffic jams or a sewage crisis, new roads and treatment plants could be built. If Dubai was criticized for its environmental incontinence, for its subservience to the car, or for its treatment of migrant workers, then it could create developments with high degrees of sustain-ability, pedestrian-friendly paths, and model housing for workers. Humanity and sustainability became new buzzwords, to be inserted in sales spiels alongside ultimate and waterfront.

And then it stopped. As the writer Mike Davis prophesied in 2007, 'the end could be nigh and very messy'. It dawned on both players and observers that there was more built and being built in Dubai than would be needed in the foreseeable future, and that property companies were financing new construction with teetering stacks of loans predicated on delusional valuations of their portfolios.

For a while, in 2008, Dubai's PR people gave a standard answer when asked whether the latest parade of skyscrapers would become reality. The wealth of His Highness, as they always call Sheikh Mohammed, was so vast that he could underwrite everything. But it emerged that the Sheikh was seeking rescue from his cousin Sheikh Khalifa bin Zayed Al Nahyan, ruler of the more oil-rich, more cautious emirate of Abu Dhabi. Family treasures, like Dubai's port business, would be put in hock. Abu Dhabi, long irritated by its neighbour's little-brother bumptiousness, would call the shots. When the Burj Dubai finally opened, early in 2010, it was renamed Burj Khalifa, in honour of the Abu Dhabian emir.

As the intoxication of endless construction subsided, suppressed doubts came to the fore. The supremacy of image had, it turned out, a cost. The Palm, so impressive when seen on Google Earth, is more ordinary at ground level, where what you see are high walls and close-packed developments that block views of the water. Owners of homes on the fronds found that they faced not so much the sea, as a suburban cul-de-sac penetrated by a tongue of brine.

It became pertinent to ask: what, actually, is so great about Dubai? Apart from its faulty infrastructure and, for some months of the year, its atrocious heat, there was also the fact that the feverish excitement of its grand projects was not matched by everyday experience. The basic elements of Dubai are those of the modern American city – mall, tower, highway, theme park, suburb – and many of its spaces are typical of such building types, for example hotel and office foyers and mall interiors, or the insides of cars. As in America, they are air-conditioned, controlled, secure, generic, clean, soothing, ideally frictionless. They carry little sense of the drama or daring of Dubai's making. Much of Dubai's fabric is made of bland, highly managed spaces connected by a tissue of semi-chaotic infrastructure. Many ex-pat business people spend their weekends tearing up desert dunes in 4x4s, in an attempt to relieve the tedium of this allegedly exhilarating city.

It would be rash to write off Dubai and declare Sheikh Mohammed's great urban adventure finished. Cities have always proceeded with hiccups and belches, and rises and falls. Much of the celebrated skyline of New York was generated by the financial frenzy of the 1920s, which was not unlike Dubai's more recent boom, and the city survived the Wall Street crash. Modern Chinese cities, after pausing during the Asian crisis of the late '90s, resumed their rapid growth. And, in Dubai, pieces of the infrastructure that were so conspicuous by their absence have started appearing, such as the first two lines of its metro system.

But it is clear that construction in Dubai's boom lost touch with what might be called sense. Observers of Dubai were intoxicated by the speed of its construction and the outrageousness of its propositions. The sheer fact of building gave the city an air of authority and purpose that obscured the possibility that this very construction might be a problem.

Buildings, such solid-seeming things, made a front for illusion, speculation, pyramid-selling of the future. This financial adventure could only have happened because of the power of construction to excite and convince, to represent, to stand for the things it contains. Dubai establishes the power of illusion in architecture, the paradoxical intimacy between fantasy and dream, and the weight, heft, and calculation, the fact and substance of building.

In lurid colours, in 3-D, wide-screen, computer-animated form,

Dubai makes a simple point: architecture is not a thing of pure reason or function, but is shaped by human emotions and desires, and shapes them. It was generated by the ambitions of the Sheikh – for power, for glory, for pre-eminence – and drew in the desires of others – for money, glamour, or excitement. As its forms emerged, they inspired further emotional effects, such as awe, shock, emulation, and fantasy, which heightened the urge to build more.

Architecture starts with desire on the part of its makers, whether for security, or grandeur, or shelter, or rootedness. Built, it influences the emotions of those who experience and use it, whose desires continue to shape and change it. Desire and emotion are overlapping concepts, but if 'desire' is active, directed towards real and imagined ends, and if 'emotion' implies greater passivity, describing the ways in which we are moved, architecture is engaged with both. Buildings are intermediaries in the reciprocation between the hopes and intentions of people, in the present and the past. They are the mineral interval between the thoughts and actions that make them and the thoughts and actions that inhabit them.

Most people know that buildings are not purely functional, that there is an intangible something about them that has to do with emotion. Most towns or cities have towers or monuments of no special purpose, or public buildings and private houses whose volumes are larger than strictly necessary, and structures with daring cantilevers or spans that are not perfectly efficient. These cities have ornament and sculpture, also buildings whose construction drove their owners to ruin, or which never served their intended purpose, or which outlived their use but are preserved. A home might contain pictures, mementoes, vases, antiques, light shades not chosen for their function alone. It might be a centuries-old house with obsolete standards of thermal insulation, draught exclusion, and damp control, for which nonetheless its owner pays a premium. If Dubai seems preposterous, it is only an extreme version of the decisions people make in extending, building, remaking, or furnishing their own homes, which are rarely guided by pure function. If it attracts attention, it is because it presents to us urges that are familiar, but in a way that seems uncontrolled.

But to say that there is emotion in architecture is a bare beginning. What forms does it take, and by what weird alchemy do cold materials absorb and emit feeling? What transformations happen? Whose feelings matter more: the clients', the architects', the builders', or the users', those of a commissioning government or corporation, or of casual passers-by? What complexities, indirections, and unintended consequences arise, and what epiphanies and farce?

Building projects are usually justified with reference to measurables of finance and use. When we acknowledge the intangible it is often with vague words, such as 'inspiring', or perhaps 'beautiful', an honourable word which nonetheless leaves much unsaid, such as beautiful to whom, and in what way? We might resort to personal taste, or to some idea of what is good or bad derived from aesthetic standards whose origins and reasons we probably don't know.

In commercial and public building the intangible is usually confined to adjectives like 'iconic', or 'spectacular', which parcel it with blandness and discourage further exploration. Such words also convert this troubling, unruly, hard-to-name aspect of buildings into something that aids marketing – since 'icons' can help sell a place or a business – into, that is, another form of use.

Yet if emotion in building is intangible, it is also specific. Particular desires and feelings drive the making of architecture, and the experience of it, and are played out in particular ways. Hope, sex, the wish for power or money, the idea of home, the sense of mortality: these are definite, not vague, with distinct manifestations in architecture.

This book explores the ways in which these concerns of the living interact with the dead stuff of buildings. It will challenge easy assumptions about architecture: in particular that, once the builders move out, it is fixed and complete. It turns out that buildings are unstable: if their fabric is not being adjusted (and it usually is) they are prone to tricks of perception and inversions of value. This instability might feel disturbing, but it is also part of the fascination of architecture.

If buildings were 1:1 translations of human urges, my study would be short and boring: if, for example, they were monosyllables made physical, where a pitched roof = home, something soaring = hope, big = power, or phallic = sex. Where things get interesting is when desire and built space change each other, when animate and inanimate interplay. Paradoxes arise, and things that seemed certain seem less so. Buildings are powerful but also awkward means of dealing with something as mobile as emotion, and usually they create an opposite or at least different effect to the one they set out to achieve.

To look at emotion and desire in architecture is not to discount the simple fact that most buildings have a practical purpose. But that practical purpose is rarely pursued with perfect detachment, or indifferent calculation. To build and to inhabit are not small actions, and it is hard to undertake them with coolness. Rather the play of function, of decisions on budget, durability, comfort, flexibility, and use, is one of the expressive properties of architecture.

Definitions are required. 'Architecture' is seen not just as the design of buildings, more as the making of spaces: it includes the design of landscape, interiors, and stage sets. A building is seen less as an end in itself, more as an instrument for making spaces, together with whatever else is around, both inside and outside. 'Architecture' can also include fictional and cinematic places, which sometimes reveal as much, and differently, as those you can touch.

'To build' is used in its usual way, as the action of contractors and workers, and of clients, architects, and other consultants, leading to the making of a physical construction. But the verb will also be used metaphorically, to describe the ways in which the people who use and experience buildings – that is, almost all of us – inhabit and shape, physically and in the imagination, the spaces we find.

This book is not a manual. It will not tell you how to decorate your home, or architecture students how to set about their work. Still less will it tell urban planners how to make wise decisions. Should it have an influence, I dread an outbreak of 'emotional' architecture, with sales guff from developers talking of 'feelings'. Catastrophes will be described, and successes, and works somewhere between; also projects that started well and finished sadly, and vice versa. But the idea is not to make a score-sheet of good and bad, rather to see the many ways in which human impulses are played out in building. This book tries not to instruct, prescribe, or moralize. Its aim is to show, examine, and reveal.

I like to imagine, however, that this book could have some useful effect. Failures of architecture and development often occur because emotional choices come disguised as practical ones. If I can make it a little easier to discern what is going on in such situations, one or two disasters might, conceivably, be mitigated.

A leading character will be Lina Bo Bardi, an Italian-born Brazilian who for long was the most underrated architect of the twentieth century. She is here because, like the promoters of Dubai developments, she spoke of desire. For her, however, the word did not mean billboards of speedboats, or sail-shaped hotels. She liked bold gestures, but she also had an understanding that is hard to find in Dubai: she knew that buildings act not alone, but reciprocally with the people and things around them, that they have to be open to chance, time, and life. She knew when to be dramatic and when to hold back, creating a stage for others.

In describing Dubai, one runs with the idea that desire in architecture equates with craziness in the external shapes of buildings: they might be insanely large or bizarre, and consecrated as 'iconic'. So, up to a point, it does. There is a buzz to be had from contemplating the cumulative incongruity of a whole city. You might, as a resident or a visitor, share in this excitement, or feel pride. If you are an architect (ever, as architects tend to be, in fear of your own insignificance), you might get a thrill that your profession could assist in such feats.

But the question is, whose desires are we witnessing? Whatever thrill might be had from large and unusual objects is experienced above all by the developers and architects who design them and get them built. Everyone else is a spectator, a passive gawper. Extravagant skylines leave the spaces in which most people spend most of their time untouched. There is little interplay of their lives with the frozen computer games above their heads. Instead the generic spaces of malls and atria request that you leave your memories outside the door. Identity, desire, and stimulation become things you have to buy, as clothes, restaurant meals of calculated diversity, and rides on the ski slope or up the Burj Khalifa. You are not invited to contribute, except as a consumer.

The eye is engaged but not the body. Mostly, you are not invited to move through these works, unless by lift or escalator. Climate is an awkwardness, to be banished by air-conditioning. Similarly smell: this can be repurchased as perfume. As you enter from the heat and dust outside, you are lightly gripped by mechanical clamminess, in a transition we now treat as normal. It tells us that the air and temperature have been paid for, and that we agree to the terms and conditions of the people who have paid for them. As the architect Rem Koolhaas says, conditioned space is conditional space.

The wackiness of the skyline becomes an accomplice. The outward gestures of genius, suggesting ecstasy and fervour, are distractions. If they were not there, the tedium of the rest would become too apparent. Architectural forms on the outside collude with controlled and laundered atmospheres on the inside.

Lina Bo Bardi, by contrast, placed four 'subtle substances' at the centre of her work: air, light, nature, and art. She was interested in the movements of people through spaces, in the ways they reacted with each other and with nature, and in their desires and memories. Look, shape, external appearance, and the hard stuff of which buildings are made came second. Her works look distinctive, but their ultimate purpose is not to be striking. They are devices that make possible new experiences, or intensify existing ones, or excavate or recover lost sensations. 'Until man enters the building,' she said, 'climbs steps, and takes possession of the space in a "human adventure" which develops over time, architecture does not exist.'

Photographs of her show a searching gaze, sharp features, and a lean face thickening over time. She had, of necessity and inclination, a restless life. 'I never wanted to be young,' she said. 'What I really wanted was to have history. At the age of twenty-five I wanted to write memoirs, but I didn't have the materials.' By the time she died in 1992 she had plenty. Never satisfied only with designing buildings, and sometimes lacking the chance to do so, she wrote, illustrated, and painted, made theatre sets, exhibitions, and furniture, and agitated and cultivated political debate.

She was born Achillina Bo in Rome in 1914, worked for the architect Gio Ponti, and then set up her own practice in Milan which, never prospering, ended when its premises were destroyed by bombing in 1943. She joined the underground Communist Party, assisted the Italian resistance, and edited the magazine *Domus*, where one of her editorials on urbanism attracted the attention of the Gestapo. After the end of the war she toured Italy, chronicling the damage caused by the fighting.

'The years', she said, 'that should have been ones of sunshine, blue skies, and happiness, I spent underground, running and taking shelter from bombs and machine guns.' But 'I felt that the world could still be saved and for the better, and that this was the only task worth living for, the starting point to be able to survive.'

In 1946 she married Pietro Maria Bardi, an art critic, dealer, and self-confessed adventurer, 'whom I had admired ever since I was a bobby-soxer in the Rome Artistic Lyceum', and sailed with him to Brazil. In the same year he met the Brazilian media mogul and buccaneer Assis Chateaubriand, who invited Pietro to help him build the collection for a new museum he was founding in São Paulo.

Compared to Europe, Brazil was 'like a lighthouse shining over a field of death . . . It was something marvellous.' It had the 'dazzle of an unimaginable country with no middle class, just two great aristocracies: that of the land, of Coffee, of Sugar Cane, and . . . the People.' It was a country defining its own version of modernity, which had avoided the worst of the war, and prospered. It had the freedoms of a new country, expressed in the modern architecture of Lucio Costa, Oscar Niemeyer, and others, which would eventually lead to the flamboyant monuments of the new capital of Brasilia. It also had the legends and customs of an old country, multiple, varied, and particular to different places and races. Its flora and fauna were rampant and vivid. Lina Bo Bardi loved it. She said: 'when we are born, we choose nothing. I was not born here, I chose this country to live. This is the reason why Brazil is my country twice. It is my "Chosen Nation" and I feel a citizen in all of its cities and towns'. It gave her opportunity and inspiration, but its political fluctuations, its turn to military dictatorship and slow crawl back to democracy, would also create long barren periods when she was out of favour.

She designed a house for herself and her husband, called the Glass House. It would be both their home and a social centre, an 'open house' whose visitors included the film director Roberto Rossellini, the artist Alexander Calder, and the musician John Cage. It was in the Jardim Morumbi, a former tea farm on the edge of São Paulo and a nature reserve whose life she joyously inventoried: 'ocelot, armadillo, small deer, cavy, opossum, sloth . . . It was also a bird sanctuary, where during the day time one could see the squirrel cuckoo, *peitica*, rufous-billed thrush and slaty thrush, smooth-billed ani, great kiskadee, tinamou, white-tipped dove, the Cariama cristata, and at night, the long-trained nightjar, ferruginous pygmy-owl, and other night birds. Many frogs and toads could be heard croaking at night. There were some very beautiful snakes and many cicadas.'

The front part of the house was a glass-walled box perched on high stilts, crowning a hill. It was spare in detail, but extravagant in the volume captured beneath its raised floor. It was penetrated by a square court, which brought sunlight down and allowed a tree to grow up through the middle of the building. Next to the court, a stair ascended from the ground, pausing at a quarter-landing to offer a view of the landscape, before turning back and taking you up, past a mosaic by Giorgio di Chirico, into the living space. Here, too, the structure was slight but the space ample, and beyond its skinny-framed glass enclosure the hills and forests formed the walls of the room.

The room contained the Bardis' collections: paintings, some gilt-framed religious oils, and unframed abstracts; furniture, some in

tubular steel, some to Lina's designs, some in old wood, thick, gilded, and dark, that seemed heavier than the building itself. There were carvings and odd objects, both man-made and natural; plants, patterned carpets, books, a classical statue of Diana (above lifesize), a golden sphere. Or, as a pupil of Lina's described:

> A cheap glass bottle in the form of the Jules Rimet football cup rubs shoulders with a baroque angel: a little peasant's bench keeps company with a chaise longue by Le Corbusier, a little plastic car, a child's birthday present, rests at the feet of a sculpture by Ernesto de Fiori, and so on.

Full-height vinyl curtains, coloured cream, permitted the closing-off or opening-up of the view. The floor was in mosaic tiles, in the blue of both swimming pools and a Tiepolo sky.

Deeper into the house, further rooms could be found: the kitchen, bedrooms, and, since her version of Communism did not preclude these, servants' quarters. Here the house was no longer glass or floating, but almost traditional, with solid walls, green-shuttered windows, and a hidden court. In Lina and Pietro's bedroom are a Renaissance *Madonna and Child* above a spare metal bed, and the trunks, much labelled with the names of destinations, which carried their possessions across the Atlantic, as if they were still in transit. The building turns out to be two houses in one: solid, traditional, and nocturnal at the back; light, modern, and diurnal at the front.

The house echoes some of the most celebrated works of twentieth-century architecture. As a glass box, it is like Ludwig Mies van der Rohe's Farnsworth House, a small temple of crystalline perfection in Plano, Illinois, completed like Bo Bardi's house in 1951. As a building on stilts, it recalled Le Corbusier's Villa Savoye, completed outside Paris in 1929. In the way it embraces the tree growing up its middle, it uses an occasional motif of Frank Lloyd Wright.

But it is different. Unlike them, it is not a self-sufficient work of art. In the Farnsworth House every detail is expensively perfect, making inhabitation incidental, in fact problematic. The Villa Savoye is also an artwork, in which each movement through the house, and each view, is a conscious composition of building, furniture, people, and landscape. In Frank Lloyd Wright's work, his artistic personality is omnipresent, in every chair and door handle. For all his undoubted talent, and for all that he is the most revered of American architects, it is easy to be oppressed by the insistent buzzing of the diminutive genius that emits from every surface. The Farnsworth House, the Villa Savoye, and many of Wright's houses also required the sacrifice of their clients, as the projects ended with blown budgets, lawsuits, and disillusioned misery for the people who paid for them.

The point of Bo Bardi's house is that its form and structure are not ends in themselves. Striking though it is, the main purpose of the architecture is not to make you look at it. 'Neither decorative nor compositional effects were sought,' she said. The fusion of glassy front and solid rear is an inconsistency Mies would not have tolerated, nor any architect for whom the unity of the artwork is paramount. Instead the Glass House is an instrument that enables other events and experiences to happen. The purpose of the glass walls is to create a relationship between two forms of life, the flora and fauna outside, and the people, art, and objects within. Both verdure and contents grew over time, so the spare house is now enveloped and populated by lushness, natural outside and human within. Early black-and-white photographs show it standing brightly against the landscape; now it is engulfed with green. Like a person growing old, it has changed, while remaining the same.

The passage of time does not embarrass the architecture, as it often does the pristine works of modernism. Berthold Lubetkin, whose Penguin Pool in London Zoo and Highpoint Tower were the most dazzling buildings in 1930s Britain, once told me that he hated to revisit his works. 'It is like seeing an old girlfriend,' he said, 'who was beautiful, but has become wrinkled and lost her teeth.' For Bo Bardi, change was foreseen and welcomed. Her house got better as it got older.

In her early sketches of the project she drew its architecture with light, thin lines, such that people, plants, and objects, which are rendered with more fullness and detail, stand out. They anticipate the future of the house, that it would recede beneath the things in and around it. This does not mean that the building is neutral: it guides the arriving visitor on a route through shadows to light; it proposes relationships and gives a spin or a flavour to them. If the house were different, so would the perception of the objects and the surroundings. But the ambition of the architecture is to become less conspicuous over time, like sculptor's wax melting from the mould that has formed around it.

The architecture holds with its thin lines volumes of air – three dimensions retained by strokes of one dimension – within which life happens. Even the treads of the stairs are designed with open space between them. The mosaic floor, defined at its edges as if cut by a knife, is a plane (two dimensions now) of celestial or aqueous colour. Here the air (or possibly water) is imaginary, but delineated with the uncanny precision you find in dreams.

When still in Italy, Lina Bo Bardi had written about 'airborne architectures', illustrating her article with images, strikingly combined, of the Villa Savoye and of an airship. The Glass House is a fulfilment of this idea, but it is not literal. It does not make gestures of soaring, or mimic the shapes of aircraft. It is not a fantasy. It does not oblige you to accept its imagery. It still knows it is a house, and a building, which has to stand up, be plumbed, withstand weather, contain things. As she put it:

the idea was to have a house that gave physical protection from the wind and rain, but shared this with poetry and ethics, things that can be found even in a storm.

By 'poetry' she meant such things as the ability of the house to seem airborne and grounded at once, or the rapport she created between artefacts and vegetation. Early in its life the house was visited by the artist/illustrator/cartoonist Saul Steinberg. He, like Bo Bardi, knew how to conjure the four dimensions of time and space with a line. He said the Glass House was, as she had intended, 'a poetic house'.

The promotions for Dubai properties use words like dream, inspire, imagination, humanity, passion, vision, and legendary. Their imagery is about desire. The developments themselves exploit the power of dreamlike inversion and incongruity, of which the giant palm trees, laid flat on water, are the most obvious.

Similar words were used by and of Lina Bo Bardi, if not with identical meanings. Her blue floor, as a piece of sky you can walk on, is dreamlike: it is her subtler, smaller version of the Sheikh's Palm. Imagination and passion are plainly at work in her designs. Where Dubai estate agents profess 'humanity', she said of her later work that it was 'for the greater wellbeing of the people'. If they talk of the 'legendary', she immersed herself in the legends of Brazilian peoples.

Both the Dubai developments and the Glass House borrow richness from outside themselves. In Dubai they plunder imagery, of Venice, the Chrysler Building, of sails, flowers, and old Arab towns. They import marble and exotic fish. In the Jardim Morumbi, Lina Bo Bardi opened her design to the outdoor territory of ocelots and kiskadees and, inside, to the baroque angels, Corbusier furniture, and plastic car. Sheikh Mohammed considers it important that people know he is a poet; Bo Bardi, seconded by Steinberg, considered her house poetic.

These two poets, the Sheikh and the architect, play with the emotional power of buildings, but they do so in opposite ways, and with different results. The Sheikh's architecture comes down from above. It communicates almost exclusively through the most distancing, least intimate sense, sight; it is 'visionary', a thing of vision. It subjugates what is external: climate, nature, the memories and identities of the people who witness it. Whatever qualities there might have been in the sites of Dubai developments – and every place always has something – were wiped clean, so that 'the new reality' could come. Similarly with the stuff that the buildings were made of. Construction materials and techniques have characters, can create atmospheres, and the way they are used shapes the beauty or otherwise of a building. In Dubai materials and technique were means to an end, valued only for their ability to achieve size and spectacle.

The Glass House welcomes what Dubai architecture suppresses: place, stuff, people, growth, weather, chance, the passage of time. It is not passive, inert, or especially gentle. It is forceful, and makes something new, but the new thing it makes is formed with the things around it.

It is not an equal comparison, a big city formed almost from nothing in a desert, and a house for a singular couple in a delightful sub-tropical spot (although, as will be seen, Bo Bardi also knew how to work for less privileged people and at an urban scale). But taken together the two places show, if we are speaking of emotion or desire in architecture, how varied and opposite its manifestations can be.

2: The fixed and wandering home

An architect used to tell a story. Invited by a couple to design an extension to their house, he dined with them, listened to their needs and desires, heard his and her versions of what they wanted. At the end of the evening he gave his professional advice. 'You don't need an extension,' he said, 'you need a divorce.'

It is advice that could have saved the software entrepreneur Larry Dean tens of millions of dollars. Dean grew up in a house without indoor plumbing, overcame his early poverty, and became a millionaire many times over. In 1992 he and his wife Lynda completed the biggest house in Atlanta, Georgia, a mansion of 32,000 square feet, the colour of salmon mousse. According to its architect, Bill Harrison, each square inch of it was given the attention to detail of 'a Fabergé egg'. The interiors were designed by their son Chris, then a design student aged twenty-one. The Deans' dream, it was later reported, 'was to raise their four children here in an atmosphere like *Dynasty*, only happy.'

It is hard to do justice to the extravagance of Dean Gardens, as it was called, and the promiscuity of its inspirations and appropriations. To use the words of others:

Inspired by the dome of Florence, Italy's Brunelleschi Cathedral, the Rotunda is perhaps the mansion's most dramatic element. Three and a half stories high and capped with a circular skylight, the Rotunda sets an elegant tone for this exceptional home.

Or:

The Grande Salon's glass wall looks out the back of the home onto the shell-shaped swimming pool, the formal gardens, the three-acre man-made lake and the river beyond. The French Empire furnishings here set a comfortable, yet formal tone for the entire home.

Or:

At the end of this east wing of the main floor is the octagonally shaped Peacock Room. With its baby grand piano and cappuccino bar, this unique space is perfect for entertaining large groups. The room has 11' x 15' arched windows which weigh some 12 hundred pounds each. From the center of the ceiling, 43 feet above the floor, an eight-foot tall 'pendant' lighting fixture is suspended. The ceiling mural was painted by James Chadwick of Atlanta. The table in the center of the room is carved from English limestone and weighs four thousand pounds. It sits atop a steel beam buried in bedrock under the home.

And these are only a few plums from the feast that was Dean Gardens. There were also the Moroccan Rooms, the Egyptian Suite, the Oriental Suite, the Hawaiian Art Gallery, the Game Room got up as a 1950s diner, the Malachite Bathroom, the Silver Suite, the raspberry-coloured kitchen, the Old English Bedroom whose en-suite bathroom 'is quite masculine with fixtures reminiscent of a fine locker room'.

Dean Gardens is a variation on the theme of *Citizen Kane*'s Xanadu, or its real-life inspiration, William Randolph Hearst's Hearst Castle. Like them, it is a compendium of lootings across history and geography. Its architecture reaches across millennia and continents to assemble a microcosm, an image of the world for the personal enjoyment of its owner. The only parsimony shown by Dean, relative to Kane and Hearst, is that he did not seize whole chunks of historic buildings and have them imported bodily to his home. He only had them mimicked.

A distinctive feature of Dean Gardens was the contribution of young Chris, the interior designer, whose appointment echoes less Xanadu than Kane's purchase of an opera house as a showcase for the singing of his mistress turned second wife. Familial love eclipsed clear perception of talent. For Chris could no more make a room than Susan Alexander could hold a tune: Dean Gardens, the first of two commissions before he wisely ended his design career at the age of twenty-four, proceeded arrhythmically and out of key.

Clichés of opulence mingled with spasms of student surrealist angst. It was oysters in ketchup, double-fudge-caviar-and-Tabasco ice cream. There were tritons unicorns dolphins jukeboxes water-jets topiary astrolabes chinoiserie tassels flounces marble damask leather abstraction trompe l'œil statuary four-posters leopardskin zebraskin pediments Corinthian Ionic Doric palms stars moons mosquelights neon globes stripes peacocks pianos chandeliers chandeliers chandeliers gold gold gold royal-blue putti lions and a decorated camel. There was a tortured sculpture: a mannequin torso in glossy black, images of cats and sea creatures crawling up its skin, its severed head green-eyed and half-feline, perched on an extended elbow. In the Game Room a giant anthropomorphized cone of French fries gave a sinister wink. The parental bed, 'crafted by North Carolina artist Jane Goco', was engulfed by writhing

turquoise vegetables, with terminations like crab claws, and by gooey blossomings the colour of vulvas.

With the benefit of hindsight one can guess that Chris's designs were an unconscious commentary on the state of his parents' marriage. It turned out that Lynda would be only the first of Larry's three, to date, ex-wives. She and he separated in 1993, shortly after moving into the house, and there followed a seventeen-year struggle to sell the place. In 1994 Michael Jackson was said to be interested: perhaps sensing that this was a temple to problematic matrimony, he wanted to buy it as a surprise present for his fiancée, Lisa Marie Presley, until news leaked and his plan was ruined. 'He that is of a merry heart hath a continual feast' was written, quoting Proverbs 15.15, in the fresco above the dining table, and as time passed the words sounded ever more hollow. The nursery, with carousel horses prancing across one end, and a table set for a soft toys' arid tea party, became a thing of desolation.

The house cost $25 million to build, and a further $18 million in upkeep. In 2010 it was finally sold, with the help of the estate agents' encomiums quoted above, for $7.6 million. The contents were auctioned for charity. The buyer was the producer and actor Tyler Perry, most famous for his drag act as Madea, the vast, aggressive grandmother in *Diary of a Mad Black Woman*, *Madea's Family Reunion*, *Madea's Class Reunion* and *Madea Goes to Jail*. His plan was to demolish Dean Gardens and build something 'sustainable' instead. Larry Dean, to his credit, frankly admitted that he had made a mistake, while telling the *New York Times* that he still considered himself happy and successful.

One can also guess that whatever brought down the Dean marriage was already incubating when the house was conceived and developed, that the house was intended as some kind of remedy, but exacerbated the ills it was supposed to cure. The frenetic accumulation of motifs can be seen as a way of covering a void. In which case Larry and Lynda would be very far from the first people to imagine that homebuilding can fix relationships, and be proved wrong.

At the heart of this enduring syndrome is the double meaning of the word 'home'. It means the physical residence, but also the family that inhabit it. It means building, people, and relationship. It is easy to imagine that by fixing the bricks and mortar, one is fixing the flesh and blood, the more so as buildings seem easier to sort out than people. The results are more tangible, measurable, demonstrable. Because they are expensive and effortful, construction projects offer the appearance of serious attempts to fix something, even if they are irrelevant to the matter in hand.

If Dean Gardens ranks high in the annals of follies, it comes lower in the history of architectural masterpieces. Yet there are many treasured houses where human troubles have motivated the creation of a dream home, of an architectural cosmos where ache is healed, and disorder ordered. Often they have failed in their aim, but they are still preserved, restored, chronicled, and opened to the public. One is Sir John Soane's house and museum at 12–14 Lincoln's Inn Fields, London, built in stages from 1792 to 1824, with further adjustments after that.

Soane, born the son of a bricklayer in 1753, fell from fashion following his death in 1837, but is now widely considered one of the most brilliant and original of British architects. He worked in the classical tradition at a time when it was challenged by travel and archaeology, which revealed a richer range of styles than had previously been imagined. He responded in two ways: by trying to find a more essential form of classicism – more primitive, and stripped of extraneous ornament – and by absorbing Gothic and other non-classical influences.

His grandest building was the Bank of England, largely destroyed in the 1930s. Here clerks shuffled paper in halls vaulted like Imperial Roman baths, only delicate and bubble-like compared to the massive originals, thanks to Soane's techniques for lightening the structure of his buildings. At the Dulwich Picture Gallery he designed top-lit galleries that have been a model for museums ever since. In the twentieth century the K2 and K6 red telephone boxes, which once covered Britain, were directly inspired by Soane's architecture.

As the historian John Summerson recorded, he could be 'courteous and gentle, even with a spice of humour', but these pleasant touches were overwhelmed by what a pupil called:

> an acute sensitiveness, and a fearful irritability, dangerous to himself if not to others; an embittered heart, prompting a cutting and sarcastic mind; uncompromising pride, neither respecting nor desiring respect; a contemptuous regard for the feelings of his dependants; and yet himself the very victim of irrational impulse; with no pity for the trials of his neighbour, and nothing but frantic despair for his own.

Soane started by building no. 12 Lincoln's Inn Fields, before acquiring and remodelling another house, Pitzhanger Manor in Ealing, for himself, his wife, Eliza, and his two sons, John and George. He had dreams of founding a dynasty, and Pitzhanger was conceived, as Summerson put it, as an 'ideal environment for a classic breed of architects'. He started collecting art and antiquities, and installed them in exquisite rooms, of his own design, for the boys' inspiration and instruction.

In 1808 he bought no. 13 Lincoln's Inn Fields, and over the next few years he rebuilt it as both his main family residence and as a museum. He brought his collection from Pitzhanger (which he sold in 1810) and continued to grow it, still holding to his dream of an edifying environment. In 1823–4 he redeveloped no. 14, expanding his museum to its rear and rebuilding and reselling the house at the front.

Put like this, Soane's creation sounds like the outcome of four decades of steady productive work, and of a happy and balanced union of professional and domestic life. The reality was different. His sons disliked architecture and, George especially, warred with their father. Both married unsuitably – to spite their parents, George said; he would also get his wife's sister pregnant, publish an anonymous attack on his father's architecture as mediocre and plagiaristic, and enter a debtors' prison. Eliza died in 1815, which Sir John blamed on George-induced stress. John junior died in 1823, while George lived on as an embittered and unsuccessful novelist. In 1833 Sir John arranged a private Act of Parliament, a more certain and final instrument than a mere will, under which his house and its contents would become a national institution. It was a device to make absolutely sure that, in what the writer and MP William Cobbett called 'so unnatural an act', Soane's son would be disinherited in favour of a wider posterity. For a quarter-century, then, the buildings at Lincoln's Inn Fields, now a monument of domestic architecture, were the home of a widower, alone with his collections, and his ruined hopes for his family.

A painting of 1794 suggests some causes of the troubles to come. It is a view of the breakfast room at no. 12, by J. M. Gandy, the artist Soane preferred for representing his work. The four people in the picture are shrunk, relative to the architecture, to make the little room look bigger than it is. Seen through the window is a lusher landscape than would ever have been possible in what is a narrow London court at the rear of the house. The room is lined with edification: books in glazed cases, framed pictures, antiquities in niches. Furniture is kept in place against the wall, except two chairs in use by the diminished figures of the architect and his wife, as they take a stiff breakfast. The design is characteristically Soanic, with thin, incised lines or reeded decoration, and a shallow vault, lightened with a ceiling decoration of painted trellis and flowers, as if this room were really outside.

Gandy renders it with a ruthless if naive single-point perspective, with Soane's rectilinear architecture converging on a vanishing point placed dead centre, on a horizon line above the human heads. And within it are the two boys, identically dressed in smart, adult-looking britches and tailcoats, scuttling about like mantises inside the elegant but rigid grid. One is drawn bending over a toy, so as not to obscure a view of a piece of furniture. Eliza makes a small gesture of tenderness to the other. John Senior, seen from behind, seems to stare ahead over his teacup. All the shrivelled figures, especially the children, fit awkwardly into the composition, and you sense that the artist would be happier if they were not there. Gandy's picture, in other words, can be seen as a picture of young George and John imprisoned by architecture, from which they would make a violent escape.

The image is also a premonition of the architectural themes of the later stages of the house. The decorative style is already there, as are the improving cultural artefacts. The breakfast room demonstrates a form of miniaturization that would reappear. Not only does Gandy's view through the window make a park out of flowerpots, but the space borrows motifs from grander buildings; the arches and vaults are forms from masonry construction, when really they are made of wood and plaster.

In later stages the artefacts multiplied. Spaces were encrusted with plaster casts of the *Apollo Belvedere* or of fragments of temple entablature, and genuine antiquities like the alabaster sarcophagus of Pharaoh Seti I. Like Larry Dean, Soane was ravenous for history.

There was a 'Monk's Parlour', and displays of Medieval, Renaissance, and oriental objects. Paintings and portraits from Soane's own time jostled with images of the ancients. A set of Hogarth canvases hangs in the picture gallery, part of the later development of no. 14. These can only be seen in full by opening a succession of shutters on which they hang, in an erudite striptease, the last of which reveals a statue of an undressing nymph. There was an impressive collection of architectural drawings and models, for the education of future generations of architects.

Into this relatively small site Soane compresses the plans and forms of palaces and Roman baths. He derived concealed lighting effects from the high altars of baroque churches, and applied them to bourgeois interiors. Roman ruins and monuments, which he had studied on a travelling scholarship when young, are reduced and brought indoors.

The Soane Museum is mostly interior. Its facade is fairly sober, telling you nothing of the artificial landscape within. Once inside, you lose sense of the world you have left. Instead you are taken into Soane's universe of architecture and archaeology, an effect heightened by his constructional devices. You see little of the sun, but rather indirect lighting from hidden sources: light, that is, arrives on his terms. He uses mirrors, screens, and openings to create layers of space and dissolve the boundaries of rooms. You are always looking from one place into another, into another. The limits of the building's standard London plots melt. You are disoriented, until Soane's architecture, with its little domes, axes, and framing pairs of columns, restores your sense of direction: as with the light, on his terms. The mirrors, sometimes distorting and sometimes true, give you a strange sense of yourself: you keep being arrested by fragments and warpings of your reflection, enmeshed in the architect's many-layered collage.

It's possible that Soane was more unhappy than Larry, but like

Dean Gardens his house is a personal cosmos, an image of a world he would have rather had, than the one in which he found himself. Both houses are examples of an enduring metaphor in architecture, of the building as a microcosm of the world, to be found in the Palace of Agamemnon at Mycenae, or in Hadrian's villa in Tivoli. Or in the writings of the fifteenth-century architect and theorist Leon Battista Alberti, who said that a house is a miniature city, by which he meant that both are links in a chain of resemblances that runs from the human body to the universe. When Leonardo da Vinci drew his famous image of a naked man, arms stretched, and inscribed in a circle and square, he wanted to show the underlying proportions of the human body, which were also thought to structure all things.

The idea of home as cosmos can be expressed abstractly, as a geometrical order underlying all things, or physically and explicitly. It is present in Renaissance theory, and in the fantastical structures hand-built out of broken china and other debris by untutored obsessives that occur rarely but persistently around the world. It is in the gathering of family photographs and mementoes on a mantelpiece, and in the promise made by interiors magazines: choose the products shown in articles and advertisements, and you can form them into your own personal universe.

The common wish is to dream up a world, of which the maker is master, where everything is as he or she wishes it. The same wish drives children to build homes out of cardboard boxes and impose entry conditions, and it is a powerful reason why, functional questions apart, clients commission and architects design buildings. As people and cultures learn more, the ambitions of these cosmosmakers increase, to include in their spheres as much knowledge, history and geography, science and religion, as they can from small to large.

But if homes aspire to the cosmic, they can also be nomadic. If one desire is to create a static, rooted image of perfection, another is to migrate, to colonize and adapt different places, to make a home out of a city or a landscape.

A significant portion of humanity lives or lived on the move: Bedouin, Masai, Romanies, pedlars, salesmen, migrant workers, the ever-airborne businessman played by George Clooney in *Up In The Air*. People live in tents, boats, caravans, igloos, boarding houses, and hotels. For sailors, according to Joseph Conrad, 'their home is always with them – the ship; and so is their country – the sea.' Many in cities have come from somewhere else, and are, or hope to be, on the way to another place. It is normal for most city-dwellers to have several different homes during their lives.

People who inhabit through motion include desert-dwellers, obliged to move with herds in search of feeding-grounds and markets. Also the flâneur, the nineteenth-century gentleman stroller of cities in search of fascination, of whom Charles Baudelaire was the archetype. A flâneur, in one description, is 'the deliberately aimless pedestrian, unencumbered by any obligation or sense of urgency, who . . . wastes nothing, including his time which he spends with the leisurely discrimination of a gourmet, savouring the multiple flavors of his city.' For him the city, to quote another, 'opens like a landscape and encloses him like a room'.

One could include someone like the surrealist writer and 1920s flâneur Louis Aragon, who frequented glazed arcades 'rather disturbingly named *passages*, as though no one had a right to linger for more than an instant in those sunless corridors.' Here he explored a world of shops selling books and umbrellas, cafes, dubious boarding houses, and an erotic theatre. In such transitory places, in 'a light ranging from the brightness of the tomb to the shadow of sensual pleasure', Aragon wanders, sampling their delights and deciphering their signs, such that he 'shall once again plumb his own depths'. In these 'sanctuaries to the cult of the ephemeral', he finds himself, and makes his home.

Some distinctions should be made. There is a difference between the desert nomad and economic migrant who wander to survive, and the dandified poet in search of diversion, between necessity and choice, and between escaping hunger and escaping boredom. If wandering peoples have often been marginal and despised by settled society, if 'vagrant' and 'vagabond' are usually insults, poetic travellers tend to rely on an infrastructure of privilege and superfluity. But all show an ability to construct space out of the tracks they follow and the landmarks, whether a shop window or a sand dune, that they see. They do not need a house to make a home.

In *The Songlines* Bruce Chatwin speculated about the invisible pathways laid by aboriginal Australians across the country. Their 'Creation myths', he said, 'tell of the legendary totemic beings who had wandered over the continent in the Dreamtime, singing out the name of everything that crossed their path – birds, animals, plants, rocks, waterholes – and so singing the world into existence.'

Aboriginals re-enacted these myths by going on walkabout, tracing the lines with the help of songs that connected geography to myth. 'In theory at least, the whole of Australia could be read as a musical score. There was hardly a rock or a creek in the country that could not or had not been sung. One should perhaps visualize the Songlines as a spaghetti of Iliads and Odysseys, writhing this way and that, in which every "episode" was readable in terms of geology . . . Anywhere in the bush you can point to some feature of the landscape and ask the Aboriginal with you, "What's the story there?" or "Who's that?" The chances are he'll answer "Kangaroo" or "Budgerigar" or "Jew Lizard", depending on which Ancestor walked that way.' Social structures, the definition of territories, of groups and individual identities, were formed by the patterns of the lines. At their most practical, they help navigation. They are a way of making a home out of desert.

With the songlines as an example, Chatwin, a restless traveller, translated his personal wanderlust into a universal human condition. 'All the Great Teachers have preached that Man, originally, was a "wanderer in the scorching and barren wilderness of this world" – the words are those of Dostoevsky's Grand Inquisitor – and that to rediscover his humanity, he must slough off attachments and take to the road.'

Another book, *Journeys*, by the Canadian Centre for Architecture, describes migrant inhabitation in more concrete terms than Chatwin's. It mentions how, for example, Inuit place names describe locations in terms of their wind direction or the shape of their snow drifts, so that they can find their place and way in the seemingly baffling and shifting Arctic landscape. It tells how in Newfoundland, Canada, fishing communities once lived in timber-framed homes which with pitched roofs and glazed windows looked as stable and settled as most houses, but which sat lightly on the ground. When dwindling stocks required them to seek new fishing grounds, they would take whole villages with them, house by house, dragging each one across ice and snow, or floating them on the sea. When, from the 1950s to the 1970s, government policy encouraged them to move to more central, better serviced towns, many took their houses with them, and grounded them in empty lots. Each house would bring with it mementoes, furniture, some modest equipment such as a stove, and memories and associations, but its relationship to the landscape and to other houses would be new.

In south-east Amsterdam, an enormous housing development called Bijlmermeer, or the Bijlmer for short, was planned in the late 1960s. It aimed to be the ultimate example of the internationally recognized Dutch genius for planning, and an attempt to apply with breathtaking consistency and determination the theories of the time. Homes for a hundred thousand inhabitants were created in almost identical ten-storey concrete blocks, whose walls and windows were mass-produced in factories, laid out on a hexagonal grid. Parks and lakes filled the spaces between the blocks, and roads were built on viaducts, to separate cars from pedestrians. The architects, inspired by Soviet models, planned collective facilities – bars, daycare centres, hobby rooms – to stimulate communal life and serve the new society of almost limitless leisure time that modern technology would soon create. Five-room flats, of reasonably generous dimensions, were designed for the needs of a typical Dutch family. An overriding principle was the avoidance of danger or discomfort: covered walkways meant you could get from car to flat without getting wet, vehicular traffic was separated from people, flats were designed to catch the maximum sunlight and fresh air.

Although it attracted optimistic and idealistic early residents, problems arose. A promised metro line to central Amsterdam did not materialize, leaving the Bijlmer cut off. Nor did the provision of adequate shopping come to pass. No one had worked out who would pay for the communal facilities and the maintenance of the parks, meaning that the latter degenerated and the former stayed closed, except when opened by residents' initiatives. The construction cost more than expected, so rents went up to recoup costs. Flats emptied, or were never occupied.

Then, in 1975, Holland ceded independence to its colony Surinam, on the north coast of South America. Citizens were entitled to a Dutch passport, with the result that soon there were nearly as many Surinamese in Holland, in search of economic opportunities, as in Surinam. With inevitable logic many moved into the vacant flats of the Bijlmer, despite official attempts to stop it becoming 'Holland's first ghetto' by rationing the provision of homes there to

immigrants. The prices remained high, leading to overcrowding, in one case twelve adults and twelve children in one flat.

The new residents adapted the flats, designed for typical white Dutch families, to their own needs. They knocked through walls or floors to make larger homes for their extended families. Many were from rural backgrounds and lived as they had in tropical villages, only adapted to a colder climate. Livestock was kept in flats, camp-fires lit indoors, and rubbish thrown from balconies to the ground, rather than down chutes into bins. Catholic churches were set up in disused parking garages, and flats became part-time temples to the Surinamese religion of Winti. Bird-singing contests were held in the parks, with betting on which brightly coloured bird would sing the longest. A petting zoo and farm were set up, and for a while a Bijlmer cheese was made. The architects' dream of communal activity came true, but not in the orderly form they had imagined.

The estate's original problems of disconnection and poor facil-ities remained, with the result that more stable and better-off families left when they could. The Bijlmer declined, crime grew. The walkways, products of the original ambition for complete safety and comfort, became dangerous, and ground-floor lock-ups became brothels and drug dens. The estate's bad name, acquired when the first residents started complaining about its defects, got worse. Racists called it 'Negro-ghetto' and 'monkey mountain'. Masterplans for its improvement by leading architects came and went unrealized. In 1992 an El Al cargo-carrying 747, trying to return to Schiphol Airport after two of its engines had fallen off, crashed, made a ten-storey gash at one of the 120° corners in one of the hexagonally-planned blocks, and killed forty-three (or possi-bly more, as the large numbers of unregistered immigrants made it difficult to be certain). It was a random catastrophe, but confirmed Bijlmermeer's image as a place of ill omen. Following the aero-plane's lead, the authorities later started demolishing the blocks, to the point where they have now mostly gone. Meanwhile, however, the blighted place began to show glimmers of success.

The residents, who included Hindus, Antilleans, Ghanaians, and white Dutch as well as Surinamese, had organized themselves into a community group substantial enough to get itself heard by official bodies. A thriving weekly market started. A cultural festival, 'Blij-met-de-Bijlmer' (Happy with the Biljmer), was set up and, perhaps burdened by the forced upbeatness of its name, closed after sixteen years. A more successful festival, called Kwakoe, grew from a series of informal soccer matches into an event of music, dance, sport, and food that came to attract four hundred thousand people. Crime started to fall and, if the Biljmer did not become paradise on earth, it ceased to be the sink of despair it was once thought to be.

The point of the Bijlmer story is partly how an obsessively planned development could be thrown off course by the unexpected: the independence of Surinam, a plane crash. It is also about the way in which a migrant population can, not easily but with some success, make a home in an unpromising location. It is hard to imagine anywhere less domestic than the huge repetitive blocks of the Bijlmer, or more alien to the incoming Surinamese. They offer almost no prompts or signs, few suggestions as to how to inhabit them. They are as desolate, in their stacked-up engineered way, as the Australian desert or the Arctic wastes, with the difference that Aboriginals and Inuit have had many generations in which to learn how to make the most of faint traces and drifts in dust or snow. The population of the Bijlmer had to discover, in a few decades, how to inhabit a place through adaptations, actions, successes, and mistakes. It is the opposite of the Deans and Soane, who invested everything in the fixed fabric of their homes. The residents of the Bijlmer make their universes around and in spite of the fabric.

•

John Berger, novelist, writer on art, artist, and partly disillusioned communist, described the idea of home-as-cosmos as fundamental to humanity, as essential to making sense of the world. In 'traditional' societies, he said,

> without a home at the centre of the real, one was not only shelterless, but also lost in non-being, in unreality. Without a home everything was fragmentation.

Being nomadic did not exclude this cosmic idea: nomads could establish a sense of home wherever they pitched their tents. But, for Berger, this life of mobile rootedness was not the experience of displaced people in the twentieth century, of those forced by economic pressure to uproot themselves and move to alien cities. To emigrate 'is always to dismantle the centre of the world, and so to move into a lost, disoriented one of fragments'. To find a new centre and preserve their identity, city dwellers have to resort to actions rather than physical form. They have to make a 'substitute' home that

> has little to do with a building. The roof over the head, the four walls, have become . . . independent from whatever is kept in the heart and is sacred . . . The displaced preserve their identity and improvise a shelter. Built of what? Of habits, I think, of the raw material of repetition, turned into a shelter. The habits imply words, jokes, opinions, gestures, even the way one wears a hat. Physical objects and places – a piece of furniture, a bed, the corner of a room, a particular bar, a street corner – supply the scene, the site of the habit, yet it is not they but the habit which protects.

Man was born rooted, in other words, and is everywhere in motion. He has been ripped out of the ground in a distant past, to which he might be returned in the distant future, when the communist society of which Berger dreamed might arrive. Meanwhile he has to console and compensate himself with the personal rituals and gestures with which he occupies spaces in the impersonal city.

Berger was talking about 'the masses', the dispossessed and underprivileged, and specifically not the 'bourgeois, with his town house, his country house, his three cars, his several televisions, his tennis court, his wine cellar'. But his words could still illuminate the bourgeois Dean Gardens. Larry Dean, having done whatever 'dodging, picking up, hustling' was necessary to make his space in the poor streets of Atlanta, escaped them. The building of his house can be seen as scrambling to find the centre of the world. It failed, because this centre could not be found, and because the project invested too heavily and too literally in the physical fabric, the walls and roof. This house built as cosmic became nomadic, or at least transitory. The Deans' stay there was only a little longer than in a hotel room.

Berger can mythologize too much. His opposition of 'traditional' people to the soulless metropolis seems too polarized, as it does between the 'masses' and the 'bourgeois'. But he eloquently describes the nature of dwelling: that it aspires to rootedness, but also includes transience and mobility. That it promises to immerse us in or connect us to what Berger calls 'the real', that is, the sense of oneself in relation to the world. That dwelling does not perfectly correspond with the physical object of a home, its walls or its boundaries, but may also consist of patterns of behaviour, or appearance, and may take place in a city or a landscape.

The static and mobile aspects of home are of equal weight. Indeed, they are different versions of the same thing, both attempts to rearrange the bewildering world, so as to find your place and way in it. And a home will always be in some way imperfect. It won't quite stabilize. It won't give utter wholeness. The more so if we live in cities, in streets and buildings built for us by people we don't know, and sharing them with other people, most of whom we also don't know, also in search of their personal cosmos. The desires of these different people, both the builders and the fellow residents, will never fit together perfectly.

For architects and city builders, the nature of dwelling (should they care about it) presents some problems. They can't build nothing. They have to make some kind of armature for existence, which people might inhabit physically and psychically, but in ways they can't predict. And, as dwelling does not precisely match the measured, constructed form of a building, they will in some sense get it wrong. They will have to make shapes, which predict particular ways of living more than others, which carry some idea of propriety, or status, or social order, or some dream of domestic bliss. But whatever they do, lives will take place in and around these buildings, exploiting, subverting, misusing, and ignoring the forms that have been provided for them.

Indifference is an option, and one often taken by property developers and speculators. Much city-building is by people without a great deal of love for those who will inhabit them. But if profit is the motive, it makes sense to pay at least some attention to the needs and desires of potential buyers and tenants, and to the extent that cities are shaped by planners and politicians, they represent ideas of collective decorum, of how things should be. The most successful attempts at creating space for multiple dwelling are not indifferent, but do not prescribe, either. They propose, suggest. They also include an element of chance.

One such success is the Victorian expansion of West London. In *Soft City*, of 1974, Jonathan Raban wrote:

> . . . the city goes soft; it awaits the imprint of an identity. For better or worse, it invites you to remake it, to consolidate it

into a shape you can live in. You, too. Decide who you are, and the city will again assume a fixed form round you. Decide what it is, and your own identity will be revealed.

Raban was giving his idea of cities in general, but he was thinking of London in particular. He admired its ability to contain multiple versions of itself, which enables appropriation and adaptation by the people who live in it. Lack of fixedness, and prescription, is essential to this 'softness', although this is not the same thing as neutrality. The London he describes is suggestive, offering many forms of appearance and disguise.

Fred Scott, an architectural teacher and writer, recounts the creation of the districts of Kensington, North Kensington, Notting Hill, and Notting Dale, from the 1840s to the 1860s. He considers this, the making of thousands of new houses, as a wonder of the world, a feat of construction equal to the Pyramids. It is also remarkable for making successful new neighbourhoods out of nothing, on previously undeveloped land. This is a notoriously difficult task, the history of planning being littered with disappointed attempts to make new towns from scratch. Yet these districts of West London are now among the most desired and expensive in the world, which is one measure of success.

Their houses were designed for large and prosperous families, with servants. They had many rooms, hierarchically and functionally differentiated, from pantries to drawing rooms. Their stucco facades calibrated with scale and decoration the relative social importance of the people and activities behind them. Yet over one and a half centuries these houses have been carved up into flats, sometimes becoming slum tenements; accommodated immigrants, bohemians, and students; become respectable again; been undivided back into houses; and in some cases become the property of some of the richest people in Europe. These houses, so specifically created for one set of circumstances, have accommodated change, social, economic, and technical.

Their assets included a degree of superfluity, redundancy, or generosity. Rooms were bigger and more numerous than necessary, and with high ceilings; also simple – oblong and arranged around a readily intelligible plan – but with variety in their sizes and aspects. These houses were not of the highest construction quality, nor did they require the lowest possible maintenance, but they were built of forgiving stuff: stucco and plaster that could be patched and repainted, wooden floorboards that could receive different coverings, bricks, timber-framed partitions that could be hacked about and altered. All that was required was skill in a few not-very-difficult building trades. The buildings were yielding and their spaces slack, not over-defined or over-prescribed.

The decoration contributed. Following Georgian precedents, terraces were composed as if they were the unified elevations of Palladian country houses, emphasized in the centre and framed with projecting bays at each end. They looked like stately homes that happened to contain numerous homes, in a bourgeois appropriation of the imagery of aristocracy. The classical detail is competent enough but not scholarly or rigorous. These facades are sketches: of dignity, of house-ness, of a connection with history and antiquity. They are not too specific, allowing different users to read them in their own way.

They also make a sharp distinction between front and back, visible at the ends of terrace as if drawn with a ruler. Symmetrical stucco, which aspires to look like stone, becomes undisguised brick, which is permitted to ramble and climb into back extensions, susceptible to additions and modifications, with little thought to the composition of the whole. The formal front permits informality behind. It is partly a mask, a disguise, a face shown to the world, formed not to suppress interior identities but to help them to flourish.

These districts' success is external as well as internal. Their builders felt the need to build streets of sufficient breadth to allow large plane trees to grow, and sufficient flexibility to allow the multiple uses of a city – domestic, retail, social, functional. They created generous garden squares, and laid them out on simple but effective plans of streets, squares, and crescents. Over time these rapidly built areas became part of the collective idea of London: few Anglo-American romcoms are complete without a shot of speculators' stucco seen over the shapely shoulder of Gwyneth Paltrow, Julia Roberts, or Scarlett Johansson.

This collective marvel was not the work of a guiding genius, or of great architects. It was created by property developers in pursuit of their self-interest, real or perceived. Houses, streets, and squares were built according to established patterns, which evolved in response to the preferences of the market. Architectural details, descended from ancient Rome via the Italian Renaissance and the Palladian houses of eighteenth-century aristocrats, were copied and pasted on. Surviving drawings are few, because few were ever made, and economical.

There was also chance. The development of these areas proceeded through booms and bankruptcies, Darwinian struggles in which relative innocents lost fortunes to the sharper-elbowed. Sometimes the torrent of construction stopped, leaving half-built terraces abandoned. What are now some of the most expensive districts displayed, according to an account in 1861,

> the melancholy vestiges of the wreck . . . The naked carcasses, crumbling decorations, fractured walls, and slimy cement-work, upon which the summer's heat and winter's rain have left their damaging mark, may still be seen on the estate . . . . With misfortune came insult, and the opprobrious epithet of 'Coffinrow' was fixed upon the dead street, where the windows

had that ghastly form. The 'Stumps' was a term given to another range of what was intended to be gentlemen's residences. The whole estate was as a graveyard of buried hopes.

By the late 1860s, in outer edges of this explosion, supply outran demand. Values plummeted. Some houses remained empty for years, and many were subdivided into smaller units, as over decades the area continued to sink, eventually falling victim to the exploitation of slum landlords: the most notorious of all, Peter Rachman, operated in Notting Hill in the 1950s. This swathe of West London formed a Bijlmer of sorts, where failed ambitions created space for appropriation, for the unexpected, for disasters and experiments, for race riots and carnivals. (And the possibility should not be excluded that, had it been allowed to survive, the Dutch concrete monster would have eventually seemed as marvellous and attractive as West London would become, thus prompting analysis of the architectural wisdom that made it all possible.)

The Victorian terraces were soft, in Jonathan Raban's sense, who in the 1970s singled out dilapidated Notting Hill for its 'fierce heterogeneity' and 'messy prolixity', 'a place where anything is possible, a nightmare – or paradise, perhaps, for some – of chance and choice'. 'The streets around Ladbroke Grove,' he wrote, 'with their architecture of white candy stucco, are warrens of eccentric privateness; they are occupied by people who have taken no part in the hypothetical consensus of urban life – the poor, the blacks, the more feckless young living on National Assistance or casual jobs on building sites or bedsitter industries like stringing beads or making candles.'

Then messiness acquired real estate value. University graduates came to like the area where they bought their drugs, and bought their first flats there. Prices rose. By the 1990s Notting Hill, which in 1963 had been the sleazy setting for scenes in the Profumo

affair, hosted another political scandal. This time it revolved around the fact that Peter Mandelson, the most fascinating minister of his age, owned a house whose price seemed far beyond his salary. Those romcoms were made, and turned Raban's 'ruined Eden, tangled, exotic and overgrown, where people see signs in scraps of junk and motley' into a place sweet and clean as Jane Austen's Bath.

It became the nursery of a plump young Conservative government, whose leading lights formed something called the Notting Hill Set. Smug books were written about living there, by people who lived there. It became inhabited by people who were more and more rich, until its expense began to encrust. Stucco, whose nature includes perpetual dilapidation, became fixed with always-new paint. Security systems locked up this ex-bohemia. The soft city became hard, carapaced like its residents' coiffures and 4x4s. It became the posh place it had been supposed to be when built. Which, even if a certain envious resentment is the natural reaction, can be seen as another stage in the adaptability of these buildings.

The makers of these streets had notions of dignity and order, but were not prophets of the lives that would take place in their creation. They had little theory of the future, of city-making, of architecture, of what they were doing. It was automatic architecture, made with limited vision or intent, which yet reflected the needs and desires of its future users, both those who would live in the houses and those who would pass through its streets. It allowed the semi-nomadic dwellers of cities to form their multiple, overlapping universes.

In cases like Dean's and Soane's the idea of home can seem a pathology, and it eventually consumed Soane so much as to make him, as Cobbett said, 'unnatural'. He lived at a time when the architects were converting themselves from elevated craftsmen into organized professionals, and an important purpose of his house was to store, celebrate, and disseminate architectural knowledge. It was a personal institution, a prototype of the Royal Institute of British Architects, the professional body which was created by others towards the end of his life. Soane has been described as a 'father' of the profession, which is striking, given his unsuccessful parenthood of his sons. One could argue, at a stretch, that the British architectural profession was incubated by personal dysfunction. You might say that part of its DNA is to miss the human point; to make expert, occasionally beautiful, evasions or consolations like the Soane house and museum. Certainly such a theory would explain many architectural mishaps of the last century and a half.

The multiple meanings of 'home', its ability to contain in four letters concepts of family, life, building, belonging, longing, house, village, land, property, shelter both physical and spiritual, both container and thing contained, lend it to exploitation. It can be used, for example, in political rhetoric: John Berger has pointed out how it justifies dubious ideas of domestic morality or, in 'homeland', of belligerent patriotism.

The density and portability of the word – its ability to mean so much with so little – has made it attractive to architects who want to add significance to their work. Many architects with fraught domestic arrangements have set themselves up as prophets of the home. Ludwig Mies van der Rohe and Frank Lloyd Wright both left trails of marital failures and abandonments through their lives. Both made manifestos and masterpieces out of singular houses, such as Mies' Farnsworth House or Wright's Fallingwater. These are amazing things, dazzling essays on space and structure, and on man and nature, which borrow power from the idea that they are homes. They would be less interesting if they were abstract sculptures, if you could not imagine living in them, yet they would be inhabited only for a few decades, or years. Soon they became scheduled monuments, carefully restored after intensive fundraising campaigns, and opened to public tours led by eager interns. They would become museum pieces in the open air, exhibits on the theory of home.

And then there was Le Corbusier. He stayed married to one woman, Yvonne Gallis, for thirty-five years, but it was a relationship complicated by his infidelities, her alcoholism, their childlessness, and his formidable mother. In 1934 Corbusier and Yvonne moved into an apartment and studio on the top floor of a block he had designed in a street named after two aviators, Nungesser and Coli, near to the Roland Garros tennis stadium in Paris. It remained their home until they died, she in 1957, he in 1965. It is an unconsciously eloquent summary of Le Corbusier's feelings about his life.

It is, generally, beautiful, opening up to daylight and views of Paris, with moments of intricacy and shadow. Areas of colour are composed with the eye of someone who, as Le Corbusier did, painted every morning. A stair of medieval simplicity winds up to a favourite Corbusian feature, a roof garden, via a glass pavilion where inside and outside overlap. The studio, where he painted, is ample, high, and vaulted, with bars of sunshine running across the exposed rough stone of the party wall.

The bedroom, meanwhile, is cramped and unsettled. Le Corbusier loved modern appliances, as pure products of industry, and as means to a hygienic life, and here sanitaryware becomes a form of artillery. Two washbasins, a bath, shower, bidet, and toilet bombard the space, exposed or partly concealed by partitions. Fixed cupboards further crowd the room. The bed is a broad board, perched high on thin steel tubes, so as to allow a view over an external parapet. A place of repose, or Eros, or tenderness, it is not. (And the other marital beds Corbusier designed were even worse. At the house he built for his mother on Lake Geneva he

provided a pair of Spartan bunks, one over the other, for himself and Yvonne; in his Cabanon, the tiny retreat he built at Cap Martin on the French Riviera, there is only a hard single bed. Yvonne had to sleep in a cafe next door.)

The serene splendour of the studio, compared with the nerviness of the bedroom, suggests someone who was more at ease with work than home, and documentary evidence bears this out. Yet Le Corbusier did not only, as Mies and Wright did, make private houses into famous artworks. He also proposed plans for cities of the future where homes, arranged in towers and blocks, were the main shaping and organizing element. It is not inevitable that homes are the primary stuff of cities: earlier grand urban plans centred on public spaces and monuments, for example the net of boulevards that Baron Haussmann laid in Paris in the 1850s and '60s, or the avenues that Pope Sixtus V had cut through Rome in the late sixteenth century.

Le Corbusier chose to make homes his main ingredient because he saw redesigning the home as the key to re-forming society. 'The problem of the house', he said, 'is a problem of the epoch. The equilibrium of society to-day depends upon it. Architecture has for its first duty, in this period of renewal, that of bringing about a revision of values, a revision of the constituent elements of the house.' A house should be as practical, efficient, and beautiful as a machine ('one *can* be proud of having a house as serviceable as a typewriter'). Then, 'if we eliminate from our hearts and minds all dead concepts in regard to the houses and look at the question from a critical and objective point of view, we shall arrive at the "House-Machine", the mass-production house, healthy (and morally so too) and beautiful in the same way that the working tools and instruments which accompany our existence are beautiful.' This was not a purely functional idea – the 'animation that the artist's sensibility can add to severe and pure functioning elements' was part of it. Illogic, waste, confusion, and sentimentality were, however, excluded.

The destiny of Le Corbusier's theories is one of the most-told stories in architecture. When post-war reconstruction demanded the rapid building of huge numbers of homes, European governments and contractors found much to like in his idea of vast, repetitive blocks and towers. Certain crucial elements of his plans got lost, however, to issues of time and money, and to indifference. The well-kept parks and sports grounds that he imagined in the spaces between his towers usually failed to materialize. The 'artist's sensibility' was rarely to be seen. His ideas of efficiency were adopted; his visions of beauty were not.

It also turned out that Le Corbusier had misread human nature. He had thought that 'a well mapped-out scheme, constructed on a mass-production basis, can give a feeling of calm, order and neatness, and inevitably imposes discipline on the inhabitants'. But humanity was not as ready to abandon the sentimental as he had hoped. There was no inevitable link between rational design and disciplined living. Rather, the public housing projects that loosely followed his theories were soon reviled as inhumane and soulless, and as havens of vandalism and crime.

This story is over-simplified. One can point to estates of Corbusian towers that are happy and peaceful, as one can point to traditional streets where life is vicious and troubled. But it is fair to say that he was proved wrong in his belief that society would be transformed for the better by the building of 'healthy and beautiful' homes. Like Dean and Soane he overrated the redeeming power of the physical object.

It is easy to see the absurdity of a belief in the healing power of masonry – it is a superstition, animism – but people fall for it again and again, and they are not entirely wrong to do so. For if it is a mistake to think that a house can mend a family, the opposite is also false. That is, the built background to our lives is not irrelevant, either. To put the case negatively, the wrong kinds of buildings can inflict misery and frustration. A world in which the dwelling becomes a purely technical question is not appealing.

We want buildings to embellish, beautify, dignify, distract, or divert. We want them to propose and to enable: to suggest what could be, to make things possible, to give freedoms. The passion that Dean, Soane, and the Surinamese put into inhabitation shows how much this matters. The idea of home, whether expressed as stable cosmos or as nomadic wandering, shows a basic truth, which is that the space we occupy is not neutral to us. We cannot look at it with detachment. We are in it, we make it, and it makes us.

What are mysterious are the ways in which physical surroundings interact with our desires. If Dean Gardens or the Corbusian mass-produced house seem over-determined and clumsy, where exactly do they go wrong? How might a builder or an architect make a happier relation of stuff to humanity?

The assumption behind Dean Gardens, or the Soane house, or Le Corbusier's theories, is that there is a close alignment of form and content: that if a mansion represents happy family life such life will take place within it, or that orderly design will lead to orderly people. (Similar conceptions have played their part in the global economy, when the illusionary solidity of owning a home contributed to the American sub-prime crisis. As the US Secretary of Housing and Urban Development Shaun Donovan put it, 'the built environment helped create the economic crisis'.)

The Surinamese colonization of Bijlmermeer almost proves the opposite of Dean's assumption: it suggests that people can make their home anywhere, without or despite the contribution of built form, albeit with considerable struggle. The Notting Hill story suggests that the planning and design of cities can after all make a difference to the futures they will contain, but with luck and unpredictable events along the way.

The disappointments of Dean, Soane, and Corb show that they misjudged the power of form, and imagined a too-direct connection between the inanimate and the animate. If there is cause and effect in the relations of minerals and people, it is more circuitous and reciprocal, and less linear. If there is truth in architecture, its shape is not immediately obvious.

3: The true fake

That 'home' can mean both container and thing contained shows that buildings are both symbols and instruments. They represent a purpose, and they serve it. If 'home' holds this doubleness with exceptional compression, it also occurs in other types: office, school, and church can be both building and use.

That buildings are both symbols and instruments makes architecture deceptive and fickle, sometimes comic. It is possible for a building to look as if it is doing something when it is not, or is even obstructing its apparent aim. This is what Larry Dean so expensively discovered. His home (the building), far from strengthening his home (the family), contributed to its dissolution.

The joke is that architecture is supposed to be practical, but it keeps tripping over its pretensions. Raine, Countess Spencer, stepmother of Princess Diana, would summon the architect of her house in Bognor Regis each time a light bulb needed changing, which he did, until she belatedly paid his bill. Hers was one, highly functional, view of the role of an architect, which is not shared by many in the profession: generally they think their job is to contribute an added something to the question of shelter. An architect assumes a certain dignity, and an air of mastery, but can be made a fool by physical fact. What buildings are supposed to do is one thing; what they actually do is another.

The British architect Richard Rogers once said:

one of the things which we are searching for is a form of architecture which, unlike classical architecture, is not perfect and finite upon completion . . . We are looking for an architecture rather like some music and poetry which can actually be changed by the users, an architecture of improvisation.

Rogers designed the Lloyd's Building in London and (with Renzo Piano) the Pompidou Centre in Paris, whose aesthetic was based on this idea of improvisation and change. The two buildings, completed in 1986 and 1977, had pipes, lifts and escalators placed on the outside to leave unobstructed space inside. In theory these elements could be unclipped, replaced, and rearranged to suit the changing needs of the buildings' users. In the case of the Pompidou Centre they enabled flexible galleries where partitions and displays of art might be rearranged at will, while the escalator that climbed the diagonal of the main facade invited the public to enter and explore. Still glowing with 1960s ideas of freedom, the Pompidou Centre aimed to be the opposite of the traditional idea of a museum as treasure house, fixed, fortified, and stern. The Centre promised liberation, flux, and flow.

The pipes and tubes also looked arresting. In the orderly, bone-coloured streets of Paris they made an apparition of colour and life, a statement of revolutionary intent. In London their forms were burnished and exaggerated, to create an intricacy that one critic compared to a motorcycle engine, another 'to the vision of Gaudi'.

But, according to the American writer and environmentalist Stewart Brand, the Pompidou 'requires prodigious amounts of maintenance' and was 'an exorbitant scandal of rust and peeling paint'.

Lloyd's was

one of the most expensive buildings ever made. A 1988 survey showed that 75 percent of its occupants wanted to move back

to their old 1958 building across the street. The vaunted adaptivity in the building was all high-tech and at a grandiose scale, oblivious to the individual worker and workgroup.

(At least, this is what he said in the American edition of his book, *How Buildings Learn*. His British publishers, under pressure from Rogers' lawyers, replaced them with tamer passages, about other buildings by other architects.)

In other words, Brand claimed, the look of flexibility was one thing, the reality another, and another statement of Rogers' on Lloyd's revealingly blurs look and use:

> the key to this changing juxtaposition of parts is the legibility of the role of each technological component which is functionally expressed to the full . . . Each single element is isolated and used to give order. Nothing is hidden, everything is expressed. The legibility of the parts gives the building scale, grain and shadow.

Rogers shuttles unconsciously between function ('technological component') and appearance ('scale, grain and shadow'). The exposure of the pipes, explained at other times as an aid to flexibility – that is, as something useful – is here a matter of 'expression' and 'legibility'. The building is a sign of flexibility as much as its instrument.

While pricking the claims of high architecture like Rogers', Brand extols the virtues of 'low road' buildings, modest practical structures that can be extended or altered easily, and are often adapted to uses unforeseen when they were built. A garage becomes a clothes shop, a shipping container becomes a library. The designers of such structures are often unknown and/or without professional qualifications, and their aesthetic ambitions are limited, but over time they inspire affection.

His definitive comparison is between two buildings at the Massachusetts Institute of Technology, Building 20 and Media Lab. Building 20 was 'a sprawling 250,000 square foot three-storey wood structure . . . constructed hastily in 1943 for the urgent development of radar, and almost immediately slated for demolition.' Media Lab was purpose-built in 1986 to house 'people collaborating on deep research in fast-evolving computer and communication technologies'. It was designed by I. M. Pei, who a few years later was voted 'the most influential living American architect' in a poll of the American Institute of Architects.

Building 20 was eventually demolished in 1998, decades later than first planned, having become, according to one user, the 'best experimental building ever built'. Also called the 'plywood palace' or the 'magical incubator', it housed some of MIT's greatest achievements, in communications, linguistics, nuclear science, cosmic rays, acoustics, food technology, stroboscopic photography, and computing. Its users said its secret was that it was 'a very matter-of-fact building' where 'one never needs to worry about injuring the architectural or artistic value of the environment'. Researchers could move partitions, knock holes in walls, nail things to the structure, and open windows when they wanted. They could adapt it to their practical needs, and make their corner of it personal. Building 20's other great asset was its spreading, horizontal layout, which encouraged chance meetings and impromptu collaborations.

Brand accused Media Lab, by contrast, of '$45million pretentiousness, ill-functionality, and non-adaptability' whose 'vast, sterile atrium' 'cuts people off from each other'. 'From nowhere can you see other humans in the five-storey-high space. Where people might be visible, they are carefully obscured by internal windows of smoked glass.' The building's rigidity made 'growth and new programmes nearly impossible' and its planning exacerbated 'academic turf battles from the first day'.

Brand is persuasive: few, given the choice between down-to-earth wisdom and pretentious folly, would side with the latter. Except that, taken to an extreme, his thesis could lead to a world where all buildings are like Gap khakis: practical but dull. The role of appearance, of illusion, dream, symbol, and imagination, is little discussed.

This becomes clear when he described the fifteenth-century palazzo Ca d'Oro in Venice. Here he admired the flank wall of the building, a brick history of adaptations with Brandian qualities of responsiveness and flexibility. Rightly so, but he gave less attention to the building's main facade, a curtain of marble hung above its reflection in the Grand Canal, embroidered with carving. This was lavish and relatively unchanging, and not much to do with practicality. Originally its details were decorated with gold leaf and ultramarine paint, even though these flourishes would soon flake away in the salty Venetian air. The owners knew they would, and ostentatious wastefulness was the point. It is the wilfully expensive facade, not the pleasingly adaptive brick flank wall, that makes the Ca d'Oro famous, and brings millions of tourists to see it. Brand's arguments do not explain such an apparition.

At its most obvious level, the symbolic nature of architecture can be described in terms of display and propaganda; buildings are used to send out messages, true or not. The Ca d'Oro was built for Marino Contarini, whose family over the centuries supplied eight doges to Venice, and as the historian Deborah Howard puts it, its 'preposterously extravagant gestures' were 'a demonstration of his wealth and status'. She guesses that it may also have been a memorial to his wife, who died young. The palace was therefore ceremonial as well as residential, and was designed accordingly.

The Pompidou Centre was created by a conservative client, President Georges Pompidou, who wanted to look progressive. Taking office the year after the student riots of May 1968, his main task was to restore order, and if he decreed that an avant-garde palace of art should rise from the paving stones that had so recently been ripped up and thrown at policemen, his purpose was not to celebrate revolution but to tame it. If the building's long-haired young architects looked, as they did, much like the student rioters, so much the better. The building might look alarming to traditionalists. It might even create some genuine pleasures and freedoms, and allow people to occupy and enjoy the old city in new ways, such as the famous ride up its external escalator. But radical architecture was better, from the Gaullist president's point of view, than radical politics. The piazza formed in front of the Centre would allow young performers to juggle balls and eat fire, which improved on hurling stones and Molotov cocktails.

Lloyd's of London, the insurance market begun in 1688, was also a conservative client and, afraid in its own way of seeming too antiquated, also wanted the look of change. With both Pompidou and Lloyd's, when Rogers conjured the dazzling appearance of modernity, he was fulfilling part of his brief. And what he achieved was more than propaganda: the Pompidou Centre really does change the experience of the Marais, where it sits, and of Paris, even as it leaves the political status quo intact. It is a negotiation, a deal, between the establishment and the young architects, where each got something of what they wanted.

To see how thoroughly buildings can mislead, you can visit the gilded pavilions of the All-Union Agricultural Exhibition, which covers an area larger than the principality of Monaco, in the Moscow suburb of Ostankino. It is one of the more outstanding examples of deceitful construction in the country that gave the concept of the Potemkin Village to the world. The exhibition was conceived in 1935 as a celebration of the abundance of Soviet agriculture, two years after the greatest of a series of famines induced by communist policies had killed between six and eight million people. It also celebrated the fraternity of the sixteen republics of the Soviet Union at a time when regional identity was being murderously suppressed.

The original idea was that the project would open in 1937, for the twentieth anniversary of the revolution, but slow progress delayed it until 1939. Then there was disappointment – the temporary wooden structures were considered underwhelming. For this crime, together with an unlucky choice of political patron, the exhibition's architect, Vyacheslav Oltarzhevsky, served four years' exile in the Gulag city of Vorkuta.

The exhibition was reinvigorated after the Second World War, untroubled by a further famine in 1947, which killed one to one-and-a-half million. It was finally completed in 1954, a campus dotted with declamatory structures in the manner of World's Fairs and Great Exhibitions. Each republic had a pavilion, as did important branches of agriculture – grain, meat, rabbit-breeding – and the buildings mattered more than their contents. In the Pavilion of the Mechanization and Electrification of Agriculture a huddle of combine harvesters was out-dazzled by a glass dome mounted on filigree gilded steelwork. The machines were dwarfed by a statue of giant sturdy labourers, flanked by trumpeting children, ascending towards a golden banner and radiant five-pointed star.

Unlike World's Fairs and Great Exhibitions, the architecture of the Agricultural Exhibition made little attempt to look to the future. London in 1851 gave the world the Crystal Palace, Paris 1889 the Eiffel Tower, and Brussels in 1958 a building in the shape of an atom. The Moscow show was the fulfilment of Stalin's twenty-year search for a truly Soviet architecture, which turned out to be a form of Greek and Roman classicism, made fantastical with Asiatic details, and made mighty with the scale of American skyscrapers.

This style had diminishing interest in the future, or the modern, but drew its motifs from architecture of the past.

Party statements said that the aim was 'mastery of heritage', also 'clarity and precision . . . which must be easily comprehensible by and accessible to the masses', also 'art as stunningly simple as the heroism we find today in the Soviet Union'. As time passed the desire to impress the masses trumped the duty to simplicity. As in Moscow's famous metro stations, mosaics, marble, chandeliers, and rococo scrolls, the decadent stuff of aristocratic ballrooms, came to decorate the collective and functional spaces of the city. Like Stalin's public persona, this architecture combined force with charm, the twinkling eyes with the mailed fist.

At the Agricultural Exhibition the pavilions were only minimally constrained by their function of sheltering exhibits, and their style tended towards the delirious. Architects, perhaps mindful of the penalty Oltarzhevsky paid for dullness, let rip. Greece and Rome are evoked, and Babylon and Assyria. Buildings typically establish close-packed rhythms, through crowded ranks of columns, banners, statues, carvings of crops or Soviet stars. This is the part that speaks of force, with military repetition and arrogant redundancy. The columns are bigger, denser, and more numerous than needed to support whatever they are supposed to carry (often, not much). They tell you they were built by a power that could spend what it wanted.

Then there is the charm, delivered with fanciful skylines of pinnacles and cupolas, parapets frilled with ornament, and carving explicit as a child's picture book. White and gold dominate. Embrasures are fecund with plump carved produce, maize, sunflowers, pears, grapes, pumpkins, almost unbearable in their superabundance. Statues are noble and handsome, and wholesomely clothed. Carved into the pediment of the Karelian-Finnish pavilion, lumberjacks hew trees with chainsaws, to get the stuff – timber – of which the pavilion is made.

Literalism reigns, but with lacunae. Bulls surmount the capitals of the Pavilion of the Ministry of Meat Production. A farmer, hunter, shepherdess, and miner help carry the entablature of the Siberia Pavilion, with no hint of the inmates of forced labour camps, who then formed the majority of the republic's population. A frieze on the Pavilion of Rabbit-Breeding shows bas-relief lagomorphs at frolic, presumably pre- or post-coital, although the sculptor was too coy to show the eponymous breeding in progress.

A central avenue is staked out with great fountains. One, the Stone Flower, heaps up basket-loads of fruit and vegetables, jugs, and water-spewing geese. In another, the Friendship of Nations, sixteen gold women embody the republics of the Soviet Union. Their colour is electrically bright and sweet as syrup, and their arms spread in gestures of peace. In the centre a gilded sheaf of wheat rises, crowned with spumes of water that echo the nodding ears of corn.

The exhibition ground was later renamed the Exhibition of National Economic Achievements, and themes such as space exploration were added. It continues to this day as an underpopulated ground for trade shows, where the silt of commerce gathers: cubicles selling woollens, phone parts, and souvenirs lap at the bases of giant columns; suburban show homes appear next to the white-pillared pavilions; hawkers sell the opportunity to be photographed with SpongeBob SquarePants and characters from *Shrek*, with an old bronze Lenin ignored and impotent behind. The place is too grand to be demolished, but too big to be useful.

The obvious lies of the All-Union Agricultural Exhibition, told by its buildings with such energy and persuasion, were that Soviet agriculture was productive, efficient, and abundant, and that the republics of the Union were happy and fraternal. There was a further one: the exhibition is a statement of Stalinist authority, expressed in an extreme form of the styles developed under him for Moscow's skyscrapers and metro. It is a bubble in time, indifferent

to the modern styles of architecture to be found then in almost every other country in the world. Looking at these confident structures you would have no sense that Stalin died the year before they were completed, and that his cult was on the verge of decline. As is often the case in architecture, it celebrates the almost gone.

At the same time there is, if you know how to look, a truth. The most glittering of the pavilions, centrally located by the Stone Flower fountain, is the Ukrainian, decorated with rapidly repeating verticals to recall a field of wheat, and a crown-like superstructure. Its grandeur reflects the wishes of the First Secretary of the Ukrainian Communist Party, who declared a previous pavilion inadequate. If you detected political ambition in a man who wanted to outshine his comrades' structures, you would be right. This First Secretary was Nikita Khrushchev, who would become leader of the Soviet Union after Stalin's death, and lead the campaign of de-Stalinization. As a document of the power politics of its time, the exhibition is, to this extent at least, perfectly honest.

The theme of architecture as propaganda is rich. A personal favourite is Kijŏng-dong, a prosperous- and harmonious-looking North Korean town in sight of South Korea, which turns out to have no glass in its windows nor rooms behind its walls, where the lights are turned on and off from time to time to give an appearance of inhabitation. It also has the second-highest flagpole in the world (the tallest is in Azerbaijan) in order to outdo anything the South Koreans might erect. Buildings are powerful tools for saying black is white, and persuasive ways of presenting fictions as reality. It is an important, but limited aspect of architecture.

The use of architecture to make political points is a sub-set of a larger group, of buildings as PR, as boosterism, as selling, as message. Over the last two decades the idea of the iconic building has grown, where a spectacularly shaped building is thought to attract tourism and investment to a city, with the 1997 Guggenheim Museum in Bilbao being an early example, and still the best known. The idea has proved remarkably persistent, despite scepticism expressed by critics early on, and despite the obvious fact that it is a currency that devalues with overuse: if Milwaukee *and* Middlesbrough *and* Guadalajara *and* Chengdu have their icons, each is as interesting, or as boring, as each other.

When architecture is used to deliver messages it tends to resemble language. A building becomes a word or a sentence. Sometimes the idea of building-as-word is taken to an extreme: the critic Charles Jencks once celebrated hot-dog stands shaped like hot dogs and doughnut stands shaped like doughnuts. He also drew attention to imaginary projects by eighteenth-century French architects, such as the cow-shaped cowshed of Jean-Jacques Lequeu, and a phallus-shaped brothel by Claude-Nicolas Ledoux.

But the moment the message of a building is translated into words, it is drained of life. Construction allows only ponderous sentences, compared to writing or speaking, and if its expense and labour only goes to state clumsily what could be written – 'buy a doughnut', 'Stalin rules', 'invest in Bilbao', 'here be cows/sex' – it hardly seems worth the trouble. There is a minor genre of imitative architecture, which included Jencks' hot dog, but it remains minor because it is an idea that only gets you so far before you discover that there is not very much to say.

Lequeu's cowshed and Ledoux's brothel are engaging, but only if they are seen as deliberately absurd – you stop and look because you can't believe someone has done something so literal-minded. Why would you want a giant inanimate cow, when you have the living, breathing creatures to hand? Among other things a giant built cow is nothing like a real one: they have nothing in common – not life, scale, smell, or temperature – but shape. In the end, a

Fig. 174.

L'Etable à Vache tournée au midi, et sur la fraîche prairie

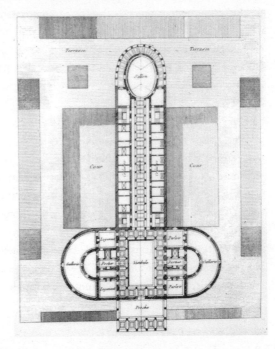

doughnut you can eat gives more pleasure than one you can only look at.

The thing about buildings is that they are built. They are works of time and stuff, of materials drawn from the earth, and hewn, cut, woven, melted, baked, soaked, purified, and electrolysed, and made to stand in weather and light. Materials have their own properties, limits, beauty, and recalcitrance. Their assembly requires force, skill and labour. Buildings involve risk and danger: construction can kill and maim, projects can bankrupt people. They are decorated and furnished, and re-decorated and re-furnished, usually by people with little connection to the original construction and design.

They are made through collaboration and competition. They are commissioned by clients, financed by banks, regulated by planners, designed by architects and engineers, built by contractors and sub-contractors, sold by agents. Lawyers write the contracts, plumbers fix the pipes, and critics write the reviews. Buildings engage, as few other creations do, lives of divergent wealth, interests, and comfort, from the labourer digging a hole to the financiers paying the bills. It is unlikely that all will like, understand, or even know each other, but they have to make something together. Every building is part Babel.

Then they are inhabited and used. One, quite rare, form of inhabitation is the client living in the house he or she has had built. More often people buy or rent homes commissioned by developers who live somewhere else, or are long dead. A school is inhabited by teachers, pupils, janitors, and visiting parents and governors, each of whom use it and see it in a different way. A building will also be part of a city or a landscape, and will be experienced by passers-by and neighbours. It will form part of the background of their lives.

Users and uses change: staff coming and going at offices and factories, annual intakes of schoolchildren, patients at hospitals leaving for their home or the grave. A Tudorbethan suburb, built in the 1930s to suit the tastes of Anglo-Saxon clerks, might be settled by a south Asian middle class. A school might become flats, a power station an art gallery, a church a mosque. A building might be altered or extended. Or, even if its fabric is untouched, perceptions of it might change. Its style might go out of and into fashion. A structure seen as oppressive by one generation might be loved by the next.

Buildings, seemingly so fixed, are always in motion. From conception to demolition, they are negotiations between the people who make, use, and experience them. They age and weather. They are propositions about the lives they might contain, always subject to revision. They are prone to nemesis and slapstick: the stone portico of a bust bank, the palace of a deposed dictator, a bridge to nowhere.

Construction contracts are usually about certainty and completion. They are about reaching the point where all parties can agree that the job is done, and can go off and do another project. With few exceptions the creation of architecture requires people to delineate, measure, divide, and fix. Buildings are also described in magazines and history books as finite and immobile. They are photographed at their most pristine moment, often in the very early morning, when the balance of light and shadow is easier for cameras to handle. Extraneous matter – road signs, other buildings, often people – is generally excluded. The primacy of the architectural object is stressed.

Yet buildings are always incomplete. Or rather, they are completed only by the lives for which they are the setting. From this paradox comes much of the fascination and misunderstanding of architecture.

All of which gives architecture a particular relation to intention, and truth. A building is not a sentence, which in principle has the ability to match and express a thought closely. It is not linear, like language. Compared to the fluidity of words, a building is atrociously clumsy, but it can be lived and inhabited as books cannot be.

A building that sets out with one intention is prone, thanks to the many people and accidents that will shape it, to end up with different, opposite, or multiple effects. It creates a reality different from its stated aim, and allows future, as yet unknown, realities to take place within it. This is a quality of architecture – the way it transforms – and one definition of bad architecture would be buildings that deny its special form of mutable complexity, that try to behave too much like words. A luxury apartment building that decides to look like a diamond, for example. A museum dedicated to a sheikh who loved falconry, which claims to look like wing feathers. Works like this do violence to their medium.

There is a public laundry in southern Portugal – possibly was, as the ultimate victory of the washing machine may have caused its demolition. Externally it is as basic as a bus shelter, a long oblong with one open side, with white plastered walls of concrete block, and a shallow monopitch concrete roof. A single central pillar props the roof above the open side. It has no windows, doors, or glazing. It stands on the border of a dusty road, among untended vegetation. It has no insignia to say what it is: no one from outside its village needs to know, and its purpose is self-evident.

Beneath the roof is a tank of water whose surface – unless churned by washing – is smooth as lacquer. A precise rim, rounded and level, holds it, and is punctured in one place to allow a trickle out. Two pipes project unevenly from the wall, crude valveless taps from which water enters. Beneath and around them asymmetric clouds of damp spread on the plaster wall. On a hot day

the shadowy tank is a pool of relief, a poor person's Alhambra. Its depth is hard to fathom, as the water reflects both the rough concrete soffit of the roof and a slot of sky which, bleached when viewed directly, becomes a richer blue.

A channel runs outside the rim, outside which is a concrete shelf, sloping inwards. The shelf is punctuated by squares of marble, on which clothes can be scrubbed, spaced far enough apart to give enough room for one person to work at each slab. The structure as a whole is scaled to allow room to move around the tank, and around others working at it.

This functional building is attuned to climate and society. It would not work in the same way in a colder place, and it is the artefact of a community where working together at laundry is (or was) normal, and where there is sufficient collective organ-ization to create this communal facility. It is scaled around the actions of washing. Materials – concrete, marble, water – are used as needed. Details are rough or precise as the occasion demands. It is hard to know how self-consciously it was designed, but its guiding principle is graceful economy. It is austere, but accidentally sensual.

Advertently or not, it makes connections. It connects people to climate, being an architecture of temperatures that run from the cold water to the hot dust outside. This anonymous work creates an ambiguity of inside and out of a kind for which famous works of modernist architecture are celebrated.

It represents. It is in an interruption in space and time shaped by and giving shape to certain values. It is completed only by the actions that take place within it, and they by it. It is without words. It does not mimic: the laundry does not try to look like clothes, but shapes and is shaped by the activity it serves.

It is easy to imagine that a building should look like its contents, that an art museum should look like an artwork, for example, and be 'creative' and 'sculptural', or that an airport should look as though it is about to take off. Or that the development of deprived areas should take on soaring lines of hope. But it is hard to overstate how bizarre this idea is, even if it is the basis of some large and expensive buildings by much-praised architects. A little contemplation of Lequeu's cow-shaped cowshed might help to reveal its absurdity: there is almost no reason why a container should look like the thing contained. A building built like a means of transport is as dumb as a ship made of bricks; you don't have to eat strawberries off strawberry-shaped plates.

What both buildings and crockery can do, depending on the way they are made and of what, is change the physical and social experience of things they serve. A meal off bone china is not like one off plastic, or off a white plate or a yellow one, or one decorated with gilded sprigs, or with a picture of Peter Rabbit eating radishes. Chopsticks and forks imply different cuisines and different etiquettes. It is similar with buildings: they complement, they reciprocate.

Between two watery works, the Portuguese laundry and the Friendship of Nations fountain, runs much of architecture. Both represent, but one through use and the other through signs; one through doing and the other through looking. Most buildings do something of both. The Asamkirche in Munich, also known as St Johann Nepomuk, tends towards the fountain's end of the scale more than the laundry's – it was built to convince – but it would be too simple to call it propaganda. It is a good example of the mutability of truth in architecture.

Built from 1733 to 1746, and set just away from the city's centre, it is the expression of devotion, to God and architecture, of the brothers Egid Quirin and Cosmas Damian Asam. Between them

they shared the skills of architect, sculptor, stuccoist, and painter, and together they made themselves famous as the creators of hallucinatory churches in eighteenth-century Bavaria. Egid Quirin then bought a plot himself and spent his own money on a church where, unimpeded by the whims of clients, the two could build exactly what they wanted. He bought a house next door, added a new facade, and lived there. A window in the party wall between house and church allowed him to look into his and his brother's creation from his home.

The Asamkirche is in a similar category of obsessive personal cosmos to Sir John Soane's house and museum, or Dean Gardens. At the same time, it has a public use, in that congregations can worship there, and it was part of the culture in which it sat. The Asams' careers were spent serving a society presided over by the Electors of Bavaria, who with the help of the Catholic Church were intent on preserving a view of the world that was still partly medieval. By then the scientific revolution had come, the Industrial Revolution was coming, and the Enlightenment was soon to come, but the Asams, and their patrons and rulers, wished all away. Their church is a confident, or desperate, assertion of the old order.

It swells and froths into a street of flat-fronted six-storey houses and upwards through their cornice line. Apart from white, its colours are pink, liverish purple, orange, a submarine or malachite green: they are secondary colours not primary, not pure but made by mixing. Stucco fruit is strung in swags through space, virtuosic in their realism and fragility, and capturing clear air. If the fruit were any more detached from the building it would fall off. A spume of ribbons, fronds, and angels spreads onto the facade of Egid Quirin's house next door, enlisting it in the church's rapture. Most strangely, a rockery breaks out at pavement level, as if the church was fastened against an Alpine slope. The rocks' naturalism makes them the more unreal, as all the evidence of the surrounding environment is that you are not in the Alps (which, on a clear day, are visible from the city).

This is just the facade, the throat-clearing before the interior. But before I describe the *horror vacui* reigning inside, which demands that surfaces wriggle with ornament, like gorgeous bugs beneath an upturned stone, it is worth introducing a thought from another century and another part of Germany. 'Architecture', said the twentieth-century Frankfurt thinker Walter Benjamin, 'is experienced as background or not at all'.

At first this sounds sad, or at least a call to sobriety. It seems to suggest that architecture's role is to stand behind the actions and dramas of life, to be discreet and reticent. At different times architects and writers have urged just such an architecture of dignified anonymity, the opposite of the Asamkirche. As Ludwig Wittgenstein, philosopher and occasional architect, said of Dublin's plain brick Georgian terraces, such architecture 'has the good taste to know that it has nothing very important to say'.

On further reflection, Benjamin's remark turns out to be less limiting. The Alps can be a background, as can the Rio carnival, the Manhattan skyline, or even a battle, and all have been backgrounds in plays or films. Some films – *Metropolis*, *Blade Runner* – are defined as much by their settings as their stories. If architecture is background, it can colour, shape, inhibit, or enhance the events of our lives. Most memorable things are bound to the place where they happen, and cannot be imagined without their setting, which is why people like to choose where they are married, or commemorated, or celebrate birthdays, and usually remember where they were when they fell in love, or heard of calamities. If architecture is background, it becomes more important, not less.

At a simple level, the choice of stainless steel or oak panelling or velvet drapes or Formica helps define the nature of a restaurant, and of what happens there; wall tiles seem normal in a

bathroom, strange in a dining room, unless that dining room is from seventeenth-century Holland, or is Iberian.

If architecture is background there are consequences. The first is the need of all architectural space, however magnificent or perfect, to be completed by something outside itself, even if this might sometimes be no more than a private thought by a single person passing through. Buildings whose architects forget this, that strive to be all foreground and allow no room for completion, fail.

And if architecture entwines itself with experiences of life, it has to be asked how dumb building materials do this. How can the effects of inert matter be described without resort to notions of action-at-a-distance such as those used flailingly by scientists before magnetism or gravity were understood? How, too, to avoid cod psychology, of the kind that dwells on the uprights and orifices of architecture?

There is no quick answer, but to find a slow answer it helps to go back to the Asams, to what they thought they were doing – what truths they believed were embodied in their architecture – and to what they actually did. The Asams assumed possibly without question that a building could represent a reality beyond itself, and at the simplest level their church was what churches had been for centuries: an image of heaven, rendered in explicit works of sculpture and painting. Thus the interior takes you towards an altar lit by a sunburst of divine illumination, and to a ceiling cracked open by illusionistic painting to an infinite sky, into which St John of Nepomuk is transported on clouds and angels up from the scene of his martyrdom in the Vltava River. A crucified Christ hangs in the space between altar and vault, joining the upper and lower worlds. A cast of saints hovers in attendance. Strong horizontals – balustrades and cornices – define boundaries between you, an earthbound mortal, and the celestial vision above, boundaries that can only be transcended by the intercession of the man on the cross, with the help of the Church.

So far so clear, but also so fairly boring, as there is little in this description to distinguish the church from a theological tract, or the 'Rapture' books that describe imminent Armageddon. It is an account of beliefs. What makes the church interesting is that it has to represent its imagery using physical stuff, in a specific time and place, and that it will be inhabited by human beings. If the idea is simple, the progression from the mortal to the celestial, its realization is anything but. The substances and techniques known to the Asams are exploited, and the multiple properties of materials are mined. There are resonances, reversals, and surprises.

The church follows an old and basic pattern whereby a hall is enclosed by walls, with columns helping to support the roof, and define subsidiary spaces, except that here expectations of weight and structure are confounded. The walls are made by thin mouldings to look papery and insubstantial, while the palpably substantial columns are thrust into space, seemingly unsupported and supporting nothing: deprived of their correct and industrious role as supporters of a building, they become decorative adjuncts, like construction workers in a fashion shoot. The rule seems to be that anything that looks heavy and rounded must fly, while walls sustaining the building must look light and flat.

Games are played with appearance and reality. Some of the marble is real and some fake, but it is not always easy to know which. Sometimes, in the pews and the confessional booths, wood is clearly wood; sometimes it is sculpted beyond recognition into garlands of fruit and flowers. Daylight is augmented by yellow glass and by gilded, carved sunbeams. The ceiling contains painted architecture, which continues the three-dimensional stuff below.

Echoes start to yodel across the space: the S-curves of sculpted

ribbons with those of turbulent cornices, with those of angels' drapery, and those of vegetal ironwork. Two long painted plumes of smoke continue the upward twist of barley-sugar columns below them, stone becoming vapour, before becoming the clouds that carry the ascending saint. In the ceiling a crowd of citizens are shown witnessing the miraculous event, standing in a city (Prague, the scene of the saint's martyrdom) with recognizably central European towers. Although they are placed in the heavenly zone, above angels and saints, they are mortals, and echo the living congregation standing below them.

It begins to seem as if the church is made of a single foam, into which the identities of individual materials and images disappear and reappear. It only begins to seem like this, however: for all the church's fever of motion and illusion, the Asams continue to articulate differences and hierarchies. They do not want you to forget the difference between animals and objects, or people and God. The aim is not to melt all knowledge, but to create a space between experience and appearance in which the unseen can be revealed.

The immaterial – heaven – is rendered in matter, and in a place which contains the shuffling, smelling, imperfect bodies of the congregation. It is reached by a vestibule and a door off Sendlinger Strasse, a journey from the pavement of only a few feet. It is a vision of heaven made in Bavaria, 1733–46, a time and place with its own views of where it stands in relation to other times and places, and which can only create buildings and artefacts with its own imprint; which cannot do otherwise even if it wanted.

The Asamkirche is therefore an impossibility, a date-stamped eternity, infinity with party walls, heaven with street numbers. Perhaps the Asams could have depicted their paradise purely as a picture, utterly separate from the physical space of the viewers. They could have put them in blackness, like spectators in a cinema, so that their presence is minimized and a zone of disconnection formed between the image and the quotidian exterior. But they still could not have removed the incongruity of their idea, of meeting the saints almost as easily as you would a shopkeeper. Nor could they escape the fact that their image would have to have been made out of stuff: sloppy plaster hardened into fresco; hidden armatures of timber cut from forests; metals dragged from rocks and formed with heat; stones cut and moved with sweat and cursing. Their heaven had to be lit, whether by natural light from a window, which would in turn require construction, or by string and animal fat formed into candles.

The Asamkirche yearns to convince. It is as vivid as the available technology of illusion allowed. But the design lets you glimpse the stage machinery. The rocks at the entrance are real, unlike much of the pasteboard interior, but are palpably artificial in this location. They are the most real and the most fake elements in the church. They signal from the start that you are about to be offered an illusion.

The trompe l'œil paintings in the ceiling integrate with the architecture of the interior, with columns and arches in the painting apparently growing out of the physical construction of the church, but only when seen from one point. At others the vanishing points of the painted and the physical spaces differ, which is the immutable joke of illusionistic perspective: the more brilliant it is, the more strangely distorted it looks when seen from the wrong angle. No one would think that they truly were contemplating heaven, or that they were supposed to think they were.

The Asams wanted to represent their truth, but they did so with the help of fakery. To make the fake completely plausible would have been a lie, but they occasionally revealed the fictional nature of their illusion. Truth and fake flirt. Their consummation is a space which could be called a true fake, and it is the play of the two that just (barely) keeps the church from being kitsch. Compare it with depictions of heaven in movies or fundamentalist Christian writing. These are more certain about their abilities to convince even though they should be less so. Their vision is prescriptive and oppressive, leaving no room for the mind of the viewer or reader.

If the Asams wanted to create a personal universe, they risked imposing the tedium, and worse, of imposing private fantasies on others. Hearing other people's dreams is usually boring; living inside them is more so, and imposing them is a notorious vice of architects. Yet it is an architect's job to make worlds, and one who brings only indifference or neutrality creates another kind of tyranny.

Overwhelming though it is, the Asamkirche leaves a space to be occupied by the imagination. It is only finished by the movements, actions, readings, and imaginings of worshippers and viewers within it. This is one sense in which it is incomplete, or background, and it is so in other senses: it was designed as the setting for religious ritual and actions, and music, words, incense, and candles are part of the totality. If parts of it, like the ceiling, can be inhabited only by the eye and mind, others engage the whole body, and all the senses. It is specific to its time, and its gestures – an unconventional use of a conventional detail, a motif borrowed from another recent building – would have had particular meanings that are lost on modern viewers.

It is not however wasted on us, who look at it now. I am not an eighteenth-century Bavarian. I regard the miracles depicted in its paintings as no more probable than that the sun is pushed around the sky, as the Egyptians believed, by a giant dung beetle. Its sumptuousness is potentially repulsive to the Protestant/agnostic/modernist taste with which I grew up. I visit it as a tourist, a spectator, a writer on architecture. It has become an historical object, requiring an effort of imagination to animate it. My experience of it is more detached than that of eighteenth-century worshippers, channelled mostly through eye and mind and less, as it was for them, through body, movement, and other senses than sight. But it is not pointless for me. It does not leave me cold.

I appreciate its endeavour and virtuosity. More, there is the sense of being taken into something, into a proposition about people and our place in the universe. For the Asams this proposition was *the* truth; for me it is *a* truth, as in a play or painting. I do not have to accept literally and completely the authors' beliefs to be taken into the work, and moved or illuminated by it. This is because it is not verbal but built, and unfolds in matter and making, not in a message. It is not a sermon or a billboard but a space, which I can inhabit. I can move around in it, and change my experience of it through my movement.

The Asams' is a theatrical version of truthfulness, in which illusion and artifice are used to create a form of reality. There is another, almost opposite, idea of truth in architecture, which grew up in the nineteenth and twentieth centuries. It has variants, but the common theme is that buildings should honestly display what they are. Illusion, fakery, and dressing-up became taboo. To call a building a 'stage set' became an insult.

In *The Seven Lamps of Architecture* of 1849, John Ruskin wrote:

> Do not let us lie at all. Do not think of one falsity as harmless, and another as slight, and another as unintended. Cast them all aside: they may be light and accidental; but they are an ugly soot from the smoke of the pit, for all that; and it is better that our hearts should be swept clean of them, without over care as to which is the largest or blackest.

Rather he wanted artists and craftsmen to be faithful to the 'Lamp of Truth', which meant honestly revealing the materials and techniques with which a building was made, from which beauty would follow. Ignoring truth would lead to decadence and decline.

He thought there were three kinds of 'Architectural Deceit': the falsifying of the structure, the materials, and the craftsmanship of a building. He hated columns that supported nothing, the 'green and yellow sickness of false marble', and machine-made ornaments that imitated the handmade. 'Exactly as a woman of feeling', he fumed,

> would not wear false jewels, so would a builder of honour disdain false ornaments. The using of them is just as downright and inexcusable a lie. You use that which pretends to a worth which it has not; which pretends to have cost, and to be, what it did not, and is not; it is an imposition, a vulgarity, an impertinence, and a sin. Down with it to the ground, grind it to powder, leave its ragged place upon the wall, rather; you have not paid for it, you have no business with it, you do not want it.

The rewards of truthful architecture were great, and the penalties of false architecture were greater. For Ruskin medieval architecture reached a fateful turning point in the fourteenth century when, on 'reaching the place that was nearest heaven', builders started to abandon their true principles. The main crime came when 'the bars of tracery were caused to appear to the eye as if they had been woven together like a net'. This might seem harmless enough, and modern tourists find equal delight or boredom in works before or after the great fall Ruskin describes. They might for example like King's College Chapel, Cambridge (bad), as much as they like Chartres Cathedral (good). For Ruskin the difference is absolute: once stone was carved to look like weaving, it started to pretend that it was something it was not. Once medieval architecture made this error, 'its own truth was gone, and it sank for ever . . .

the error of zeal, and the softness of luxury, smote it down and dissolved it away'.

This is borderline bonkers, ranting of a distilled and exquisite kind. To see apocalypse in architectural detail makes hardly more sense than the sandwich board, for years carried up and down Oxford Street by a dedicated fanatic, that claimed that lentils caused lust. Yet this is one of the most influential texts of architectural history, underlying a recurring theme of modern architecture, that buildings should be 'true' to function, materials, structure, and the spirit of the age. In time the argument would lead to the elimination of ornament, as being a form of concealment, and the celebration of industrial materials, as being truthful to the age of machines. Ruskin would have loathed both developments, but from his words eventually derived office buildings that frankly displayed their steel or concrete frames. When Richard Rogers chooses to reveal the pipes and tubes that make a modern building work, he has a debt to Ruskin.

Ruskin ties himself in knots. Having proclaimed that the difference between truth and falsehood is absolute and inviolate, he proceeds to recognize some grey areas. Gilding, for example, is allowed, on the grounds that everybody knows that it is not solid gold but a film laid on something else. The painted pieces of architecture in Michelangelo's Sistine Chapel ceiling are permissible because you can see they are not really real. His modernist descendants performed similar contortions: Le Corbusier designed buildings that looked as if they were in the truthfully modern material of reinforced concrete, but were actually of plastered blockwork; Mies van der Rohe's Seagram Building in New York has vertical steel beams stuck to the exterior to symbolize the frame, unseen behind fire-proofing, that is actually holding the tower up.

Ruskin hated iron construction, which stopped him seeing that it should, by his reasoning, be exposed as much as stone or wood.

He rationed the material's right to be seen: 'it is evident that metals may, and sometimes must, enter into the construction to a certain extent, as nails in wooden architecture and therefore as legitimately rivets and solderings in stone.'

He went most awry when he attempted to convert his fervent personal experiences into immutable laws, when, using almost biblical language, he tried to issue commandments for the future construction of all buildings, and to judge, as at the last trump, between the blessed and the damned among architecture. Yet he commands attention, for the acute perception and sensitivity he brought to buildings. He invested the materials of construction with an emotional intensity few have matched, and seen through his eyes they become vivid, if also morbid. For example this, in *The Stones of Venice*, of the Basilica of Saint Mark:

> . . . and deep-green serpentine spotted with flakes of snow,
> and marbles, that half refuse and half yield to the sunshine,
> Cleopatra-like, 'their bluest veins to kiss'.

His writings on Truth have this much truth: that the ways buildings are built, and of what, are not neutral. Different stones, or timber frames, or ornament pressed in moulds as opposed to carved by hand, have individual properties. A granite block in a bridge abutment is used for its strength, a marble veneer in a hotel bathroom for its ease of maintenance and suggestions of luxury. The intricate carving on the palazzo Ca d'Oro intimates the wealth of the patron; the unvarying yellow M of McDonald's speaks of a corporation with the will and power to impose itself across the world. There is politics in stuff.

It is possible to celebrate material properties, or play with them, or to abuse and do violence to them. A rose carved out of soap, or a concrete cow, are striking because they are such unexpected uses for their materials, but for the same reason they verge on kitsch.

If a Palladian front is slapped on a modern office building, such that grids of fluorescent lights can be seen through the sash windows, the effect is uncomfortable. Palladian architecture usually implies a certain form of masonry construction, which requires cellular rooms that align with the windows on the elevation, so it is unsettling if an open-plan office is revealed. If thin pieces of wood are stuck to a brick house, to make it look vaguely like a Tudor structure of solid oak, or hand-made wooden mouldings are mimicked in extrusions of glass-reinforced plastic, the effect can also be cheap and nasty. If a column is pretending to hold something up, but its proportions or materials are such that it cannot be doing anything useful at all, it can look painful.

Then again most people admire, as Ruskin did, the elevation of the Ca d'Oro onto the Grand Canal, where heavy stone is made to look light and almost cloth-like. Effects of marble or wood grain in paint or plastic can have charm, especially if they are patently unconvincing. The Doric order of classical architecture, than which it is hard to get more august, is based on the imitation of wooden construction in stone, down to the laborious recreation of rows of pegs, called guttae, that in the timber originals held beams in place. As the Asam brothers showed in an extreme example, an architect might play with the apparent and inherent properties of construction – things that look like marble, or as if they are holding a building up, and in reality may or may not – in order to create a theatrical form of truth. It doesn't always have to be as extreme: the stucco house fronts of West London also have some qualities of theatre. They are a form of mask or make-up or dressing-up, a recognition that, to be yourself, you need some disguise.

There is no rule, just a sense that construction has a character that can be either respected or ignored. It can be respected in a Ruskinian way, which is to cherish and bring out its inherent qualities, or in the way of the Asams, which is to exploit these qualities to create illusions. What matters is that whatever is done, is done with awareness: with the sense that plaster is one thing, steel another, and we have perceptions and expectations of both. No final balance can be found between one way and the other, and there is no certainty as to what are right and wrong approaches.

Because buildings are both symbols and instruments, confusion arises, as in Richard Rogers' works in London and (with Renzo Piano) in Paris. These symbolize freedom and change but, because Rogers is a descendant of Ruskin, via modernist architecture, he cannot permit himself the theatrical fakery of the Asams. He has to use the exposed pipes and equipment as symbols, as props and stage sets, while still acting as if – probably himself believing that – their primary role is as instruments, as things that truly make, in practical terms, the Pompidou Centre and Lloyd's much more flexible and liberating than other buildings. There is not much evidence that they do, which exposes Rogers to Brand's ridicule. The double role of a pipe, like a plumber dressed in doublet and hose, or a Cleopatra dressed in overalls, can get a little absurd. If it is a practical aid to hygiene why is it coloured and exposed, such that it has to be expensively insulated against the cold? If it is a thespian flourish, why not get something less mundane to play the part?

At the level of image, Pompidou and Lloyd's work, brilliantly so. They have such visual verve, delivered with virtuosity and self-confidence, that their sheer retinal effect changes the perception and experience of their two cities. It is also more than visual, at least in the case of the Pompidou Centre. The forms of movement, and the physical relationships created by building, piazza, and escalator, change the experience and perception of Paris.

I would rather have a Rogers than a Brand design a palace of art in a great city, but to rely so heavily on the power of look cuts out much of architecture: the other senses, for a start, and the range of expression and appearance of which materials, light, and space are capable. To scramble symbol and instrument, to try to use one as the other, sets up pratfalls: this scrambling tends to require sacrifices of function to look. But use and theatre, or instrument and symbol, do not have to be antagonistic.

Symbol in architecture is not like a word, a sentence, a road sign, or an advertisement, or a sculpture or a painting. It is more elusive. It emerges over time, out of the fact that buildings are both built and inhabited, and through the interaction of material, space, light, image, movement, and use. A building's meanings and uses are unstable and ungovernable, despite which architects have to impose fixity and certainty in order to get anything built at all. A good building is decisive but not rigid, which is one of the reasons why architecture is difficult.

The instability of architecture is also its grace: it is the reason why places shaped with the help of corruption, tyranny, greed, fear, megalomania, or repression – which includes many of the most admired public spaces in Europe – can be beautiful and liberating. It is the reason why clients and architects can create something richer than their narrow ambitions would suggest.

4: The inconstant horizon, or notes on the erotic in architecture

'But your Countess . . . ' she said, stopping.

I was about to reply when the doors opened; my answer was interrupted by admiration. I was astonished, delighted, I no longer know what became of me, and I began in good faith to believe in magic. The door closed again, and I could no longer see from whence I had entered. All I could see now was a seamless, bird's eye view of a grove of trees which seemed to stand and rest on nothing. In truth, I found myself in a vast cage of mirrors . . .

In Vivant Denon's *Point de Lendemain*, the young hero is seduced, over an evening and night, by the beautiful Mme de T—. Events unfold in a series of interiors, from adjoining boxes at the opera, to a moonlit carriage ride, to a frosty dinner with old M. de T— in his chateau, to the chateau's garden. Although outdoors, this too has the qualities of an interior, enclosed by night.

Events proceed by way of a terrace thickly planted with trees, a grassy bank, and a little pavilion. There are delays, when Mme de T—'s 'principles of decency' erect gossamer barricades, and the tricky subject of his lover, the Countess, comes up. But eventually 'our knees buckled, our weakening arms intertwined and, unable to hold each other up, we sank down onto a sofa . . . The moon was setting, and its last rays soon lifted the veil of a modesty that was, I think, becoming rather tiresome'. Then they notice the lapping of the River Seine, which borders the garden, and which seems in harmony with their beating hearts.

From the opera box to the pavilion, space is an accomplice to seduction. It offers shelter, intimacy, distraction, suggestion, and disguise, as well as timely and practical assistance in the form of the grassy bank and the sofa. It stimulates the senses, with the sound of waves and the magical effects of moonlight. Nature and artifice alternate from the opera to the moon to the chateau to the river.

After the pavilion there is a hesitant pause. Then the couple make their way back towards 'an even more charming room' in the chateau. They pass through a 'labyrinth' of unlit stairs and hall-ways, a secret door, and a small, dark corridor, a journey which the narrator compares to an initiation rite. Just before they enter, Mme de T—'s scruples momentarily reappear:

'But your Countess . . .' she said, stopping.

The effect of the seamless room stops his answer, as he is overwhelmed by the illusionistic grove of trees, and the 'cage of mirrors'. Light sources are mysterious and concealed, there are incense burners, a flame on an altar, flowers and garlands, statues of Cupid and other deities, a temple of light-hearted design. There is a dark grotto, whose carpet imitates grass, and 'a canopy under which were piles of pillows with a baldachin upheld by cupids'.

At one point the hero confesses that 'it was no longer Mme de T— whom I desired, it was the little room'. But the inevitable hap-pens, or starts to happen, in the mirrored space, 'and in that instant, because the couple we formed was repeated in its every angle, I saw that island entirely populated by happy lovers'. They enter the grotto, where a cleverly contrived spring propels them onto a mound of cushions. In due course she asks about his Countess again, but once again his reply is interrupted, this time by a trusted servant announcing that day has broken, and they have to leave.

He finds himself back in the garden, where daylight dispels the magic, and the room now seems like a dream. 'Instead of an enchanted nature, I saw only an innocent nature', he says. He meets, unexpectedly, 'the Marquis', who is Mme de T—'s regular lover. He works out that the previous night was part of an elaborate intrigue involving himself, the Marquis, and the husband, one of which only she had the whole picture, and over which she had control. He has been an actor without knowing it in a play without an audience (except, that is, for the readers). The theatrical performance with which the story starts, which they leave after the first act to pursue their adventure, is continued in different form through a series of scene changes to the end of the story.

The little room is of course fictional, a literary contrivance which if made real, with its magic spring and fake grass carpet, would be laughable. But Denon describes qualities and effects of erotically charged space that can be found outside the pages of a book. His world is almost all interior, including the garden, a flow of spaces and atmospheres from the theatre to the secret room in which roofs, facades, masonry, and other external features are barely mentioned.

This world is multi-sensory – the sound of the river, the smell of incense, the softness of the cushions, the optical confusion – and experiences cross from one sense to another: the light is soft; sighs – things of sound – express sensations. Artifice plays with nature, and the intensely artificial room evokes with its decoration groves, flowers, and arbours, its images 'so artistically painted that they produced the illusion of all the objects they represented'. Although it is internal and windowless, the room is a compressed, more urgent version of the garden where the couple's earlier dalliances took place. Boundaries of in and out dissolve.

Denon's spaces unravel perspective and gravity. There is never a horizon, but a fading into shadow or into uncertain edges. Trees 'seem to stand and rest on nothing'. The room is disconnected from the world, unmoored from it, with a labyrinth of hallways necessary to reach it, and its door disappears once closed. Here the lovers have to make their own horizons, their own gravity and their own nature.

They are witnessed by gods and cupids, and mythological figures painted on the ceiling, adjuncts to the erotic that have slightly gone out of fashion (but not entirely: classical Venuses can be seen marking the entrance to London strip clubs, or brothels in Shanghai). In Denon they seem to serve a safe exhibitionism – the lovers are seen, but not by real people – and a euphemizing or authenticating purpose, by placing the lust of that moment into the eternal realms of classical deities. A less elegant modern equivalent might be the practice of making love to a background of porn films. It takes the personal into some version of the universal.

The lovers are also witnessed by the mirrors, an enduring staple of spaces for sex, as in the mirrored ceilings and headboards of brothels or the lairs of studs. I have seen a much-mirrored bedroom in a flat in Miami, which once belonged to a Latino singer known as the Puma, and I have also seen a 1970s extension to a Sussex farm-house palpably designed for swinging. Here, with the excruciating ugliness of Callaghan-era sensuality, there is a disco/bar in brown brick and brown leather, a swimming pool whose windows are edged with pink, lacy, knicker-like frills, a sauna, and, in case you don't get the hints, lighting fixtures decorated with pictures of wind-swept Scotsmen, beneath whose up-blown kilts, in the place of the penis, is the switch waiting to be flicked. Here the café-au-lait Jacuzzi is faceted with multiple mirrors, like an inside-out disco ball.

'Desires are reproduced by their images', says Denon, and this is part of the power of mirrors. They allow lovers to see themselves entire and from outside, just when they are engaged in Picassoesque collage, to be within and without the moment. Mirrors give them glamour, making them stars of their own show, of which they are also the audience. They make their actions eddy outwards to form part of the space they are in, and beyond that a wider world.

Actual, non-literary versions of Denon's secret room might be found in Japanese love hotels, where rooms can be rented by the hour, to serve a population often deprived, in densely inhabited cities, of domestic privacy. Or, according to an alternative explanation, they answer the needs of a society that divides more than most the public respectability of marriage, and private desire.

Distantly descended from Geisha teahouses of the Edo period, they provide floating worlds, with no sense of an exterior, and obscure connections to the city outside. Some have particularly discreet stairs for people who don't want to be seen, some have automated check-in to avoid any human contact on the way in. They have silky, shiny, and furry surfaces and, again, plenty of mirrors. Some play on the theme of artificial nature: trees in the corridors, ocean scenes in the bedrooms.

They have, where Denon did not, equipment: wooden Xs with handcuffs for spread-eagled bondage, chains, ingenious seats and swings, cages, dispensers of vibrators and lubricants. Some have adjoining rooms with windows between them, where consenting couples can view each other in action. Above all, they are themed. So, in a way, was Denon's room, with its faux garden and classical mythology, but love hotels are more literal. There are prison cells, Roman baths, 'cathedral style' rooms with stained glass, spaceships, a subway train, a 'naughty nurse playroom'. Infantilism is a pervasive theme. You might find a carousel, or a 'Hello Kitty S and M room', or a schoolroom. Transgression is embraced, as with a Christian-looking cross, painted black, with manacles for wrists and feet. Grotesquerie too, with wilfully hideous images of animals, and repulsive combinations of colours and surfaces.

The reasons for the fervour of the theming are a little obscure. One Japanese writer, Natsuo Kirino, claims that 'when Japanese have sex they need a sense of unreality accompanying it. Rather than sex itself, they love the fantasies that go along with it.' (In which they would resemble Denon's hero, in the moment when he desires the room more than the woman.) Perhaps it could be said that the theming contributes to the sense of escape; that, like the lack of windows and the obscure access, the role-playing architecture removes lovers from the daily world. At the same time the kitschery and the cartoonish imagery reduce threat and fear. They draw some of the power out of sex by treating it as a big joke.

The decor could be considered as a form of courtliness. Talking and writing about sex is usually sparing in its naming of acts and parts, preferring the light disguise of suggestion and indirection. So it is with the theming: the assiduous pursuit of a theme becomes an analogy for the pursuit of lust. The identity of a theme (outer space, ancient Rome, Hello Kitty) is less important than the persistence with which it is realized, as it is only standing in for something less easily named.

It is unclear is how aphrodisiac all this paraphernalia really is. There is not, as far as I am aware, any peer-reviewed research as to whether images of spaceships heighten pleasure and performance, compared with a plain bed in a home or a conventional hotel. Some of these interiors, so ambitious to excite, communicate a kind of desperation. They are prone to bathos, as when banal objects like waste bins and air-conditioning units intrude on the fantasies.

The bedrooms of love hotels are signs of sex, more about the idea than the reality which, *in flagrante delicto*, loses the need for interior design. They remind me of something an English property developer told me. What really sells a flat, he said, is not a beautiful kitchen, as had been the case until recently, but a shower big enough for two. I suspect, although again scholarship on the subject is minimal, that here too the idea matters more than the fact. After a flat is bought, and the erotic possibilities of the shower are explored a few times, it resembles a neglected exercise bicycle, an object more about intention than use.

Although they physically exist, love hotels seem as contrived and unreal as Denon's fictional room. Both are over-scripted and over-prescriptive, as Dean Gardens was for family life. Usually, sex doesn't need architecture to write its script. It can happen anywhere, an alley, a park, a kitchen, an aeroplane, a truck stop, on the Internet. Most of the time, for most people, it is less important to have a naughty nurse playroom than a jug of wine, a loaf of bread, and thou.

In a series of photographs called Wonderland an artist called Dean Sameshima recorded the exteriors of gay sex clubs in Los Angeles. They are blank, low buildings, bathed in the city's ubiquitous sunshine, with windows that are either blocked or absent. Things of the night, they are shown blinking in the daylight. Each is coloured, because they have to have some kind of surface, in a single hue, quite randomly chosen: the deep green of pine trees on one, an off-raspberry, sand. Their oblong elevations are linear and horizontal, like most buildings in that city stretched by cars.

Their blankness is almost industrial or, as factories usually carry signs, beyond industrial. Muteness is taken to the point where it becomes an advertisement. With nothing else to contemplate each front door, also blank, becomes suggestive and charged. The power of the images lies in the absence of the sensual, which is indicated only by the titles Sameshima gives them. For example: *Untitled (12 stalls, 1 leather bunk bed, outdoor garden, 1 water fountain, 1 barber's chair, glory-hole platform, Chinese decor)*. If love hotels are like Dean Gardens, these sheds are like the Bijlmer, examples of the human ability to colonize unpromising places.

Sameshima has also photographed a site of sex in a public park. As with the clubs the image is depopulated, and its power is in

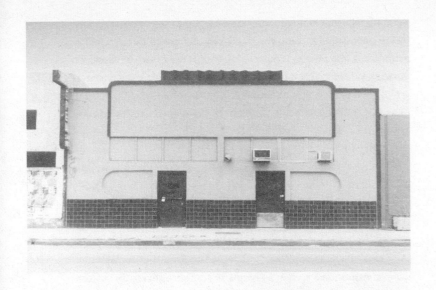

what is not shown. There are scrubby trees, some conveniently dense undergrowth, some weed-like yellow flowers through which a track has been worn. A path through flowers might be innocent enough, except that this has been beaten down with some purpose, while heading nowhere but a shadow in the undergrowth, in front of which lies a fallen trunk. A thick rope is draped over this trunk, whose use can only be guessed at.

This park is not designed for sex, but its accidental features have been appropriated by the ingenuity of desire. Nor were the buildings housing the gay clubs made for this purpose, even if their internal furnishings, described in the captions, take us back to the specificity of love hotels and Denon. The relation of design to desire can run from the most explicit to the most indirect.

Sex challenges with unusual force the idea that architecture can be customized to the activities it contains, given that it can happen anywhere. The fact that I resort to fiction to find a room designed exclusively for love-making reveals that such places are esoteric. The example of love hotels suggests that attempts to make erotic space can become weirdly over-programmed, and miss the point.

Yet it is untrue that setting is irrelevant. It can suggest, provoke, inspire, encourage, dishearten, impede, or enable. For most people, most of the time, the requirements are quite simple – certain qualities of comfort, light, privacy, and atmosphere – with more detailed specifications required for specialist tastes, but these requirements are nonetheless still there. Often the role of architecture is to suggest one thing, such as propriety, in order that the opposite – passion, danger, transgression – can happen. If architecture is background, this is particularly true in relation to sex. It is also true that the relation of setting to action is in this case exceptionally oblique, and subject to inversions and surprises.

•

On 29 July 1981 His Royal Highness the Prince of Wales rode in an open landau from St Paul's Cathedral, along Fleet Street and the Strand, across Trafalgar Square, beside St James's Park towards Buckingham Palace. At his side was his beautiful twenty-year-old bride, Diana, who was generally accepted to be – and this detail seemed terribly important at the time – a virgin. They were accompanied by cheering crowds, six hundred thousand strong, and ecstatic television coverage.

What the couple may not have known is that two centuries previously this route was London's main line of vice. In the eighteenth century it was an active business thoroughfare, linking the City of London to the City of Westminster, which created opportunity for prostitution. It was a thronged zone of transaction and transition, of display and sale. Little capillaries, alleys and courts, ran down from the artery to the Thames and provided settings for the consummation of deals done in the main streets. So did the dense-packed buildings where prostitutes rented rooms, and the nooks and bushes of the park.

As the historian Dan Cruickshank has recorded, the shape and organization of the city provided the content and form of the sex trade, from the publicity of the Strand and Fleet Street to the privacy of the alleys. It laid on the clientele in large numbers, and gave them the spaces they needed. In 1787 *The Times* reported that

> the indecencies practiced by the crowds of prostitutes before Somerset-House every night, not only put modesty to blush, but render it absolutely dangerous to pass.

James Boswell, the famous man of letters, gave the john's point of view. He wrote how he

> picked up a low brimstone, called myself a barber and agreed with her for sixpence, went to the bottom of the Park arm in

arm, and dipped my machine in the Canal and performed most manfully . . . In the Strand I picked up a little profligate wretch and gave her sixpence. She allowed me entrance. But the miscreant refused me performance. I was much stronger than her, and nolens volens, pushed her up against the wall.

The route was used by the gay as well as the straight, especially around the church of St Clement Danes, in the surroundings of St Paul's Cathedral, and at the Royal Exchange, at the eastward end of the axis. Here dock workers, or 'water rats', were an attraction, and a writer of 1699 tells that he found himself

jostled in amongst a parcel of Swarthy Buggerantoes, Preternatural Fornicators, as my Friend call'd them, who would Ogle a Handsome Young Man with as much lust, as a True-bred English Whoremaster would gaze upon a Beautiful Virgin.

Not that Georgian London's sex trade was limited to the Strand–Fleet Street line; it is almost more difficult to find parts of eighteenth-century London that were not actively exploited than those that were. As Cruickshank describes, prostitution was a significant part of London's economy, with its proceeds invested, among other things, in property development. The squares and terraces of Georgian London, now much admired for their taste and discretion, were partly the work of money-laundering by pimps and brothel-keepers.

The sex trade generated its own architecture, such as the bagnio, a building type almost lost to London's architectural history. These were steam baths, sometimes designed in an exotic Ottoman style, where ablution was to a greater or lesser degree a front for prostitution and illicit liaisons. There was Vauxhall Gardens on the south side of the Thames, a place of assembly and entertainment where sex was a major, but not the only attraction. It was

an alternative version of the brick city across the river, a grid of foliage and shadows where the stages of seduction were served by open spaces for display, which led to semi-private restaurant boxes, and again into dark groves and wooded alleys.

There was also Carlisle House in Soho Square, a seventeenth-century building enlarged and decorated by Theresa Cornelys, an Austrian-born singer, actor, dancer, prostitute, and ex-lover of Casanova. Its purpose was to be the setting of masquerades, musical masked parties where disguise eased seduction, assignation, and prostitution. Contemporaries described Carlisle House as a 'Fairy Palace', whose magnificence, the 'splendor of the illuminations and embellishments', formed part of the erotic effect. Its interior was a sequence of rooms, some mirrored and decorated with rococo plasterwork and chandeliers, some in a Chinese style, one evoking a wilderness with trees around the walls. The connection of role-playing architecture to sex, to be explored further in Japanese love hotels, was already established. It was all interior: the outside was as plain and proper as a boarding school.

For the most part, however, the sex business in eighteenth-century London did not occupy bespoke buildings, but took over spaces designed for other purposes. The typical Georgian town house, with its staircase efficiently serving its several rooms, could make a convenient brothel. Windows became advertisements, with women placed visibly within them, sometimes naked, sometimes with obscene gestures and poses. And sex appropriated the open spaces, the streets, alleys, and parks. These were the places where Boswell found his blunt pleasures, far from the long-drawn-out refinement of Denon.

The same distance can be found between the frantic images of the Londoner William Hogarth and the paintings of Jean-Honoré Fragonard, born in France a generation later, in which child-like aristocrats flirt and intrigue in exquisite gardens. In Fragonard, as in

Denon, there is a conspiracy of space and desire: roses chime with blushes, and pretty swirls of foliage with those of petticoats; human and natural twist in shared delight. They are bathed in a ubiquitous softness, of light, shade, fabric, and flesh, which even the stone statues seem to share. Hogarth shows convulsions of lust, an incessant groping and snogging in busy streets, where couples probe and grapple amid others striving for dignity, or a livelihood, or oblivion in drink. Spots and corrosions of disease spread indiscriminately across the faces of posh and common, and the amorous and seemingly chaste.

There are, as in Fragonard, some echoes of desire in inanimate objects. A rod, a spar, a truncheon, an obelisk, a drooping sign-pole become suggestive, or an oozing crack in piecrust, or the opening lid of a tankard, or a basket of fish. A girl toys meaningfully with a key in her lap. The more you look, the more tumescent becomes the atmosphere, yet there is not the harmony of flesh, feeling, and space you find in Fragonard. The setting is formed by the brick oblongs of eighteenth-century London, indifferent to the bodies they contain, and hard and ugly – like, one imagines, much of the sex it contained.

Fragonard's characters roam in generic boskiness; Hogarth's scenes are in specific, identifiable parts of London, albeit sometimes adjusted for effect. One, *Morning*, of 1738, might delight architectural historians: it shows the porch of Inigo Jones' St Paul's Church in Covent Garden, a striking essay in the Tuscan order, and Russell House, a rare work by the dazzling but wayward baroque architect Thomas Archer. Hogarth, however, is more interested in a wooden shack in front of the church, its eaves fringed with icicles, a violent rabble visible through its door. In front is a mound of humanity, with a beggar at its base and a woman warming her hands at a fire, surmounted by a kissing couple, and a man sliding his hand over a girl's breast. Occupying a pool of space untouched by debauchery, and looking straight ahead as if she cannot see it, is a bony, prim-looking woman, possibly a well-known retired prostitute, followed by a sour but obedient boy, whose day is starting as the revellers' night is ending.

The wooden shack is Tom King's Coffee House, relocated for the purposes of this picture from its actual location, which was to the side of that shown. Here men of all classes could gather, drink, find prostitutes, and sometimes fight. It grew in response to demand, but the architecture of this place of pleasuring was always basic.

It stood in Covent Garden Piazza, laid out by Inigo Jones about a century earlier, and the first and best of London's residential squares, the prototype for many re-workings of the idea in the following centuries. It was built in conscious imitation of the Place des Vosges in Paris (originally called the Place Royale), which was started in 1605. Both are rectangular spaces, lined with arcaded orderly elevations, with a centre intended for some form of public activity. The piazza, in its name and architectural style, also evokes Italian versions of formal public space.

The difference between the two is that the Parisian example was commissioned by the King of France, whereas the piazza was a commercial property speculation by its owner, the 4th Earl of Bedford, on the grounds of his family home, Bedford House. Like most property development, it wasn't quite what it seemed, with the investment in quality directed where it would be most visible. Both the houses and the church of St Paul present impressive and solid stonework to the piazza, but become much more basic behind. And if the project was sold on the promise of Jones' symmetrical plan, this did not mean the plan would be completed. Its southern side, in a characteristic victory of private interest over architectural order, was omitted, as it would have encroached on the Earl's garden more than he liked.

The houses of the Place de Vosges were designated for courtiers,

and its open space was designed for the specific, articulated activities of the court, including tournaments and pageants. The houses at Covent Garden were for whoever would pay their high rents, and the purpose of the open space in the piazza was unspecific, leaving a void that would be filled by more raucous forms of public life. A short distance from the Strand, it became a reservoir for the overflow of that street's vice.

In the early eighteenth century, a later Bedford (by now a duke) moved out of the area, had Bedford House demolished, and turned over its site to developers. The rich residents for whom the piazza was built moved to newer developments, and it filled with humble and disreputable uses. The fruit, flower, and vegetable market, first installed as a money-making venture in the mid-seventeenth century, expanded. Gambling dens, taverns, and the sex trade moved in. Writers called it 'the great square of Venus' and 'grand seraglio to the nation'. Emma Hart, the future Emma Hamilton and mistress of Admiral Lord Nelson, was probably a child prostitute in Covent Garden. The piazza was now an uneven hybrid of high and low architecture, of measured classical structures in brick and stone, and of rough wooden sheds like King's Coffee House.

The arcades worked well as shelter for a flesh market, and Jones' dignified buildings were taken over by brothels, prostitutes' lodgings, and a stall selling pornographic prints. In one corner was the Shakespeare's Head Tavern whose head waiter published *Harris's List of Covent Garden Ladies*, a shameless, functional, and regularly updated directory of prostitutes. At no. 8 the Piazza was Haddock's Bagnio, a town house now containing twenty-two beds in elegantly furnished rooms, decorated with mirrors, 'India paper', and views of Venice. There was some modest provision for the bagnio's ostensible purpose of bathing, and a coffee shop where prostitutes and clients could meet. The close connection of arcade, coffee shop, and bedroom offered a more efficient and pleasant transition from public to private than that from the Strand to its back alleys.

Covent Garden Piazza was not designed for trade in sex, but it proved well suited to its purpose. In its eighteenth-century state it was a work of dignity and neglect combined, allowing both erotic havoc and, behind its architectural masks, concealment and discretion. Its range of construction, from wooden shacks to masonry townhouses and their elegant interiors, matched the people, from rich to destitute, who used the space and its attractions, or were used. The piazza, governed by lust, was an astounding, if brutal, condenser of social class.

Hogarth's *Morning* is part of a series called *Four Times of The Day*. Another, *Night*, shows a spot a short distance from Covent Garden along the Fleet Street–Strand line of vice, near Charing Cross. In the background, standing still amid fire and mayhem, is an equestrian statue of Charles I; in the foreground a chamber pot is being emptied on the head of a pompous but drunk-looking man, thought to be a magistrate hypocritically severe on disorderly behaviour. Behind them is a coach wreck. Signs on the buildings announce two bagnios and the Cardigan Head, a pub used by prostitutes.

Nothing of this scene now remains, except the statue of the King. In the early nineteenth century this area was swept away, along with a redundant Royal Mews, to help make the large, empty zone of Trafalgar Square and its surroundings. It was an act of urban cleansing, the replacement of anarchic and dangerous tissue with a formal, ceremonial space, surveyed and controlled by government, and filled with its monuments. Its fountains, rebuilt in the 1930s by Sir Edwin Lutyens, were made extra-large to reduce the space available for unruly crowds to gather.

In recent decades it has been declared a disgrace that the square is so boring, and persistent attempts have been made to invigorate it, including the expensive rearrangement of traffic and public sponsorship of festivals and art. I wish good luck to these efforts, but their promoters probably don't realize that the square is boring because it was designed to be so. It is a grand prophylactic, a bromide, a way to suppress the dangerous lust that once flourished on its site. This lust is expressed only in symbolic form, in the famous phallus in the middle of the square. ('Did Lady Hamilton', as the old joke has it, 'have a hand in erecting Nelson's column?')

Covent Garden is also tamer now, given over to street performers, tourist shops, and boutiques. The Fleet Street–Strand line begins with Goldman Sachs and ends with Coutts Bank. When the prince and the virgin rode along it, symbols as they were of wholesome and publically approved matrimony, they were consecrating a long and largely successful campaign to clean up an ancient avenue of filth.

Spaces for sex, whether designed, like Denon's room, or appropriated, like the piazza, are one manifestation of the erotic in architecture. Another is the way that any place – a house, a street, a museum, a park – might reflect the sexuality of its makers. For developers, architects, planners, and theorists have their own sexual preferences and complexities which, as they are human, influence their professional work. Even the most respectable buildings are shaped, at some level, by instincts or ideas about desire.

Most of the celebrated architects I have met, at least those of them who are men, have a conquistadorial sexuality. The wife of one was once quoted as saying that he is a plug, 'and the whole world is full of sockets'. Another once described to me an imaginary party involving himself, a client who had created a famous nightclub, 'and a hundred supermodels'. There are tales of the architect who has to buy off sexual-harassment suits from his staff, and the legendary randiness of a certain minimalist. (There seems to be a

"A BUD"
Copyright 1901 by McKenny

JAP. BY NIGHT   HUDSON STREET, N.Y.

connection, perhaps worthy of a slim but thoughtful academic study, between minimalist purity and roving priapism.)

There isn't anything new in this. Le Corbusier was famous for his comedic and sometimes impressive seductions (for example, Josephine Baker). Frank Lloyd Wright built his early career, it is said, servicing the wives of rich men while designing their houses for them. Stanford White, a phenomenally successful architect of late-nineteenth-century America, a man with penetrating eyes and a moustache lush and dense as a forest canopy, had an apartment in the Spanish-Moorish tower of Madison Square Garden, the palace of spectacle he built in New York. It was painted, as his great-granddaughter Suzannah Lessard has described, in umber, sienna, vermilion, and chrome yellow, and its decor included tapestries, animal skins, paintings, Japanese fish, and a leaping bronze nude bacchante. It had a red velvet swing on which women would entertain him. He once held a party in which white wine was served by a nearly naked blonde and red by a brunette, and a third woman jumped out of a pie, accompanied by canaries. In 1906, in the rooftop restaurant of Madison Square Garden, during a performance of the song 'I Could Love a Million Girls', he was shot in the face, dead, by the husband of Evelyn Nesbit. She was a woman whom, when she was sixteen and he forty-seven, White had seduced, or raped.

Adolf Loos was an architect in Vienna in the time of Sigmund Freud. He became syphilitic at the age of twenty-one, was married three times, had a penchant for young actresses and dancers, and was accused, but not convicted, of paedophilia. He, as Corbusier would be, was fascinated with Josephine Baker, the torch of sensuality whose dances were lighting up Paris in the 1920s, when Loos was also spending long periods there. Probably without her asking, he produced for her designs for a house, with a glass-walled swimming pool, wrapped in corridors for viewing her lithe body at

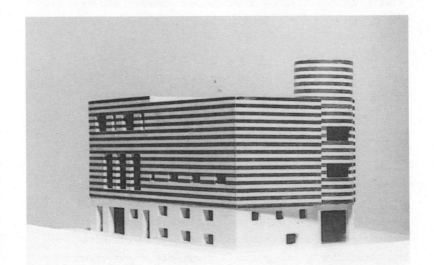

exercise. Its exterior was to have vibrant black-and-white stripes, in contrast with the plain white that Loos almost always used elsewhere, perhaps expressing a wish to intermingle his European restraint with her African-American energy. It seems to have been a fantasy that Baker did not share, and the house was not built.

He had striking views about sex and about architecture. In 'Ladies' Fashion', an article of 1898, he wrote:

> Ladies' fashion! You disgraceful chapter in the history of civilization! You tell of mankind's secret desires. Whenever we peruse your pages, our souls shudder at the frightful aberrations and scandalous depravities. We hear the whimpering of abused children, the shrieks of maltreated wives, the dreadful outcry of tortured men, and the howls of those who have died at the stake. Whips crack, and the air takes on the burnt smell of scorched human flesh. *La bête humaine* . . .

Men, in fact, are worse than beasts. Unlike animals, who only want sex 'once a year', men want it all the time. 'And our sensuality is not simple but complicated, not natural but against nature.' On the other hand, 'that which is noble in a woman knows only one desire: that she hold on to her place by the side of the big, strong man'. So she has to win his 'unnatural love':

> If it were natural, the woman would be able to approach the man naked. But the naked woman is unattractive to the man.

Thus 'the woman is forced to appeal to the man's sensuality through her clothing, to appeal unconsciously to his sickly sensuality'. She has to ornament herself, and wear long impractical skirts that stress her decorative rather than useful role. She has to keep changing her appearance to suit fashion: Loos recalls how, a couple of decades earlier, under the influence of descriptions of 'voluptuous women and scenes of flagellation' by writers like

Sacher-Masoch, the style was for 'rounded and ripe femininity'. Later, the 'child-woman came into fashion'.

At the end of the article Loos unexpectedly turns these arguments into a call for the emancipation, of a kind, of women: 'no longer by an appeal to sensuality, but rather by economic independence earned through work will the woman bring about her equal status with the man . . . then velvet and silk, flowers and ribbons, feathers and paints will fail to have their effect. They will disappear.'

'Ladies' Fashion' was a rehearsal for Loos' most famous and influential essay, *Ornament and Crime*, of 1908. Here he announced that 'the evolution of culture is synonymous with the removal of ornament from objects of daily use'. Children or primitive people might blamelessly use ornament, like 'the Papuan' who 'tattoos his skin, his boat, his oar, in short, everything that is within his reach'. But 'the modern man who tattoos himself is a criminal or degenerate'.

Ornament, he said, has an erotic origin. The 'first work of art, the first artistic action of the first artist daubing on the wall, was in order to rid himself of his natural excesses'. This first work, claimed Loos, was a cross: 'a horizontal line: the reclining woman. A vertical line: the man who penetrates her. The man who created it felt the same urge as Beethoven, he experienced the same joy that Beethoven felt when he created the Ninth Symphony.'

Loos made it clear that the modern, civilized, aristocratic man, a figure very like Loos himself, should dispense with ornament in his clothes, his buildings, and his objects of daily use. Ornament is associated with the degenerate, unnatural, dangerous sensuality he described in 'Ladies' Fashion'. The modern man must control these urges, and wear plain, well-made tailoring. He 'needs his clothes as a mask'. This is not because he has surrendered his will, or his personality, or his libidinous urge to art but because, like Beethoven, he has made them sublime: 'his individuality is so strong that it can no longer be expressed in terms of items of clothing. The lack of ornament is a sign of intellectual power.'

Loos' buildings are true to his theory. He designed houses in Vienna and Prague for businessmen, professionals, and industrialists, whose white, cubic, unornamented exteriors present themselves like masks to the world. They are not ostentatious, but they stand out, as Loos' well-suited aristocrat might stand out in a crowd. These houses are also like suits, both in their sobriety and the way Loos tailored their interiors to the lives of their inhabitants.

Loos tried to find the right size, shape, and material to suit the use and mood of every room in the house, and then fit them together like the sleeves, lining, pockets, and gusset of a suit. A living room, a study, a music room, or a bedroom would have its own length, width, height, lighting, and surfaces, whether marble, wood veneer, plaster, leather, or cloth. These spaces were explicitly linked to gender: there might be a *zimmer der dame* where women could retire while men conducted business in the living room, which would be raised up like a theatre's box with a view of what was going on. In Loos' houses, as the historian Beatriz Colomina has pointed out, there is intricate cross-fire of lines of gaze, or a dance of looks, up, down, sideways, and obliquely.

The overall effect was of intricacy, as Loos fitted the elements together into a three-dimensional whole, with many short flights of stairs and shifts of level to adjust to the different heights each space required. More than that, Loos' interiors are sensual. He might have argued, in *Ornament and Crime* and elsewhere, for simplicity, but never for austerity. If buildings' exteriors had to present a disguise, their inner selves could engage the senses.

Rather than man-made decoration he favoured extensive surfaces of natural materials, which he sliced and polished to bring out their inherent patterns and luxury. Within oblong boundaries, these materials are made to writhe with suppressed life, with veins, grain,

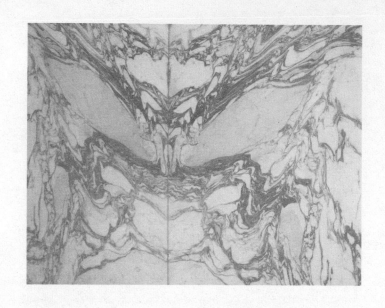

and blemishes wriggling across marble and wood, and burrs scattering like microbes across panels of walnut. Colours are strong, sometimes lurid: stones in caramellish yellow, black on white, ocean green. In a luxury apartment in Plzeň (where, as it happens, the commanding officer of the local Wehrmacht would commit suicide in 1945) you can read monsters and pudenda, as in a Rorschach test, into the grotesque symmetrical patterns of matched marble in the walls. In one memorable moment, in the Muller House in Prague, he inserted fish tanks into a wall of rippling marble, creating an assonance of mineral and aqueous, of geological and living, but in all cases cold. This is not an outdoorsy, friendly form of nature, but more strange, and manipulated by culture.

Despite Loos' disapproving words on velvet and silk in 'Ladies' Fashion', he used both, for lampshades and upholstery. He also used Delft tiles, with their pretty scenes, and richly patterned oriental carpets: permitted, under the rules of *Ornament and Crime*, because they were works of less developed cultures than Loos's, which were therefore allowed to use decoration. Loos was happy to use such decorative things, as he was to use the natural patterns of marble. It was only to attempt ornament in his own time and place that was forbidden.

His interiors are tactile and fetishistic, alternating hard and cold with soft and warm, and the stuff of exterior, like marble, with that of the interior, like polished timber and cloth. The horizon is dissolved, somewhat as in Denon's room, though with different means and effects. Views outside are limited and controlled, sometimes blocked with obscured glass. Strong internal horizontals suggest artificial horizons, but these are discontinuous. As in Denon, and Soane, the interior makes its own universe, within which, after first being disorientated, you have to form your own space.

There are mirrors. In the Steiner House in Vienna one is placed in front of a viewless window, laying a precise reflection of a dining

room in front of what you expect to frame a view out, but is only a rectangle of white light. Again, the inner landscape supplants the outer. Others are used to throw a viewer's image back at him or her, to melt the boundaries of a room or multiply its volume. Mirrors also take part in a game of surface against volume, like the marble and timber, and the obscured glass. Things of three dimensions are compressed into two, which then suggest three again. Veining and graining are evidence of depth and mass in a material that cannot be seen, and of time: the historic life of geology or a tree growth. A mirror catches a space and replays it. Obscure glass holds the sky in a plane and replaces it.

For Loos, 'the house does not have to tell anything to the exterior'. Sensuality was so potent and dangerous that it had to be placed behind masks. But it was still very much there, as is made clear by the bedroom he designed in 1903 for his first wife, Lina, during their two-year marriage. This is the opposite of the monastic planks that Le Corbusier designed for himself and Yvonne. It is a space of three surfaces, all in different degrees soft: a floor of absurdly lush fur, which climbs up the sides of the centrally placed bed, covered in something taut, such as linen, with a wall of hanging silk behind. In the only surviving photograph the bed forms a suggestively vacant rectangle, awaiting occupation by bodies. The silk recedes in the centre to form a recess for the bed, and bed and room are presented symmetrically and frontally, like a proscenium or an altar. The intention is clear: to make a setting for and celebration of the desires Loos called sickly, complicated, and unnatural, which he compared to 'pestilence' and linked to degeneracy, without which he could not live.

Loos's rants, like Ruskin's, verge on the demented. Like Ruskin, he is hard simply to dismiss, on account of his insights and skill, and his vast influence. He was a pioneer of modernist architecture, most obviously in his removal of ornament: no architect had designed buildings as plain before, as exclusively reliant externally on form and proportion. He paved the way for the younger Le Corbusier, who also removed ornament from his architecture, except that Corbusier's ideal was nakedness – the idea that a building should be like a nude body in sunlight – rather than Loos' attachment to suits and masks.

Mies van der Rohe learned plainness from Loos, and adapted the Austrian's use of gorgeous marbles and veneers, presented as pure surface, for sensual effect. This seeming negative quality, the absence of ornament, justified as a form of truthfulness, and as a way to a higher physical, spiritual, or artistic experience, became the most distinctive common feature of modernist architecture. It led among other things to gridded office buildings and apartment blocks that no longer seemed to have much connection with spiritual, or sensual, experience.

Loos' abolition of ornament later led to 'minimalism', a remarkably persistent interior-design option, most often used for sensual spaces such as luxury hotels and flats, restaurants, clothes shops, and spas. Here the properties of simple but luxurious materials are everything, and the intention is to create, through reduction and restraint, a higher order of luxury. One of the style's temples is the Cathay Pacific First Class Lounge in Hong Kong International Airport, designed by the minimalist and sensualist John Pawson. Here, within the vaulted machine of the airport building, there are intimate rooms, like cells for hedonistic monks, with plain stone, wood, and a rectangular rivulet of water running by. Here travellers can soothe and pamper their weary bodies and, conceivably, make love.

All this, the plainness of so many offices and blocks of flats, and the style of sophisticated contemporary pleasure, owe much to Adolf Loos. As his writings make clear, his views on culture and architecture grew out of his peculiar view of the erotic. Loos' personal mixture of desires, his mixture of passion, guilt, and loathing, have helped shape the world.

His is far from the only case in history of a personal sexual disposition converting into architectural theory and thence into the forms of buildings and cities. Indeed, it can seem as if architectural theory is almost always an expression of the confused sexuality of men, and would not exist without it. There is, for example, a well-known story about Ruskin's horror at his wife's body, which may or may not be true: what is known is that his marriage ended on grounds of 'incurable impotency', that he was an enthusiastic masturbator, and later became infatuated with the ten-year-old Rose la Touche. It is not hard to infer how this history influenced his fervent descriptions of buildings and building materials.

In the fifteenth century, Leon Battista Alberti wrote one of the most influential works on architecture, *On the Art of Building*, written in ten books in emulation of the Roman Vitruvius, who wrote a similar number on the subject in the reign of Augustus. In another book, *On the family*, Alberti called sex a 'vile appetite', 'lascivious and brutish', 'shameful and immodest', 'the noxious influence of Venus', and a 'bestial and merciless lust'. Of desire he said 'truly she is a master to be fled and hated'.

His revulsion governed his views on the design of houses, expressed in these two works. Women should be secluded as far as possible from visitors, in rooms 'treated as though dedicated to religion and chastity'. Men, being 'stronger' and 'of more elevated mind', could roam outside in the wider world; a woman, 'as she remains locked up at home, should watch over things by staying at her post, by diligent care and watchfulness'. Husbands and wives should have separate bedrooms, so as not to disturb each other, but with an interconnecting door so they can discreetly fulfil their duties of procreation. When a girl marries, her husband is to train her, much as he might train a dog, in the use of the house. With these theories he followed ancient Greek texts and precedents, especially Xenophon's *Oeconomicos*, and with enthusiasm amplified their puritanism.

Since, following the Renaissance imagery of microcosm and macrocosm, Alberti considered a house to be a miniature city, he applied the principles of secluding women, and the frightful desires attached to them, to towns as well as homes. It would 'hardly win our respect if our wife busied herself among the men in the marketplace, out in the public eye', he said. Alberti's ideas on city planning were much concerned with 'purity' and 'cleanliness', in channelling and separating the noxious effects of the body. He argued that 'a well-known harlot' should be forbidden from building a monument to her husband, whereas it would be permitted of a virtuous woman.

His concern with keeping desire under control informed his views on architectural harmony and the appearance of buildings, which he attempted to put into practice with buildings like his Tempio Malatestiano in Rimini. Alberti said that there should be a harmonious relationship between the greater and lesser parts of a building, which should in turn take its proper place in the hierarchy of man, building, city, and cosmos: the architect must 'consider whether each element has been well defined and allocated to its proper place'. The writer Mark Wigley has argued that by this he means that dangerous and unbalancing sensuality must be restrained. The architect, said Alberti, must 'condemn unruly passion for building: each part must be appropriate'. Sounding much as Loos would later, Alberti argued for a simple architecture clothed in white, and against buildings 'coloured and lewdly dressed with the allurement of painting . . . striving to attract and seduce the eye of the beholder', just as a woman should not be 'made up and plastered and painted and dressed in lascivious and improper clothing'.

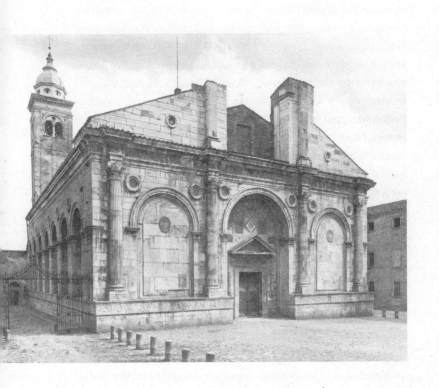

Unlike Loos, he barely relaxed his strictures on sensuality inside the house.

Alberti has helped shape the way we live now. His views on planning the home, on the grounds of moral health, anticipate the compartmentalization of houses into specialist rooms which would increase over the following centuries. His preference for form over ornament, and his views on proportion, reinforced and developed by other theorists, have become a commonplace of Western culture. You can see them realized in English country houses and town squares of the eighteenth century, in the public monuments of Washington DC, and in their imitations. Most people, if their attention is drawn to the idea that harmonious beauty comes from the proper ordering of parts to the whole, would probably find it familiar and reasonable. Le Corbusier and the Prince of Wales, usually divergent in their architectural tastes, have a common passion for what the Prince calls 'the timeless principles of harmony, balance and unity'.

Le Corbusier was more sensual than Alberti, but like him saw mathematical proportion as a tool of specifically male order. It was, for him, a procreative force. Writing on his theories of harmony, his images were orgasmic. He described the *'effect'* of architecture or art on its environment as 'waves, outcry, turmoil . . . lines spurting, radiating out as if produced by an explosion: the surroundings, both immediate and more distant are stirred and shaken, dominated or caressed by it.' A room, a city, or a landscape receives this powerful penetration by art and reacts, bringing 'its weight to bear upon the place where there is a work of art, expression of the will of man; it impresses upon that place its depths and peaks, its textures, hard or flaccid, its violence and its gentleness. A kind of harmony is created, exact like a mathematical exercise.'

He also described the unfolding measuring strip he kept in his pocket. This was marked with the gradations of the Modulor, his personal system of proportion, based on the dimensions of an ideal man, that he hoped would become universal. One day, while he was touring by Jeep the virgin soil that would bear the Indian city of Chandigarh, the strip fell out of his pocket and was lost. 'It is there now, in the very heart of the place, integrated in the soil. Soon it will flower in all the measurements of the first city of the world to be organised all of a piece in accordance with that harmonious scale.' Corbusier's magic mathematics, released from the expanding stick in his pocket, will fertilize the ground so a city can be born.

Few now, looking at a pleasant elevation, would know of the connection between the theories of proportion that lie behind it and a strange view of the relationships of men and women. Yet Alberti leaves little doubt, and other Renaissance documents confirm that ideas of harmony are bound to ideas of male dominance and visibility. Take Leonardo's drawing of a man inscribed in a circle and square, as an emblem of the geometric order of the cosmos, whose familiarity may obscure the most obvious fact about it: it shows a man, naked and well built, and would never have been a woman. In case Leonardo is too subtle, another theorist, Cesare Cesariano, reinforces the point. In his version of the same image, the man has a sturdy erection. Geometry is male, order is male, both are divine.

There is, in other words, a thing we call classical architecture. Its characteristics are symmetry, order, harmony, the precedence of exterior over interior, day over night, fixed over mobile, volume over surface, form over ornament. It prefers masonry construction and light, or white, exteriors. It likes to subdivide, make boundaries, and give things their place. Its idea of public space is as something formal, and formed by geometry, such as a square, circus, or avenue.

It is widely regarded as natural and normal, yet it is at least partly based on prejudices about sex and gender that are not. Modernist architecture, while seemingly breaking with the past,

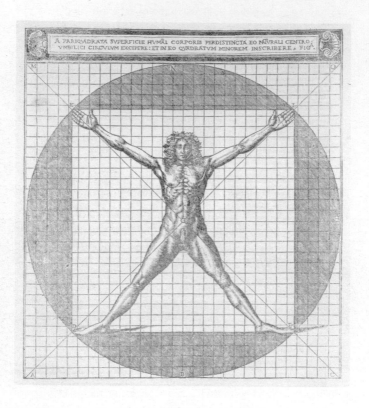

retained classical ideas of order, proportion, and propriety, and some of its theorists, such as Loos, wrote like classical architects about constraint of the sensual.

This does not mean that classical and modernist architectures cannot be beautiful, or that they must always be misogynist, and oppressive and hostile to the sensual, or that order, proportion, and masculinity are not important qualities in architecture. Because of the indirect nature of truth and intention in architecture, it is possible to inhabit and enjoy a space designed to Albertian principles, without adopting his sexual politics and his morality. The ribald history of Covent Garden Piazza is one illustration: its form mostly followed his laws, its contents (albeit misogynist in a different way) did not.

It should also be said that the classical tradition is something more complex and interesting than a series of monuments designed on Albertian lines. It includes the baroque, and the fountains and shadows of Italian Renaissance gardens, and sensuous spaces like the steam and marble of Roman baths, and the villas of Pompeii, and the dark, gleaming interiors, now all lost, of Greek temples.

But the important point is that it is not inevitable that architecture should be like this, that order, division, propriety, fixity, and daylight should be its dominant qualities and values. They are not immutable or eternal, but made by certain attitudes by certain people at certain times and places. Which makes it interesting to think what the alternatives might be. What would happen if architects listened less to the likes of Alberti, no matter how learned, and refined, and intelligent, he might have been? What might a sensual architecture be like?

Here Denon becomes interesting, less as a recipe book for making real spaces for real sex than as a description of qualities of space made marginal by the Albertian view. These include the importance of the interior, of illusion, shadow, transience, and of more senses than sight alone. Also of reflection, surface, and appearance, of artificial nature, and the inconsistant horizon – the dissolving of boundaries and bearings such that new ones can be formed.

Other possibilities are suggested by Sameshima's sex clubs and park, Theresa Cornelys' house of masquerades, love hotels, and the images of Hogarth and Fragonard. These include the discovery that spaces of desire go to extremes, of boudoir or alley, of luxury (Cornelys) or squalor (Hogarth). There is power in places found by chance, and in anonymity (Sameshima). The love hotels suggest that there is something libidinous in appropriating stuff from many different places, promiscuously.

These qualities are found in places outside fiction, and outside the specialized niche of designing spaces solely for making love. Loos' interiors, for example, employ artificial nature, the dissolving of boundaries, and the libidinous appropriation of stuff. For him such devices were private and internal, while the traditions of Alberti and Le Corbusier treat them as at best peripheral, at worst sinful, compared with the wholesome, sunlit, manly construction of fixed and solid objects. Yet there is no law, no inevitability, that one is more important than the other, that stones are more real than mirrors, or light than shadow.

Sex reveals in heightened form the more general truth about life and space, in that it can happen anywhere, without the assistance of design. Architecture is background but, as background, it can change the nature and effects of what happens, both life and sex, within it. The relation of setting to action is reciprocal – the setting changes the action and the action changes the setting – but it is not linear or direct, and can include reversals and contradictions. Often the role of architecture is as the fall guy, to provide an image of decency which is then subverted. Something unconsidered and seemingly trivial, such as the chance alignment of a window or a door, can have a more potent effect than the official intentions of an architect.

The relation of sexuality and space shows another truth about architecture, that it is usually made by one, quite specialized group of people, on behalf of another, more general one. Their desires make it, and our desires inhabit it. In this interaction of desires, in the ways they match, complement, and conflict, is a game of power. Depending how it is played out, the results can oppress, liberate, or do both at once.

5: Power and freedom

There is a photograph of Lina Bo Bardi on the construction site of the Museu de Arte de São Paulo, or MASP. She is black-clad, booted and trousered, and seated in restless contrapposto on a rough wooden chair. Her sharp nose and chin are almost in profile, but her gaze returns sideways to the camera. Her legs and the chair's rest on a rust-coloured grid of reinforcement bars, awaiting the pour of a concrete slab. Building workers stand behind in an attentive crescent, like footballers before kick-off. Above her, seemingly floating, is the underside of a concrete box. She is on an upper level, and the space between the box above and the deck below reveals a band of city and sky beyond.

She sits next to a painting which might now be worth as much as the construction cost of the whole building, Van Gogh's *The Schoolboy*. Amid the hazard of building, this treasure is mounted perilously on a single unframed sheet of glass, taller than a man, gripped only by a cube of concrete at its base to stop it toppling. Van Gogh's colours are all three primaries – red, blue and yellow – which stand out from the browns and greys of the site. Some clouds and sky from behind the camera are reflected in the glass, and the reason for the architect's pose becomes apparent. She is turning towards the boy and answering the position of his head, also in three-quarter face. His plain chair looks like hers.

The shot is from the mid-1960s, when Bo Bardi was about fifty. By then her husband Pietro, as director of MASP, had gathered the finest array of Western art in the southern hemisphere: Raphael, Botticelli, Mantegna, Bellini, Titian, Bosch, Velázquez, Rubens, Poussin, Rembrandt, Gainsborough, Turner, Goya, Delacroix, Monet, Manet, Degas, Cézanne, van Gogh, Picasso, Matisse, Modigliani, Ernst, Dalí, Calder, and Warhol. The building, designed by Lina, opened in 1968 in the presence of Queen Elizabeth II of the United Kingdom. Its purpose was to house and display the collection.

Francisco de Assis Chateaubriand Bandeira de Melo, MASP's founder and patron, also known as Chatô, also as the King of Brazil, or the Brazilian Citizen Kane, was a journalist, lawyer, media mogul, and politician born in poverty and illiterate until the age of ten, notorious for his use of bullying, lies, intimidation, and blackmail to get his way. His achievements included the introduction of television to Brazil in 1950, the development of the Miss Brasil competition, and his campaign in the 1940s to bring modern aviation to the country, which resulted in the donation of over a thousand aircraft to Brazilian training schools. When he turned from aeroplanes to art, he exploited the low prices in post-war Europe to build MASP's collection, and wielded speed, persuasion, and flattery to get his way. He would buy masterpieces by tele-gram, with Pietro Bardi as his agent, and held banquets and public parades to celebrate the best acquisitions.

Bardi later recalled that Chatô was a man of many guises:

He used to dress as a cowboy, he used to ride a mule dressed with an academic uniform to enter a masked ball . . . and he dressed in the uniform of a colonel of the military police of Minas Gerais and travelled the streets in his posh Rolls Royce. However, at a certain time, in the middle of the night, he retired to his lonely office, not to invent newspaper articles, but well elaborated programs, draw political lines, economical, educational, moral ones . . . We made the museum together;

but it was possible only because Chateaubriand invented a technique of 'squeezing' the millionaires, took off them a million cruzeiros and exchanged that amount for a billion in promotions, in help, in political favors . . . If the Museu de Arte de São Paulo exists, that is due to this builder of the future of Brazil.

Chatô was a certain type of benevolent despot, a man for whom his own elevation and that of his nation were part of the same grand theatre, and for whom exploitation and generosity were part of a single tissue of taking and giving. Other tycoons, some dictators, perhaps some criminal bosses, some Renaissance popes, have shown similar tendencies. Sometimes beauty has been the result, sometimes bombast. What is striking about MASP is that Chatô's egotism, power, and semi-legal wealth were transmuted, through Lina Bo Bardi's architecture, into something for and of the public.

The museum has three horizontal pieces, built on a site with dramatic changes of level. The lowest piece consists of two floors of concrete half-buried in a slope. The middle is an open plaza. The top is a further two storeys of concrete, wrapped in glass, that seems to hover above the plaza. MASP is therefore a sandwich, of solid-void-solid.

The lower, half-buried structure contains a library, restaurant, theatre, and 'civic hall'. The upper, raised box contains galleries, for both the permanent collection and temporary exhibitions. Thanks to the switchbacks in the existing terrain the plaza is level with the eight-lane Avenida Paulista, even though it has two floors of building underneath it. A public park, the Trianon, lies on the other side of the Avenida.

MASP stands on the former site of a public belvedere, donated to the city decades previously by the contractor who built the

Avenida, on condition that the fine views from the park were preserved. Bo Bardi's gesture, of lifting the gallery block off the ground, achieves this, by allowing the line of sight to pass through the void thus formed.

The raising of the block had another purpose, which was to help create the public place, the plaza, underneath. This place is a gift to the city, with no prescribed purpose, except as the plane from which you ascend or descend to the rooms above and below. At its simplest, it is a clearing of space in São Paulo's thickets of towers, supplied with a big rectangle of shade against the hot sun, and a concrete umbrella against tropical rain.

It is a place made extraordinary by the things around it: the view, the avenue, the park, a steep drop at the side. MASP then adds art above and, below, the theatre, hall, and library. Architects are forever offering plazas to the public and the public often treat them like a pair of Christmas socks – well meant but ignorable. Here the space has been used, for programmed and spontaneous events: concerts, a weekly antique book fair, political protests, a circus, sculpture shows, and wandering and meeting. It allows people to inhabit it how they will.

In all this Bo Bardi does not sculpt the place into funny shapes, or add jazzy paving or artistic street furniture. She did not, she said, intend 'an eccentricity to astonish people'. She just makes the void, which allows the surrounding extraordinariness to become manifest, which gives space to the things latent on the site. She does one other thing: the floating of the gallery block charges the space underneath. You feel protected, but it is also exhilarating and strange to sense the weight of this cuboid Ark above your head.

The idea of the raising-up is almost as simple as a table, but it was not easy to achieve. It required heroic engineering to hang the block off two beams, seventy metres long, which come to rest on four pillars at the ends of the building. Yet the purpose of this

engineering is not to draw attention to its own prowess, as it would in some architects' work. Its role is to make possible the intangibles of view, space, and life. Substance is enlisted to enable the insubstantial.

Bo Bardi's invention continued inside the building. In the top floor of the gallery block she made a single side-lit hall for the treasures gathered by Chatô's wealth and Pietro's guile. Here she broke with the convention that paintings should be presented as windows on a wall, and placed each one on a vertical glass sheet – like the Van Gogh in the construction site photograph – anchored at the bottom by a block of concrete. Each was now more as its artist saw it, on an easel in a studio, than as a museum curator might see it, as a specimen pinned to a surface. Her presentation brought back, as another architect said,

> the tactile reality of their painted surface, the physical existence of something actually *made* – with paint and brush, stroke after stroke – IN SPACE.

They were not just pictures – things you look at – but paintings, things made through the actions of a painter.

On the back of each glass sheet was information about the work, placed as Bo Bardi said to 'leave the spectator to his own pure unhampered observations' rather than seeing the caption first and thinking, 'You should admire this, it's a Rembrandt.' The placing also required the viewer to move around the work, from front to back to front, engaging with it actively rather than passively. The paintings became things of three dimensions, animate, inhabiting the big room alongside people and sculptures.

Together, the glass-mounted paintings formed a transparent grove through which spectators could wander, permitting simultaneous views from a Hals to a Modigliani, or a Cézanne to a Léger. Other people, glimpsed between the paintings, became part of the scene, creating a ballet of living spectators and the painted dead. Lina Bo Bardi commissioned a series of photographs showing viewers and paintings answering each other's gestures and poses, as she did with Van Gogh's schoolboy.

She broke several rules of display, as observed by almost every other museum of old masters in the world. One is that each painting should be surrounded by neutrality, so as to allow undistracted contemplation. Another is that they should be shown in even, unchanging, completely controlled light, of a kind which her high, side-lit, large-windowed room, did not permit. These rules are relatively modern, and were invented centuries after some of the works were painted. They also ignore the fact that many paintings were made for far-from-neutral settings – an altarpiece or an ornate saloon – in far-from-perfect light. They assume that a painting is essentially disconnected from the room in which it is placed, and the people looking at it. It is an arbitrary and un-historic assumption, yet it is almost universally upheld. This orthodoxy is one reason why, in the late 1990s, Bo Bardi's display was trashed, in favour of a more normal arrangement of paintings on walls in enclosed rooms.

If architecture is the mineral interval between multiple thoughts and actions, MASP is an outstanding example. It is a frame for life, that of the city that swirls round it, of the artists whose gestures are held by the paint on their canvases, of the viewers of the art, of the vegetation and water in the building's landscaping. Void counts for more than solid. The effort, skill, and force of design and structure go into making pregnant emptiness, a space in which things can happen.

It has many registers of shadow and light, from the dark undercroft to the luminous gallery, and of weight: it floats, and it is rooted. It is a building to be felt as much as it is seen. It rhymes, and makes connections. The top-floor gallery, for example, was like

a more ethereal version of the rectangle of public space directly beneath it. The floating of the paintings on glass echoes the floating of the box that contains them.

The building has a powerful presence, but it does not dictate. It is big and symmetrical, like a palace, and its plainness might be thought forbidding. But it does not have a palace's grand flight of steps and emphatic door. It avoids the distancing effects architects often use: a spectacular form that demands you stand back and admire, overly pristine details and finishes, an ever-present artistic signature. Bo Bardi said her aim was to 'eliminate cultural snobbery'. Instead she offered the immediacy with which the paintings are presented, and with which the plaza opens off the avenue. She described her approach as 'Arquitetura Pobre', poor architecture, using basic materials like raw concrete, black rubber flooring, and paving of pedra-goiàs.

It is not, precisely, a democratic building, but one offered from the top down, from the power and wealth of Chatô, mediated by the educated professional Bo Bardi, to the people of São Paulo. There was not the elaborate public consultation now considered necessary in Britain for large buildings, and the fact that the director's wife was the architect, and the director was so close to the patron, suggests that a due process of impartial selection was not followed. The photograph of Lina on the building site shows an unequal relation of power: she is in charge, privileged by her skill, knowledge, and force of personality, and the patronage of Chatô. She is at liberty to expose a Van Gogh to the hazards of a building site, if she chooses. The workers behind her have to follow her directions.

But she uses her borrowed power generously, to open up, enrich, and create possibilities. She uses money and engineering to enable the unforeseen. She uses the solid parts to serve the void. John Cage, the American composer who knew more than most about the power of the pause, called MASP 'the architecture of freedom'.

Architecture is intimate with power. It requires authority, money, and ownership. To build is to exert power, over materials, building workers, land, neighbours, and future inhabitants. To imagine otherwise is innocent or pretentious.

The placing of a kitchen in a house expresses the relative status of whoever cooks to whoever eats. You can read the degrees of authority of banks and politicians in the fabric of the City of London. A supermarket in a high street manifests the differing strengths of the owners, consumers, and the local polity.

A recurring trait of dictators is a fondness for commissioning buildings. Nursultan Nazarbayev of Kazakhstan has built a new capital, Astana, with a long central axis pinned at one end with the Palace of Peace and Reconciliation, a 62-metre-high pyramid designed by Foster and Partners, and at the other by Khan Shatyr, a tent-shaped shopping mall also by Foster. Between these poles are the Presidential Palace, a version of the White House improved by a large blue dome, and the Bayterek Tower, which, with a sphere mounted on spiky steel, represents the poplar tree where the mythical bird Samruk laid a golden egg. It is known locally as Chupa Chups, thanks to its resemblance to a well-known lollipop.

The young Adolf Hitler, to take another example, applied unsuccessfully to work for the Viennese architect Otto Wagner; he later planned to make Berlin into the mighty imperial capital of Germania, an idea that obsessed him until his last days in the bunker, to the extent that it is not entirely clear what was more important: that Germania should be created to serve the Reich, or that the Reich should be created to make Germania possible.

For their part architects – some, at least – like to flirt with power. Ludwig Mies van der Rohe lingered longer in Nazi Germany than was decent, apparently in the hope that the regime might adopt his architectural style. He proposed a design for the German national pavilion at the 1935 International Exposition in Brussels, complete with swastikas, which according to the official prospectus was to act as the symbol of 'National Socialist fighting strength and heroic will'. Philip Johnson, a young American admirer of Mies who became one of the most influential figures of twentieth-century architecture, went further: he praised *Mein Kampf*, helped found an American fascist party known as the grey shirts, and in 1939 followed the Wehrmacht into Poland, where he described the burning of Warsaw as 'a stirring spectacle'. Le Corbusier, whose efforts to secure the patronage of Soviet Russia ultimately failed, later courted the collaborationist regime of Vichy France.

It is not just an accidental or convenient relationship. Dictators and architects alike are driven by the desire to dominate and shape the world, and they like this quality in each other. Whether manifest through scale, and the sense for the spectator of being in the presence of something great, or through mastery of detail – the ability to bend materials and labour to an exacting will – some of the most admired tourist destinations in the world have as a large part of their agenda the placing of some people over others. Domination is confirmed in the language attached to architecture: master craftsman, master planner, master builder, modern master, masterpiece.

It is an uncomfortable truth that part of the thrill or impressiveness of architecture lies in its exercise of power and, sometimes, cruelty. Occasionally, in India, you can find a handful of tombs outside an exquisite monument, which honour the craftsmen who built it, slaughtered by their ruler-client so that they could not do anything more beautiful for anyone else. Today there is a revered

Asian architect who is known to beat and punch his staff, breaking noses, and to force them to sleep (inasmuch as they sleep at all) in his office, so that he can extract the greatest possible part of their lives for the service of his work, work to which he himself has given all his being. Human sacrifice and construction are old companions.

Successful architects have immense will. They need it, if their designs are to survive the many pressures applied from conception to completion: from clients, planners, and contractors, from budget, site, and brief, and from the accidents of the process of construction. And they combine force with charm: they have whatever it takes to get their way. Stanford White, the man with fire between his legs and lead between his eyes, is a case in point.

According to a contemporary, he

> was a personality of enormous power, a man of phenomenal force. He affected everyone he met. I always think of him as the embodiment of a particular period of American life – a period of effervescence, and of the sudden combining of elements that had long lain in solution and came together with a certain emotional violence.
>
> He had the vitality of a giant. He had the same divine frenzy for making himself known that great politicians are born with. He was pervasive.

He was precocious, hard-drinking, womanizing, depressive, social and generous. His idea of architecture went beyond designing buildings to creating the shows and parties within them; he was an impresario as well as a designer. He could stay up for nights and days on end to complete a piece of work, and he was ruthless with his clients, sometimes pushing them to the brink of ruin with the expense of his buildings.

He was both domineering and charming. Suzannah Lessard describes him as a 'big, inspired toddler, indulged, angelic, oblivious, tyrannical'. He also had, according to an artist friend, 'a sensitivity so great he could lose his personality'. As a young man, touring Europe, White wrote that the Elgin marbles made his 'hair stand up and then lie down again' and he wept in front of Vermeer and Veronese. 'To think that so lovely a thing could be done,' he wrote, 'and I could not do it!'

His reaction to beauty, in people or things, was first to be overwhelmed by it, and then to want to own it, consume it, and absorb it into himself. As a successful architect designing houses for the rich, he would plunder the continent that had so moved him when young. He would have ancient fireplaces ripped out of palaces and imported to America for resale at a profit to his clients. He once had the police in an Italian village paid to look the other way while its graceful public fountain was abducted. White regarded this pillage as the entitlement of a young, powerful country over an old one in decline.

His architectural work, carried out as a partner in the practice of McKim Mead and White, can be divided into two periods. In the first, which made his name before he was thirty, he designed holiday homes in Newport and Long Island for the newly leisured and the newly rich: a cotton trader retired at thirty-one, industrialists, property magnates, an art dealer. These works helped develop what would later be called the Shingle Style, where the timber-construction techniques of everyday American buildings were combined with an aesthetic sensibility, fine craftsmanship, and touches of Japanese influence. White's informal houses would dissemble their expense with light construction, usually of timber. They were, as one historian would put it, 'the architecture of the American summer'.

In the second period his clients were no longer rich, but stupendously rich. They were Vanderbilts, Whitneys, and Pulitzers, merchant princes of America's Gilded Age, for whom he designed mansions and social clubs. White and his partners also started

designing the public monuments of the time, such as Boston Public Library and the Washington Square Arch in New York. For these clients and these projects, romantic derivations of New England farmhouses were no longer sufficient. Now the models had to be the palaces of baroque Venice, or of the reign of Louis XIV, or chateaux of the French Renaissance. Some of these piles were in Newport, Rhode Island, which grew grander in step with White's career. Henry James, who had loved the place when it was simpler, lamented that, thanks to the new mansions,

> the face of nature was now as much obliterated as possible, and the original shy sweetness as much as possible bedizened and bedeviled . . . What an idea, originally, to have seen this miniature spot of earth, where the sea-nymphs on the curved sands, at the worst, might have chanted back to the shepherds, as a mere breeding-ground for white elephants!

Picturesque became symmetrical, light became heavy, and wood became stone. Cass Gilbert, a pupil of White's who went on to design the magnificent Gothic skyscraper that is the Woolworth Building in New York, identified a shift in character that roughly corresponds with the shift in style. Until his late twenties White was, said Gilbert, 'a man of extraordinary ability and the most attractive personality'; later he got 'a little sick of his arrogance, and his claiming all the credit for everything done in the office'.

It is easy enough to see how the later buildings express power. They command bluffs and promontories, and the best addresses. They are big and conspicuously expensive. They can pluck wood, stone, tapestry or carving from whatever forest, mountain, or palazzo they please, and have them freighted by ship and rail. They can hire the very best craftsmen and drive them to feats of dominion over matter. In the dining room of Frederick William Vanderbilt's Hyde Park, one immense Renaissance-style fireplace is not enough. It has to be doubled, for effect, and to heat the vast room.

They appropriate the treasures and imagery of the Old World, and then exceed them. Their Ionic and Corinthian columns, made of single pieces of marble or stone, are more perfectly regular and precise, in their fluting and the chiselling of acanthus leaves, than their European models. Then White might throw in an unexpected asymmetry remembered from the Shingle Style, a gesture which averts pomposity, but also shows that he is in charge. He has mastered the classical, and can now toy with it.

There are other, more subtle plays of power in White's work, including in the gentler houses of the Shingle Style. He had a fascination with surface, which is subjected to a refined frenzy of marking and patterning. On the outside of the earlier houses, White manipulates shingles and tiles into waves, scales, and scallops, inserts sgraffito panels, and compresses pebbles, shells and bottle glass into sunbursts and emblems. Windows are made of small panes, held by delicate grids of lead or timber. The panes are of similar scale to the shingles, and together they create an overall vibration of small things, running across wall, window and roof. Inside, wood is incised, carved and inlaid, with patterns that might be vegetal or geometric, or emulations of weaving or drapery, or rapid rhythms of lines and dots. There is a hum of innumerable pieces. Countlessness is part of the point: you are dizzied by infinity.

As well as wood, there is brass, marble, mirror, and wicker, and tiles in Mediterranean blue or Atlantic green. Glass is coloured, patterned, opaque, knotted, or clear; copper is patinated and multiply pierced. Stanford White could be unorthodox with his materials, using cork tiles in herringbone patterns, or split bamboo on walls and ceilings, or gunning doors with upholstery tacks to form patterns of suns and stars. He would mix plaster with gold dust.

There is always more of everything than you would find in the older buildings from which White borrowed his motifs. When he decided to use Delft tiles on his own house, he did not make them into a fire surround in the usual way; he conscripted one thousand of them to cover an entire wall. Like a juggler adding more objects to his airborne inventory White takes a space to a certain point, and then goes beyond it. Like a juggler, he retains his poise. These places feel obsessive rather than excessive.

White's fever of surfaces is partly a sophisticated display of his clients' wealth, as such refinement was not cheap. It is equally a display of the architect's virtuosity, and his creative ownership. There is an unspoken deal whereby the legal owner, White's client, licenses the architect to mark every surface as his, in return for a share in the genius of the magus-like maker. White never lets you forget that he is there.

There is something erotic in the fetishization of a building's skin, and the erotic for White was linked to power. In the lust nest that White made for himself above Madison Square Garden there was a connoisseurship of surface, expressed in dazzling but well-chosen colours, and in fabrics, skins, and velvet, that is close to his connoisseurship of girls, of the sommelier blonde and brunette at his famous dinner party, and of the extraordinarily beautiful sixteen-year-old Evelyn Nesbit, whose deflowering when (as she later said) drugged, would lead to White's death. It seems that wine, women, and walls were almost as one to him. Things of the senses excited a longing that had to be assuaged by mastery; in him, tyrant and epicure combined, and domination was an intimate companion of the exquisite. His mastery was not expressed as a single grabbing, but as the long-drawn-out play of artistic brilliance.

His ornament is a primal splattering executed with immaculate control. It recalls the tattooing of the Papuan that Adolf Loos described in *Ornament and Crime* and which, according to Loos, is both the expression of an erotic urge and the origin of art. Loos identified the same urge in the scrawls of 'degenerates' on toilet walls. Stanford White marked and daubed his walls too, but with taste. He turned graffiti into sgraffito.

White's ornate exteriors, especially the later ones loaded with borrowed grandeur, were the kinds of things that Loos abhorred, and sought to replace with his gentlemanly blankness. But the two men had in common the compression of space, stuff, and time into surfaces of their interiors. Both took materials and images from many origins and of great lusciousness, and fixed them into panels that advertised their flatness, or near-flatness. Both used opaque glass to hold light in the plane of a wall.

This compression is a common feature of sensuous but controlling architecture, for reasons that are not immediately obvious. Part of it is the thrill of delight against constraint, of confining life and luxury within strict bounds. Part of it is conquest and mastery, the idea of drawing things promiscuously from distant and various times and places, and exerting on them such precision that they lose a dimension of space. Like love hotels, White's and Loos' spaces are wide-ranging in their appropriations, but unlike love hotels they fuse and mutate their material into new wholes. There is also, perhaps, a fantasy of procreative magic at work. Just as an architect can conjure from two dimensions to three, from a drawn plan to a building or a city, so he can make flat walls dense with stuff and image, that intimate worlds beyond their bounds.

The signs and implements of power in buildings are many. There are scale, mass, height, and cost, which can be exploited to over-awe, or to include. A large building might be seen as intimidating or inspiring, depending whether we feel a sense of connection with its size: whether its magnificence is for them or us.

Symmetry, doubling, and repetition are signs of might. They show that client and architect had sufficient command over their workforce to get them to do the same thing, in the same way, over and over, and that the cost of duplication and redundancy can be afforded. Symmetry demonstrates a victory over the often asymmetric pressures that function and site can have on a building: rooms might need to be different sizes, while a site might slope or have irregular boundaries.

There are politics in detail. Building materials have lives and histories – ultimately natural, they have flaws and grains, and different ways of moving and changing in response to temperature and moisture – which an architect may choose to subjugate, ignore, manipulate, or cherish. For example stone, in McKim Mead and White's later mansions, is cut to a sharpness almost of steel, but the same material can be loosely piled up, undressed and without mortar, to enclose sheep fields in northern England.

The way materials and building workers are directed, with what degrees of freedom or control, is manifest in the finished building. The use of power in the making then suggests the degree of control that a building might exercise over future users. When an architect insists that parts of a building are joined in particular ways, or fails to get his or her way, it expresses the relations of power and cooperation between architect, builder, and client. Such power can be wielded generously, collaboratively, or selfishly, in pursuit of public good or personal obsession or, often, in contradictory combinations of these impulses. If an architect demands a well-made threshold or seat, or achieves beauty through persistence, it can inspire gratitude for generations, but if the purpose is only fussy egotism, it irritates.

In his essay *Poor Little Rich Man*, Adolf Loos told of an imaginary millionaire who invited an architect to 'Bring Art to me, bring Art into my home. Cost is no object.' He got his wish, and 'wherever he cast his glance was Art, Art in each and every thing. He grasped Art when he took hold of a door handle; he sat on Art when he settled into an armchair . . . he sank his feet into Art when he trod on the carpet.' The architect 'had forgotten nothing . . . everything was made by him'. Even the tram tracks outside the house were re-laid, so that the vehicles 'roll by in the rhythm of the Radetzky March'. Each furnishing had a definite place, which caused some stress: 'several times the architect had to unroll his working drawings in order to rediscover the place for the matchbox'.

Still, the rich man is happy, until he invites the architect to celebrate his birthday. The latter first berates his client for wearing shoes designed for his bedroom outside their intended place. He then flies into a rage at the rich man's wish to find somewhere to display gifts from his family: 'How do you come to allow yourself to be given gifts! . . . Did I not consider *everything*? You don't need anything more. You are complete!'

> 'But what if my grandchild gives me something he has made at kindergarten?'
> 'Then you must not accept it!'

The happy man, says Loos, 'suddenly felt deeply, deeply unhappy . . . he was precluded from all future living and striving, developing and desiring. Yes indeed. He is finished. *He is complete!'*

Loos was satirizing the architects of the Viennese secession, and of art nouveau, who sought to make every object a thing of design, and to make houses into all-encompassing symphonies of space, surface, and detail. Although this architecture was full of life, with sinuous natural forms and dazzling colours, it was liveliness lived by the architect, in advance of anyone moving in. Inhabitants could only be admiring witnesses; they could add nothing of themselves. They could look, but not dwell. Fixity or completeness of design, no matter how beautiful or intelligent, can become a kind

of death, as it was for the rich man. In its pursuit of the eternity of art, such architecture leaves little space for the living.

Such tensions between architect's vision and user's life recur beyond Adolf Loos' time and place. Historians talk of 'Palladio's Villa Rotonda' or 'Le Corbusier's Villa Savoye' as if they and not their clients owned them and, as with White's houses, there is an understanding, or misunderstanding, between the legal and creative owners as to the sense in which it belongs to each. Such deals can be harmonious or rancorous, depending whether either party feels they have to give more territory than they expected. Edith Farnsworth, the client of Mies van der Rohe's most famous house, and possibly his lover, bitterly raged against him when she found that the house was ultimately his, not hers. He was, she said, 'simply colder and more cruel than anybody I have ever known. Perhaps it was never a friend and collaborator, so to speak, that he wanted, but a dupe and a victim.'

Where architects design for a larger public than individual home owners, the tension between the intent of the work and the lives for which it will be the setting plays out in different ways. In private houses the main relationship is two-way, between client and architect. In public projects there are users and passers-by as well as a client, which might be a complicated institution of committees and officers, and a design team, which is likely to include a larger array of different consultants than is needed for a private house.

It is not always clear or predictable what form the relationships of power and interests will take. It may be that the driving force behind a building project is the wish of the client – a dictator, say, or a corporation – to impose upon a place. Architects, such as an Albert Speer working for Adolf Hitler, may see their role only as fulfilling or exceeding their patron's dreams. Others might see themselves as humanizing or civilizing tyranny, of embodying values in architecture that are not those of their dictator clients. This is the defence of European architects like Rem Koolhaas or Herzog & de Meuron when designing the headquarters of Chinese state television, or the 'bird's nest' stadium for the Beijing Olympic Games.

A desire to impose might come more from an architect than a client, as when the Catalan architect Ricardo Bofill turned blocks of affordable flats, in the French new towns Marne-la-Vallée and St-Quentin-en-Yvelines, into immense colonnaded crescents, and steroidal concrete versions of Versailles. Sometimes the play of power is not simply a matter of domination or exploitation, but includes reciprocity between users, owners, and designers, or some transmutation, as with Bo Bardi's São Paulo Art Museum, of individual might into shared freedoms.

Several modern theorists have argued that the classical tradition in architecture has inherently oppressive tendencies. In both the ancient and the Renaissance worlds classical cities had a particular version of public space, according to the writer Aaron Betsky, 'that was not part of nature and not productive, but just a place of power. It was a world conquered and emptied out by force', dedicated to appearances by rulers and aristocrats. They served and expressed not only the power of men over women, but also the superiority of citizens over slaves, lesser classes, and foreigners. The architecture that went with such spaces came to be geometric and fixed and made of stones laid on stones. It was a kind of architecture intended to be seen primarily in daylight, which Alberti would eventually promote. The dark, the unstable, the dispossessed, and the deviant were kept out of sight.

A late and famous version of such geometricized power was the system of boulevards that Baron Haussmann forced through the tangled fabric of Paris on behalf of the Emperor Napoleon III. These were instruments of control, designed to make it easier for the government to manoeuvre troops, and harder for the populace to erect barricades, in the event of revolution. They were made of stone, and had the look and expectation of permanence. They created an image of order, in their symmetry, scale, and straightness.

The illicit was banished to spaces behind the boulevards, such as the *passage* where, in the 1920s, the surrealist flâneur Louis Aragon set his autobiographical novel *Paris Peasant*. This place is doomed to imminent erasure, in order to make way for the extension of the Boulevard Haussmann, in a late fulfilment of the Baron's ideas. Local traders' campaigns for its preservation, and their 'seething fury', have been waved aside in the face of the interests of property companies, and the corrupt complicity of local politicians. For as long as it survives the onslaught of the 'giant rodent' that is the boulevard, this marginal place of poets, strange shops, and prostitutes, this 'human aquarium', is one of 'the true sanctuaries of the cult of the ephemeral, the ghostly landscape of damnable pleasures and professions'. It is one of the 'dimly lit zones' where the 'whole fauna of human fantasies, their marine vegetation, drifts and luxuriates' (and in which, to be sure, Aragon exercises his own power games, as a client of the prostitutes). Dark, unruly, and protean, the *passage* is everything the boulevard is not, which is why it has to go.

To see all geometrically ordered public spaces as nothing but sterile instruments of male power is an oversimplification. It ignores the many European and South American squares and avenues where the force of city life has overwhelmed any controlling intentions in the planning. Such places can make visible, rather than supreme authority, the people and groups who make a town. Urban populations have a way of subverting, appropriating, and overrunning whatever structures are set up to manage them. Aragon's *passage* is in fact a relic of an earlier attempt to regularize the city which, only by becoming obsolete and mortal, becomes the unstable underworld he so admires.

Avenue de l'Opéra. Derniers démolisseurs.   Portique de l'Hôtel de Tausse.

The Jamaa el Fna in Marrakesh, meanwhile, shows how unimportant regular form can be to liveliness in public. With its story-tellers, musicians, snake-charmers, magicians, medicine men, food stalls, markets, and water-sellers, its activities continuing but changing as day turns into night, it is one of the most intense and many-layered public spaces in the world. But even though it is often called a 'square', it has almost no architectural shape. It is a patch of ground with ragged edges, surrounded by low, ordinary buildings. The place is made almost entirely by the activities within it.

If a developer or architect wants to show his love of the public, he is likely to include in his proposals a vague rectangle, called a piazza, distantly descended from classical antiquity. 'Life' is then expected to appear in it, but does not always do so, or not in the way intended, which, if it is of the essence and intention of such places that they limit spontaneity, should surprise no one. It is a case of confusing form with content.

Power in buildings is manifest in one of the basic distinctions in architecture, that between object and space.

Buildings are most obviously objects, and if you look at the standard histories you will see a series of temples, cathedrals, palaces, and important modernist villas standing against a clear sky. Architectural magazines and websites also tend to celebrate the making of singular objects, photographed to minimize context and inhabitation. An architect is most often commissioned to design a thing, a building, whose boundaries are defined by legal ownership, a construction contract, and a budget. Construction workers are not paid to build, laboriously and in all weathers, an absence, but a thing of mass and hardness.

Yet the purpose of the object is largely to make or modify

spaces. It makes rooms inside and on the outside joins with other buildings to make a street, or a square, or at the very least a huddle of objects with gaps between them. The object is supposed to provide the right protection, stability, climatic control, dimensions, acoustic, lighting, comfort, and imagery for whatever might happen in and around it. If it is in a landscape, it will alter the kind of space that that landscape is, either a little or a lot. A cottage in a field changes space, as do the cooling towers of a power station.

Space allows freedoms, and qualifies them. It makes certain actions more possible or less so, depending whether it is a parade ground, dance floor, bedroom, or hillside. It changes with time. It can be intimidating or intimate, open or enclosed, unrestricted or rule-bound. It can be profoundly altered by barely perceptible adjustments. A street scanned by security cameras, for example, will look much like one that is not, but the two will be different kinds of place. Tungsten lights, or fluorescent, or neon, or halogen, or hard or soft acoustics, change rooms.

Space is something for the imagination to inhabit. Such things as material, scale, light, and ornament give a space a climate, which prompts associations, harbours memories, and provokes images. Its power lies in its multiple nature, that it is experienced through both body and imagination. Spaces, with few exceptions, are shared, and have to accommodate different people's interests and imaginings. If they are precisely tailored to a single world view, as happens in the most extreme forms of totalitarian architecture, or in the architect-designed house of Loos' poor little rich man, they become oppressive.

At the same time a space cannot be equally available to all possible uses and people; it will always belong to some more than others, mean more and have greater purpose. The absolutely blank or neutral place, that might in theory be infinitely flexible and available, is as inhuman as one that is over-prescribed. A large part of the job of an architect is, or should be, the working between these extremes, the search to achieve both openness and definition.

The object, the building, the thing often designed by architects and built by contractors, is an instrument for making space. It has an effect whether a living room has high or low ceilings, whether a shopping mall is glazed or cavernous, or whether a square is walled or colonnaded. It makes a difference whether an opera house, as it was in nineteenth-century Paris, is designed with the beaux-arts pomp of Charles Garnier or, as in modern Guangzhou, with the freeform curves of Zaha Hadid, and the difference is made both to the opera and the city around it.

A building is a powerful instrument, but it is just that – an instrument more than an end in itself – and it is not the only one. Such things as laws, light, ownership, climate, patterns of behaviour, custom, networks of communication and surveillance, maintenance, cleaning, smell and financial value can have as much influence on the nature of a space. 'When it's raining on Oxford Street the buildings are no more important than the rain', said the architect David Greene, who, perhaps because of the honesty and modesty shown in this observation, has spent more of his life teaching than building.

But it can suit the vanity of architects and the agendas of their clients to overstate the importance of the object. If a building is exalted, so is the professional who designed it. If a business or a government can point to a miraculous monument of its making, it can draw attention from actions or omissions that are less benefi- cial to the public. It is easier to build and publicize an eye-catching building than it is to keep all of a city's pavements in good order, or run a fair and effective housing policy. If London property devel- opers want to bend or break planning rules that impede their wish to build as big as they would like, they dress their plans in 'world class architecture'. If the People's Republic of China wants foreigners to talk about something other than human rights, it holds the Olympics, and commissions a beautiful stadium.

With the exaltation of the object goes an exaltation of the sense of sight. Architecture can fairly be said to be more an art of the visual than of any other sense, but it is not exclusively so. Sensation, sound, and scent also make spaces and, although it is rare outside the tale of Hansel and Gretel to taste a building, the interaction of food and space, in restaurants, markets, and shops, is fundamental to cities. In Dubai and Houston, Texas, your social status can be calibrated by the amount of time you spend in air-conditioned space, or in heat and humidity. What makes the favelas of Rio de Janeiro into slums is less their look – at a casual glance they resemble desirable Italian hill towns – than their stench.

Nor is the experience of architecture just one of standing back and looking at it, as you might a sculpture. It is more enmeshed, bodily, and temporal. Yet, when buildings are promoted or published, they are presented as pure and static images and discussed almost exclusively in terms of their visual appearance: do they look 'futuristic' or 'traditional'; are they 'spectacular' or 'elegant'; do they resemble a gherkin, a cheese-grater, a pile of cardboard boxes, or a 1930s radio set? They are represented with computer-generated images which emphasize shape, exclude weathering or time, reduce material to a generalized sheen and climate to ubiquitous blue sky and sunlight. It is of course easier to depict look than touch, sound, or smell, but it is also convenient. There are politics of the senses, as of architectural detail; air is political. Concentrating on look avoids worrying about either.

The word 'vision' is much used, as in 'vision of the future' or 'visionary architecture', phrases which hint at a quasi-divine authority, while confining architecture to the sense of sight. They usually describe an intended future reality whose rules are determined by developers and their architects, and requires as a precondition of its existence the removal of whatever might be awkward, complicated, or alive, already on the site. Instead the magical icon, conjured by the visionary architect, will through the sheer brilliance and surprise of its visible shape satisfy every possible desire for liveliness, imagination, creativity, identity, and difference. That the icon also functions as a marketing tool is all to the good: sales *and* art in one hit – it's a win-win. Shape, in fact, cannot achieve all these things alone, which is really the point. The people who commission such buildings do not want real liveliness and difference. They get in the way. It is easier to buy the look.

Consider Robert Doisneau's famous photograph *Le Baiser de l'Hôtel de Ville*, taken in 1950. A man and women catch each other with a kiss, as the photographer catches them with his lens, in the middle of a busy street. There are cars and people in comfortable co-existence, and cafe tables, one with an ashtray. Behind, as an incidental backdrop of officialdom, tilted as if by the force of the embrace, is the Hôtel de Ville, the centre of the administration of Paris. The photograph might have been posed, but it captured an idea about city life, about intimacy and multiplicity in the throng.

Now consider an equivalent spot in modern London, outside City Hall, the building completed in 2002 to house the city's mayor and the London Assembly. The British government, nervous about cost overruns on public buildings, had leased the building following a bidding process in which developers were invited to offer roughly suitable buildings, planned but not yet built, which could be modified to house the seat of the city's democracy. The idea was to be businesslike and cost-effective, and the future City Hall was, in the early stages of the bidding process, a boxy block in a proposed commercial development called More London. It was designed by the leading practice of Foster and Partners, but Norman Foster, the

leader of the business, may not have known much about it. It was a bread-and-butter commission.

It eventually dawned on both government and bidders that such a significant building should be more than just another office block. More London's main rival imported the famously creative Will Alsop to sex up their plans. Foster himself now took an interest, and doodled a visionary idea: the box would be changed to a sphere, hovering over the Thames. It would be like the much-loved London Eye, but a three-dimensional ball, not a circle, and so even better. The hovering ball proved impractical, for reasons to do with both structure and river traffic, so it was moved back onto land, warped into a sloping egg-like shape, and ringed with water, in memory of the idea that it might be surrounded by river. This ring of water then gave the potential centre of local democracy an unfortunate resemblance to a moated castle, and it was later dropped.

Foster's design made much of visibility. Glass walls around the debating chamber would allow the public to see their representatives at work, and people would ascend a spiral ramp above the chamber, up to a glorious view of the city, while looking down on the politicians. The people would be the masters. It would be a transparent building for transparent government. Foster had done something similar with the Reichstag in Berlin, with some success.

More London and Foster won the bid and City Hall was built, along with plainer blocks housing businesses like the financial advisory company Ernst and Young, but its democratizing wizardry did not work. Security considerations meant that the spiral ramp was closed to the public almost all the time. The supposedly levelling experience of seeing debates through a plane of glass could not be had without first passing through metal detectors and, in any case, there turned out to be little public appetite for watching assembly members opening and closing their mouths, soundlessly, like goldfish.

Meanwhile the spaces outside remained under the control of

More London, and managed by them in the interests of their corporate tenants. It is a well-finished, well-detailed, well-maintained world of grey granite, grey steel, and grey glass, through which well-made grey suits can come and go as they please. Should anyone wish to protest against the decisions made in City Hall, they will be moved on by security. Should they wish to park a bike or have a picnic, ditto.

And should anyone attempt a prolonged snog, and a Doisneau set up a camera to shoot them, they will be dissuaded. Inappropriate behaviour and professional photography (without special permission) are not allowed at More London. There would be no mingling of people and traffic and no ashtray on a table, because smoking is banned. There would, at least, be coffee in the cafes, if only because the cappuccino has long been an international measure of urban sensuality, a near identical shot available worldwide as a memory and substitute of the richer palette of sensations and freedoms that the Doisneau picture hints at.

A London version of that classic shot of Paris could, in other words, not be repeated. More London offers what looks like public space, because it is open and paved and contains people, but is thinner, more controlled, and less free than the real thing. For all City Hall's claims to democracy, it is really a boisterous bauble – appropriately at least for the noisy mayors Livingstone and Johnson who have so far occupied it – in the pocket of developers.

From its inception More London was billed as a new concept, a piece of city conceived as a branded product rather than a place. This is why it has its odd name, so unlike the sort of names urban districts usually have, dreamed up by image consultants. 'morelondon', as it is sometimes written (fused, lower case, web-friendly) conflates the title of the company, the place, the product, and the marketing concept. When it was being built large billboards went up showing construction workers erecting giant ice creams and dumbbells with, as good marketing practice demands, tag lines tied into the brand: 'Lick More. Enjoy the flavour; one taste and you'll want more'. Also 'Pump More. With a new gym and fitness centre it's a great place to work in – and work out'. The licking, pumping billboards suggested a sensual intensity at More London which, although you can indeed buy ice creams there, is not really on offer.

To think of a place as a brand is striking. A place offers freedoms, possibilities, and multiple identities. It is multisensory, and unfolds over time. A brand compresses content into a marketable entity, is consistent and controlled. If it permits too many interpretations or variations, it fails. A brand is essentially a thing of sight. It is not then surprising that the billboards showed visual images of a sensuality that did not materialize.

Foster's architecture also functioned in the zone of sight. In More London's rigid cloud of greyness the greatest excitement is offered by the curves and projections of City Hall. It looks striking, or at least strange. But this excitement can only be had by a passive spectator, looking. It does not engage. The curves could conceivably be called sensual, and the building was soon called the 'testicle', as a displaced companion to Foster's phallic Gherkin just across the Thames, but in truth there is nothing terribly sexy about this great distorted ball.

Above all Foster's design hoped to achieve its magic through the transparency of glass, through the effect of looking. But, as should have been quickly obvious, it is more useful and empowering for citizens to hear the words of politicians and know their thoughts than to see their physiognomies and gesticulations. And, although it is a recurring fantasy of architects that glass is transparent, often it is not. Yes, it is good at letting you see the view from inside a building, but it is also reflective of, among other things, sky and clouds. If it permits the passage of light, it is impermeable to everything else, for which reason it is a popular material for security barriers and the outsides of banks. It divides as much as it opens up. Architects like glass because it allows them to wrap up noble-sounding concepts like transparency into a single magic stuff, which concepts can then be claimed simply by specifying it. It makes them masters of philosophy when they open a glazing catalogue. Glass is indeed a wonderful material, but it is complex, elusive, and not automatically benign.

The effect of glass at City Hall and More London is the opposite of that advertised. Its reflectivity makes the building look impervious and distant, and one of the structure's many nicknames is 'Darth Vader's helmet'. Where there are glimpses of bureaucrats, local politicians, or employees of Ernst and Young, you do not feel that you share their world. Rather, their separateness is stressed.

The development is a diagram of the relative power of business, state, and citizen at a time when government had an exaggerated respect for the wisdom and abilities of the private sector. Starting from the bidding process, when estate agents were instructed to find office space of about the right size, the interests of the public were sketchily defined and weakly defended. It could in fact have been much worse, as many developers would have made more miserable and inaccessible places than did More London, who are relatively conscientious about their social responsibilities. But the end result is a cartoon of a public building, and an amputated idea of public space.

Architecture requires and involves power. The question is how that power is realized – by whom, for whom, to whom.

In a few obvious cases, such as Nazi Germany, oppressive regimes create oppressive architecture. More often, things are more complicated. Tourists to Moscow love the city's ballroom-like metro stations, not caring that they were built by slaves in appalling

conditions to serve the image of a hideous regime. The Italian architect Giuseppe Terragni was an ardent fascist, who fought for the cause on the Russian front with damage to his health that would prove fatal, yet he designed buildings of delicacy and – not an obviously fascist quality – ambiguity. Another Italian architect of subtlety and civility, Luigi Moretti, designed as one of his early masterpieces Mussolini's personal gym. Conversely, the enlightened social-democratic mayor Gijs van Hall of Amsterdam managed to commission the Bijlmermeer estate, which was seen as more oppressive than many things built by fascists.

There is no absolute correlation between the powers that shape a space and the relationships of power that that space shapes. There is no fixed form of power, no formula such as straight lines = tyranny, wiggles = freedom. Thanks to the instability of architecture, and the indirect nature of architectural truth, mean people can make generous places, and vice versa. Bullies like Chatô can commission places of freedom, like the Museum of Art in São Paulo.

Architecture sublimates. Mrs Stuyvesant Fish, one of Stamford White's clients, asked him to make a ballroom in which a person who was not well bred would feel uncomfortable, and you can still sense both his clients' snobbery and his mania in his buildings, but these are far from the only experiences they offer. They are more than a rapist's parlours. Mies van der Rohe's cruelties might be detected in the fierce rigour he applied to detail, but when converted into marble and steel they become something very different from plain nastiness. In truth, and importantly, we often like the presence of force in a building, as long as we feel it is not directed against us.

Time and chance can change or reverse the impact of a building. A Gothic cathedral would have seemed extremely menacing to anyone opposing the religion and politics that it represented – let's say a heretic whose last view of the world was of a beautifully carved portal flickering through the heat of his pyre. Now it is an object of charm to tourists. An old factory, formed for cold exploitation, can be converted into delightful lofts for young creative types. These transformations are only partly to do with design.

Buildings and spaces can however have properties that are more or less empowering. Buildings that rely exclusively on visible form, or have a completeness of detail that permits no further change, or deny the sensual, or prescribe future uses too precisely, or proclaim a single form of propaganda or branding, or ignore their surroundings, or scale, are likely to oppress. Spaces that permit accident are open to whatever is around them, and understand their role as background or instruments, are more likely to create freedoms.

This does not mean buildings should be indifferent. Shabbiness and negligence make another kind of oppression, and depression. People who build, such as clients, architects, or contractors, cannot help wielding power. They change the world even if in a small way by putting something up. They inevitably make choices and distinctions, and if they want to build well, they should make these choices well. A building is a proposition that is highly likely to be contradicted, abused, or proved wrong – architecture is often the fall guy for future events – but it is as well that this proposition is made with intelligence, imagination and awareness.

Much of the play of power in architecture is about the ownership of dreams. Manhattan, though formed by brute business, found a shape that matched the city's popular mythology of striving and display, and so came to belong to its citizens and visitors. The encrustations of its buildings allow places where the mind can take hold. It is helped by its public structure of gridded streets, parks, and museums, which frame and mediate the force of the skyscrapers. It offers places to dwell, at different scales, and many more experiences than just staring at towers.

At More London, once you have experienced whatever frisson the strange shape of City Hall might offer and enjoyed the view across the River Thames, your imagination is likely to bounce off the hard blank surfaces of the buildings. In Dubai you can experience a vicarious visual thrill at Sheikh Mohammed's dream of towers, but the ground plane of highways, barriers, and malls offers little purchase for imagining, unless through something purchased in a shop.

Loos' poor little rich man was oppressed because he had no space for imagining in a house saturated with his architect's dreams. But under-design can also eat the soul, as in the standardized design of a room in an airport hotel, or a block of flats hurled up on an ex-industrial wasteland as part of a stalled 'regeneration' project. You want buildings to stimulate, give cues, propose, provoke, engage, give evidence of a human presence, reveal what you yourself could not have imagined, and the same time offer places for your own imagination to inhabit.

This is the strength of MASP. It does not shirk its role as a building made by power. It is strong-minded. It does not ingratiate or dissemble – some indeed may look at it and see only a blunt lump. Its detail is considered and to the purpose, but not obsessive. But it uses its strength to allow freedoms and possibilities and to enrich what is already there, in the city and in the art. The object is used to make space. It is a thing to be lived, not looked at.

6: Form follows finance

A handbag is placed on the table in front of me, white and gold and tsarist, Fabergé in its intensity of ornament, but also futurist. By this I know that Zaha Hadid, possibly the most famous living architect, is arriving. The bag-carrying assistant melts away, and as I look out of the first-floor window of the Victorian schoolhouse where she has her studio, I see the architect emerge into spring sunshine out of a pearly Chrysler Voyager. She has just been driven from her airy, all-white rooftop flat, two hundred yards away.

A little later she has rejoined her handbag, and is looking at me through the piece of air which, in the days when she still smoked, would have been smoke-filled. 'They don't want me,' she says in her gravelly voice. 'You need your building. They won't let it happen with me. You should get somebody else.'

We are eighteen months into a project to create a new building for The Architecture Foundation, of which I am director. It is to be designed by Zaha. The 'they' she mentions are Land Securities, the largest company of property developers in the United Kingdom, who are to fund and build the project. It is at a point of crisis. The cost has gone from £2.25 million to £5 million, was clawed back to a theoretical £4.5 million, but is now ascending for no apparent reason to £7.5, £8.5 million, and showing no sure sign of stopping there. Something has to be done, and I am meeting her to discuss what this something will be.

Zaha Hadid first came to widespread attention in 1983 when,

aged thirty-two, she won the competition to design The Peak, a club and apartments building perched high above Hong Kong. It was a drab time for architecture, into which she made an electrifying entry. Her style was fully formed, expressed both in forms of the proposed building and in the big paintings, energetic but precise, with which she depicted it. Her idea for The Peak was to create a series of thin flying planes that overlapped and intersected, long splinters of building charged with seismic energy, like manmade versions of Hong Kong's volcanic geology. She revelled in the multi-layered intensity of Hong Kong, of which The Peak was an exalted expression.

There was no other architecture like this, and no other architect like Zaha. That she was a woman in a very male profession (it still is) was one thing. That she was an Arab, born in Baghdad, in a very white profession was another. Also remarkable was the way she carried her difference. Other woman architects went for boyish haircuts and mannish suits, but Zaha, big and rounded, flaunted her form with figure-hugging black, surmounted with capes and flying hair. Her clothes and jewellery amplified her angles and curves. Her lips were full and lipsticked, her eyelids heavy, her nose strong. She was glamorous and scary. 'Diva' became a word often attached to her, to which she eventually responded with the words worn on T-shirts by her staff at the opening of one of her buildings: 'Would they call me a diva if I were a guy?'

She spoke her mind and showed her emotions, as she still does. She rages and jokes. Sitting in the midst of her staff she discharges cajolement, using the nicknames she likes to invent for people. 'Potato' she calls her most loyal lieutenant, for reasons that are unclear. 'Licky' is her name for a well-known architectural courtier. I am 'Raw Man', later 'Low Man', after a Chinese member of staff struggles with the 'R' in my name. Another member of staff is Clinton, for reasons that might be something to do with interns.

The Peak's developer went bust before the project could get going. This started her reputation as an architect who never built, even though she began to acquire a clutch of realized projects – a block of flats, a fire station, some apartments, a bar in Japan – with which other architects at a comparable age would be happy. It would have been more accurate to say that her built output did not match the ambition shown in her drawings of projects like The Peak.

When I was trying to get a Zaha building built myself, certain phrases would bounce about my brain at times of stress. One was a saying of Harold Wilson's as he left the post of Prime Minister, quoting the Bible, that one should beware 'the cloud no bigger than a man's hand'. Another came from the founding director of the Design Museum, Stephen Bayley, at the party announcing Zaha's victory in the competition: 'This is the best bit; it gets worse from here.' Another came from my former editor Max Hastings, speaking of the role played by the writer Simon Jenkins in the catastrophic Millennium Dome: 'Journalists don't know how to *do* things.' As a writer I had made merry with the ridiculous Dome, but now I found myself grappling with my own mini-monument. My then seven-year-old daughter, who knew the foibles of a Zaha-designed table in our house, said, 'Is this a good idea?'

In 2002 I had become director of The Architecture Foundation. This was an organization with a large debt, uncertain means of support, and an unclear purpose. 'What is it?' people asked when I joined, and they still asked when I left. But it represented an aspiration, that there is something special about architecture, and that it is good to encourage this special thing with whatever means are to hand, such as exhibitions, debates, and design competitions. I shared The Architecture Foundation's aspiration.

One of my tasks was to address the question of the organization's premises. Should the Foundation have a new gallery, a permanent place where the public could come and by which it would be recognized? The feeling was that it should. I knew of a sliver of land on a large development planned near Tate Modern, designated for cultural use. I contacted the company behind the development, Land Securities. I met Mike Hussey, a man smooth of drawl and pink of cheek, in the well-laundered style of a David Cameron, which belied the fact that he had worked his way up from his East End origins to become the youngest ever member of Land Securities' board. He was riding high on a deal he had pulled off in Victoria, and was going to shake up the company's fusty image. Contemporary architecture was one of the signs and means of this new style.

We worked out a deal, whereby Land Secs (as it is known) would build the building, and the Foundation would lease it at a low rent. This would avoid the pitfalls that indigent cultural institutions usually encounter when taking on building projects. There would be no need for a grand capital fundraising campaign. The risk and the management of the project would be in the capable hands of Land Securities. The plan was elegant, efficient, and practical. We launched a competition, and excitement grew about this rare thing, an all-new cultural building in central London. Architecture dedicated to the display of architecture: this is something architects like. Over two hundred practices entered the competition, from many different countries.

Zaha was by now a celebrity, friends with the architecture-loving Brad Pitt, and had started to build substantial projects, although nothing yet in Britain. *Vogue*, and *Glamour*, and other glossy magazines, couldn't get enough of her, and *Forbes Magazine* would decide that she was the 69th Most Powerful Woman in the world, eleven places behind Queen Elizabeth II. She had just won the Pritzker Prize, which is effectively architecture's Nobel. The Architecture Foundation's building was a small project, and she might have been thought too grand for it. But she entered, was shortlisted, and presented a design to the jury assembled to choose the winner of the competition.

All the entrants struggled with the tricky triangular site, except Zaha. She revelled in it, for the opportunity it gave to play with her favourite geometry of acute and impure angles. She lifted the building's galleries into a high concrete V, hanging apparently impossibly over space. Two inclined legs, containing staircases and lifts, brought the V's weight down to earth, making it into a destabilized Stonehenge. The space under the V was glazed, forming a high, conservatory-like room that would act like a big shop window to the street. There were, as always in her work, as few true verticals and horizontals as possible. It was easy to call it 'iconic' or 'visionary', but it was more than that – it was a series of ideas about the interaction of inner and outer life, of exhibitions and street, resolved into daring and confident form. So she won.

Above this leftover piece of pavement, this residue of commercial floor space calculations, she would make an intense and dense sequence of spatial adventures. It would be like nothing else in London. But, without anyone really noticing, the nature of the project had changed: it was no longer the simple thing implied by the deal with Land Securities. We were now in the monument-building business, pursuing something that would be effortful and demanding, both to build and use. The original idea was for something like a found space which could be occupied lightly and easily, like an old warehouse, except that this happened to be a new building. The Zaha building would consume so much energy and attract so much attention that such lightness would no longer be possible. This shift turned out to be fatal.

It was obvious that her design was not the easy option. Getting people and exhibits to the elevated galleries would be one issue. The place would be demanding of curators – just sticking pictures to the walls would look feeble in such a building. We knew that the building might break the budget, but Mike Hussey, as the man who would pay for it, was happy to take on such risks. He, like everyone else in the room, could see a force in the Zaha scheme that all the others lacked. We announced the scheme, exhibited the competition entries, had a party, made speeches, did interviews with the TV news. Everything seemed set fair, apart from Stephen Bayley's admonition, like a bad godmother's in a fairy tale, and the over-floral Ghanaian shirt I wore at the exhibition opening. Teamed with a Vivienne Westwood suit in a fine houndstooth check, it suggested a dangerous light-headedness.

We came in for a light hammering from disappointed young architects, who felt that such a job was an opportunity for one of them rather than a grandee like Zaha. I could see their point, except that she was herself still in the category of under-fulfilled talent, as she had built nothing in London.

We set forth. Land Securities put an impressive team of project managers and consultants into achieving the project, under instructions to overcome all difficulties. The same contractors, Bovis, would build the office blocks next door and the Architecture Foundation's pavilion, which was about a hundredth of the former's size. Zaha put the architect she called Clinton in charge of the project. A series of meetings began to roll out at Land Securities' offices in the Strand, at which twenty or more people would explore every detail for up to two hours with exemplary professionalism. Meanwhile the Architecture Foundation's deficit had been converted into a surplus, and its programme had been brought back to life.

This was January. The cloud no bigger than a man's hand appeared in October, in a meeting with the two employees of Land Securities in charge of the project. They told me that Land Securities

would find the additional money needed to fund the, as expected, increased cost, which was good news. Some savings would nonetheless have to be made, which was fair enough. But they also informed me that Zaha's role in the project would be reduced. The design would still be hers, but Allies and Morrison, the architects of the big office buildings, would be in charge of interpreting it to building contractors. It was their way of handling the risk, which they perceived Zaha to be.

Such arrangements are sensitive with architects. It's like asking a writer to put together a plot, but getting someone else to write the dialogue, or getting painters to do a sketch and subcontracting the brushwork to others not of their choosing. Zaha felt insulted. Her practice now employed a hundred and fifty people designing buildings all over the world. The Architecture Foundation building, she pointed out, was the smallest job in the office. The implication that she couldn't handle it was absurd.

After voicing her views she then knuckled down and accepted the arrangement. But from now on the project was wounded, and lacked confidence and common purpose. Mistrust had arisen between Hussey and Hadid, who each regarded the other as disrespectful and arrogant, and between their respective companies, that never went away. Like weakened bodies, the project attracted parasites, in the form of reporters from weekly architectural magazines. These people, pallid and goggling like creatures of the lightless deep ocean, would call up with a catch of concern in their voice that failed to hide their delight at having a career-enhancing piece of bad news in their hands. I learned to expect their calls early in the week, timed close to their deadlines so as to cramp our time to respond. They would have gathered some piece of loose talk and relay it to me: was it true that Zaha was being pushed to the margins, that she was furious, that the budget was out of control?

I had to be polite, as you do with the press. I explained why there were good reasons for everything, and there was no cause for concern. But the sea creatures' dribbles of misery – which were not, indeed, wholly inaccurate – did nothing for the mood of the twenty-person two-hour meetings.

And, the more we tried to reduce the budget, the more it went up. It was heading for quadruple the original, and beyond. Cost reports became works of fantasy. Reasons were given, such as the difficulty of pouring concrete on this constricted site, and of getting trucks there through London traffic with the bespoke moulds the complex shape required.

But nothing made sense. What plots, what politics were going on? I was waking in the small hours, baffled and paranoid. One time I found myself in a lift with the people from Bovis. They looked at their shoes and mumbled that they 'really wanted to get this built'. I didn't know whether to believe them. Zaha is usually seen as exotic, but here the really strange stuff was coming from the men in suits. 'Those whom the Gods wish to destroy', I had once written of Miuccia Prada's lavish expenditure on a Rem Koolhaas-designed shop, 'they first make patrons of architecture.' It was supposed to be a joke.

I was sat down with the cost consultant, who got out his biro. 'This is what we can do,' he said, and he scrawled a parody of Zaha's design. The big glass room could be filled with floors. A prop could be put under the overhanging V, to hold it up more easily. It was too expensive to put anything useful, like galleries, into the V, but we could keep the look of it by making it into a giant ornamental parapet, with nothing behind. He had made the building into a small office block with a grotesque piece of sculpture planted, like a toupee, on top. I couldn't tell if he was serious. I couldn't tell if I was supposed to laugh, cry, or walk out.

Then I had my meeting with Zaha and her tsarist–futurist hand-bag, when she offered to step aside. 'They don't want me,' she said, and to judge by the bounce in the project manager's stride when the subject of replacing her came up, she was right. In the end she did not stand down, on the basis of PR advice of the highest quality. Zaha by now was also working on the Aquatic Centre for the London Olympics, the most splendid of architectural works of 2012, where a familiar story of escalating costs and nervous contractors was unfolding. To abandon the smaller project could be disastrous for her precarious position on the bigger one. For myself I was feeling bloody-minded. Zaha had won a competition. Yes, her architecture is not straightforward to achieve. But I refused to believe it was impossible. I agreed with the high-quality PR. She should stay.

And so we pressed on. Mike Hussey announced that he could go to £4.5 million, which should pay for a decent building, but it would have to be redesigned in steel, not concrete. On the next working day the project manager waved a page of the *Milton Keynes Citizen* at us, with a picture of a triangular tin shed in a business park. This was the sort of thing we could do, he said, with a touch of glee. The cost consultant, the man with the biro, explained the factors that pushed the cost up. This included the proportion of external wall to the internal floor space, which should be low, as external walls are expensive. Because of the dimensions of the site, it emerged, the desirable ratio was impossible to achieve. In other words, regardless of Zaha's flights of fancy, this project was never going to be on budget. The dullest, safest architect could not have made it work.

Despite this discouragement Zaha and her office returned to the task. They hammered out something new, with a simpler internal arrangement. It still had a big window and, clad in stainless steel polished until it reflected like a mirror, it would have a memorable, crystalline presence. The mammoth meetings continued, racking up consultants' fees while discussing marginal cost savings. The overall budget was minutely, strictly monitored.

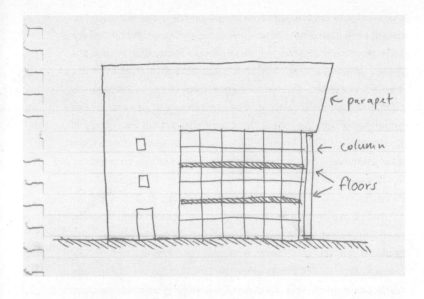

Then, again, costs started to climb, despite the simplification of the design, and despite the meticulous cost control. It headed towards £8 million again, even more mysteriously than before. The impact on construction costs of an overheated economy were blamed, along with the inflationary effects of China's hunger for steel. But the main reason for the rise seemed to be that, despite two years of coming to meetings, and despite the assurances of the shoe-gazing men in the lift, Bovis didn't want to build it. There would be easier ways for them to make money.

The Architecture Foundation acquired a new chairman, and we discussed whether to abandon the project. But he could bring in the funds to buy the building, rather than just rent it, which made it appealing again. I went to see Mike Hussey, with the Foundation's treasurer, another developer, as we did from time to time during the project. In Mike's corner office off Trafalgar Square, behind him Horatio Nelson visible on his column, he and the treasurer indulged in boys' banter, about football clubs and their womanizing managers. Mike boasted of his motorbike, which had a bigger engine than the car driven by his abstemious chief executive. Mike also came to dinner with some trustees at the house of one of our supporters, its walls hung with Bacon, Hockney, and Basquiat. There was more competitive boasting, each guest itemizing the importance of the people and the size of the budgets with which he or she dealt in their respective field.

We agreed the principle of the sale of the building from Land Securities to the Architecture Foundation, while a smaller, more willing contractor than Bovis was appointed to deliver the project at a lower cost. A purchase price of between £4.5 and £5 million was mentioned, but it somehow rose to £6 million. The chairman could still, just, raise the funds for this higher price. There would be nothing for other costs connected with the building, such as fitting it out and ensuring its programme would be well funded, but he

knew potential benefactors who would be sympathetic to supporting such a cause.

Then the stock market fell. One of the potential benefactors
said, 'This is not going to be a recession; it's going to be a depression.' The chances of finding the money for fit-out and programme
fell to nil. Faced with the prospect of a beautiful but unsustainable
liability, the Board of Trustees of The Architecture Foundation had
no option but to cancel the project. The site of Zaha's unbuilt
wonder became a bit of landscaping outside a Marks and Spencer.
A hoarding advertised the attractions of the surrounding development, wittily playing on the proximity of Tate Modern. They
presented a short checklist, with tick-boxes next to each word:

> Surrealism
> Sandwiches
> Shopping

There was a tick in the box next to 'Shopping'.

I won't bore you with all the things that went wrong. They
include the cultural mismatch between Zaha, Land Securities, and
Bovis, and several misjudgements of my own and others. I like to
think that most involved acted in good faith, and many were professional, some magnificent. Some of the press were in fact more
decent than I have made them seem.

But the question has to be asked: are Zaha and her architecture
too difficult, too impractical, too expensive, too user-unfriendly?
Window-cleaning was going to be a challenge in both versions of
the project, and at times Clinton needed reminding that the main
purpose of the building was to exhibit things, and not just be an
exhibit in itself. When the budget was ascending he cheerfully
told me it could be doubled again, if all the details he and Zaha
really wanted were included, and he cited Frank Lloyd Wright's
Fallingwater as an example of a masterpiece that had exploded

its budget. Later, at a fraught time, the PR adviser of the highest quality tried to explain that the director of another institution with a Zaha building was 'almost out of his mind' by the time it was finished. This was not as reassuring as the adviser seemed to think it would be. I did not want to be out of my mind.

We are dealing here with the Price to be Paid for Art. The beautiful building that strains its clients is an old phenomenon. Edgar J. Kaufmann, client of Fallingwater, named it 'Rising Mildew' thanks to its inadequate protection against damp. One of Adolf Loos' assistants said you could build 'a very nice detached house' for the cost of one of his rooms. Antonio Gaudí's Casa Mila in Barcelona, the pile of writhing stone that is called 'La Pedrera' or 'The Quarry', broke building codes and stepped outside its site boundary onto the public pavement, as a result of which it was threatened with compulsory demolition and incurred a fine for its owner, who then spent seven years in litigation with the architect. The monks of a baroque monastery in Bavaria refused its architect's request to be buried there, incensed by the profligate way he had spent their money on the building. Palladio's church of Il Redentore in Venice cost at least seven times its original budget (and, for good measure, has lousy acoustics). The medieval cathedrals of Wells and Salisbury have large X-shaped arches at their crossings that now look striking, but when built were expensive emergency measures to stabilize movement in the structure.

The truth is that the price of architecture can be high. This price is not only in money, and sometimes in delay, but also in risk, which includes the risk that a building may not function as intended, and that it may not happen at all. The justification for this price is that a work will be created of such great and lasting power that its budget will come to be seen as minor detail. Sometimes clients accept or even embrace this argument, or they go along with it once they find that they are so deeply involved that they have no choice.

When they make this deal with posterity, architects sometimes use their clients' money, but not their consent, as Gaudí did with La Pedrera. The building is indeed magnificent, and its value to Barcelona in tourist dollars far exceeds the costs paid out by the building's unfortunate owner, Pedro Milà i Camps. It is hard now to wish that Gaudí had been more responsible, but it was his client who had to endure most of the pain, without receiving much of the gain.

There is an unspoken understanding with contemporary architects of celebrity: by choosing them you should not expect an easy ride, but the finished building (if you get there) will be a new fragment of the world that might be extraordinary, revelatory, beautiful, perception-altering: you could call it the Masterpiece Defence. The risk does not stop there, as architects hired and then indulged on the basis of their genius, in the name of which their clients suffer torments, sometimes deliver works that are not extraordinary or revelatory, but turkeys.

Ideally, such risks are only run with eyes open, in situations where, as in building a cathedral or a rich man's house or a lavishly endowed museum, it is clear to both client and architect that magnificence and brilliance are the main aim. In the palazzo Ca d'Oro gold leaf and ultramarine paint were applied in the knowledge that they would not last long in the maritime air: conspicuous wastefulness was the point. Too often the most demanding projects are attempted by wishful thinkers, who approach them in the same spirit as the gallant amateurs who once took on Mount Everest in brogues and tweeds.

Often the supposed Great Work is a lousy deal. Those that justify the immense costs and sacrifices of their making form a tiny fraction of the world's stock of buildings, and for each work that really is great, there are many more that deploy the Masterpiece Defence, but are not. To focus too much, as history books and magazines tend to do, on triumphs of exorbitance does a disservice to the many architects who achieve much with less violence to budget and function. But at every level of building, battles have to be fought over value and cost. Cheapest and easiest is not always best or most right, a fact we accept more easily in buying clothes and food than when paying for buildings.

A building budget might seem a simple practical matter, and keeping to it a basic professional skill. It is mystifying and absurd, to most people, when construction projects exceed, double, or treble their original estimates. Yet a budget is not a thing of pure fact. It is a contested field, a form of expression, a representation of society. It is part of the rules of the game of architecture, and therefore something that can be tested, challenged, and manipulated. Sometimes it is an architect's job to point out to clients that their budgets are not enough to achieve what they want, or that the quality of a building will be so compromised by savings that they are not worth making. Sometimes it is an architect's job just to get on with whatever money is there, and make the best of it.

If the expression of magnificence and munificence is one tradition in architecture, there are others that concern themselves with extreme limitation, with making the most out of very little. Here symbol and instrument, and look and fact, can take different paths. At one extreme are works of minimalism, luxury homes and hotels which, in a sophisticated update of Marie Antoinette's playing at peasantry, lavish expense on looking simple. Rare stone and timber, sought from far places, are presented with plainness and precision that require high levels of skill. An element might be an unusual size – there may be only a few trees big enough to supply boards of a certain dimension, or a few stones in the quarry that can be hollowed out to make a monolithic bath – or exceptional engineering might be required to achieve a wide-spanning opening, which is expensive, but it is presented in such a way that you would not at first notice.

There is another tendency, where architects are working with genuinely tight budgets, and make cheapness a medium of expression. In 1925, at the Paris Exposition of Decorative Arts, Konstantin Melnikov built the Soviet pavilion in less than a month for the modest budget of 15,000 roubles, out of cheap wood and glass, assembled out of parts prefabricated by peasant labour in Russia. A British representative dismissed it as a 'greenhouse' and an American journal called it 'a practical joke' but, with its combination of dynamic diagonals and basic construction, it stole the show. Several leading architects and French magazines declared it the best in the exhibition. It reflected the fact that the post-Revolutionary nation was skint, but with its lack of frippery it also expressed fortitude and bare energy. It was about the essential, the opposite of bourgeois decadence.

Lina Bo Bardi spoke of 'Poor Architecture', which she said came from her experience of living for five years in the north-east of Brazil. Poor architecture 'eliminated all the cultural snobbery so dearly beloved by the intellectuals (and today's architects), opting for direct, raw solutions'. At MASP it took the form of bare concrete, whitewash, floors in stone and industrial rubber, tempered glass. This did not mean that her architecture was austere, but that its luxury came from space, plants, water, art, and activities.

Frank Gehry, before he became famous for spectacular confections in titanium and stainless steel, built with chain-link mesh, plywood, and corrugated metal sheet. These materials really were cheap, which allowed him to use them more extravagantly than he could more expensive materials, but they also expressed an idea about the value of things overlooked – the everyday stuff of

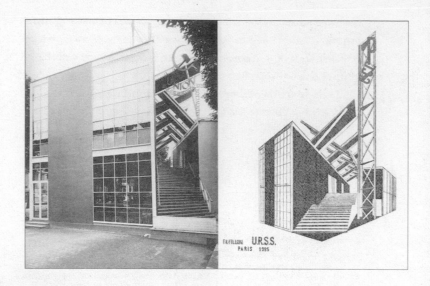

PAVILLON U.R.S.S.
PARIS 1925

the sneered-at city of Los Angeles was shown to have its own beauty.

Then there are situations where there really is almost nothing, and the artistic expression or otherwise of poverty is not the point. Writing of Mumbai, Suketu Mehta says that

> people who live without clear title in our cities are branded, en masse, as 'slum dwellers'. A slum is a matter of definition, and the weight of the word hangs heavy over the poor. What is a slum? You and me don't like it, so we call it a slum. The people in the slums of Mumbai have another word for it; basti, which means community. A basti abounds in community spaces – in the line to the toilet, in the line at the water tap, in the patches of empty ground, in front of the hundreds of little shops servicing every human need. The construction of the basti is crucial to the 'spirit of Mumbai' that saves the city time and again, through floods, riots and terror attacks.
>
> Each room in the basti is exquisitely custom-built, every detail of it, including the walls and the ceilings. Each room is different, and, over the decades, they become suited to the owner's needs. They are endlessly flexible, with partitions and extra storeys according to the number of family members that live there. They are coloured, outside and in, to their owners' taste. Look at a slum colony anywhere in the world: it is multi-coloured. Then look at the public housing that replaces it when it is demolished: it is monochromatic.
>
> . . . The moral of this story is: don't demolish slums, but improve them.

It is possible to overstate Mehta's argument – for example, slums are sometimes built, out of desperation, on unstable ground and so trigger landslides, or on sites where they destroy precious vegetation or water sources, in ways that ultimately benefit no one

– but his main point stands: there can be efficiency and wisdom in poor dwellings, born of urgent necessity. They adapt to the individual needs of inhabitants, and make the spaces for communal networks of support. Mehta's belief in the value of *architettura povera* is recognized by the value now given to rural cottages in England, made of stone and thatch simply because they were the materials nearest to hand, or by the fact that, as he says, 'we marvel at Lisbon's old city, we pay a premium to live in Trastevere, the Marais, or the East Village – all of which were "slums" a hundred years ago'.

The self-sufficiency of poor homes presents a challenge to any architect or planner who would improve them, or who would seek to address the palpable ills of slums, such as poor sanitation and overcrowding, without destroying what is good about them. In post-war Europe, as now in Mumbai, the favoured official solution was clearance and replacement of what at first sight looked like places beyond redemption. This programme is usually now seen as a mistake.

The Chilean architect Alejandro Aravena has created a company called Elemental, whose aim is 'the development of housing, public space, infrastructure and transportation projects that can perform as an effective and efficient upgrade in the quality of life of the poor'. He does not kick against the system, but tries to achieve his aims 'without changing the rules of existing policies and conditions of the market'.

In Elemental's first project, Quinta Monroy in the desert city of Iquique, squatter communities of thirty years' standing were re-housed using the standard government budget of $7,500 per home. This would pay for about 30–40 square metres, which is not very much. Aravena's idea was not to view the end product as 'simply being a small house', but 'half of a good house'. So Elemental built plain rooms, as efficiently as possible, to serve the basic minimum

of needs, with the expectation that families would build the other half themselves, just as they had built their own shelters in decades of squatting. The parts requiring the most specialist skills, such as kitchens and bathrooms, would be built in the first phase. Elemental 'included the families and the communities in the planning process, because if they were going to be responsible for 50 per cent of the built environment', it would be 'better to split tasks in a coordinated way'.

The housing took the form of rows of three-storey blocks, with gaps between each block that would filled by the residents when they wanted and were able to do so. This organization allowed a more effective use of land than is possible in one-storey shanties. It replaced their ramshackle appearance – arguably picturesque but also stigmatizing to its inhabitants – with a simple level of architectural order within which individual additions were framed. It also helped shape shared spaces for communal activities. The final results are plain, regular terraces, animated by the variety of interventions – various kinds of bays, balconies, and window shapes, colours, and decorations – that different people have made.

Often architects predict communal involvement that stubbornly refuses to materialize. In Quinta Monroy it happened, harnessing the small government grant, and the will of the residents to improve their own lot, to the maximum possible effect. It remains to be seen how widespread this model will be, but since their work at Quinta Monroy was completed in 2004, Elemental have carried out several more projects using similar principles.

Their approach is not just about financial efficiency, but about using extreme financial pressure to realize social and physical benefits, by maximizing and combining the contributions of individuals, communities, and the state. It is architectural, in the sense that design intelligence is used to create places that propose ways in which people might live. It does not just deliver units of accommodation but also offers, without prescribing, ideas about dwelling. And if architecture is always incomplete without the actions it contains, the half-built houses of Quinta Monroy prove the point with unusual directness.

In that they require a government grant, these are not the cheapest shelters possible. The point is rather that the money is directed to something built, to something physical and spatial, which, it is hoped, will support better lives for the residents.

The relation of architecture to money goes beyond the question of construction budgets. Buildings, and cities, reflect the priorities of the economic regimes that shape them. That the piazza in Covent Garden was different from its French and Italian models is due to the fact that it was driven by speculative private landowners, rather than state or monarchy; as it was designed to sell itself, architecture became advertisement, and image outran reality. Resources were directed for maximum impact. The church of St Paul declined with indecent haste from an impressive stone portico facing the piazza to a bare brick barn behind, and the houses showed a similar gradient of quality from front to back. Its classical symmetry was never completed in part because, once the place had been marketed on the promise of such a thing, its completion did not turn out to be imperative. The piazza filled with vegetable markets and prostitution, rather than the court ceremonies of the Place des Vosges, because its economics led that way.

Dubai is made of what the *Financial Times* called 'lucrative niches with their own special rules'. These are zones called 'cities', financial enclaves with individual tax and legal provisions to attract business, such as the Dubai International Financial Centre, where business is done in English, using dollars and Western regulations. There are Media City and Internet City, where state censorship and control of content are suspended. The Harvard Medical School has lent its expertise to making the $6 billion Healthcare Village. There is Humanitarian Aid City.

There are also the luxury hotels, where prohibitions on alcohol and skimpy clothing are suspended, and laws on adultery are usually overlooked. There are gated residential developments, golf courses with restricted membership, and the oceanic shopping malls from which Indian and Pakistani migrant workers are excluded. And, least visible of all except when revealed by Western newspapers, are the work camps on the fringes of the city, where the migrant workers have slept up to twelve to a room, sometimes without air conditioning and with inadequate sanitation and water supplies.

You can find maps that show the city's icons and theme parks, both real and hoped-for, but you cannot find a map that shows all the zones. Yet these zones are essential to the functioning of an emirate whose demography is made in unequal parts of migrant construction and menial workers (who form the majority of the population), expatriate business people, tourists, the super-rich, scatterings of Beckhamesque celebrities, and, at less than one-fifth of the total, native Emiratis. Dubai works on the basis that its different social groups are allowed different rights, privileges, and restrictions, an arrangement made possible by its division into zones.

Nods towards Islamic law can be combined with unlimited boozing and whoring for visiting businessmen. The use of zones creates security for residents of gated communities, and insecurity for the people in the work camps. They allow media freedom when it is good for business and not when it is threatening to authority. They allow business to be transacted at different levels of legitimacy and transparency, from the respectability of the Dubai International Financial Centre to the gold and diamond souks, the 'houses of barter and informal cash-transfer storefronts' where, according to the *Wall Street Journal*, 'black-market operators, arms dealers, terrorist financiers and money launderers have taken advantage of the freewheeling environment'.

Above all, the zones are good for business. In Dubai, as Mike Davis has said, 'the state is almost indistinguishable from private enterprise', government 'is really an equities management team', and it is led by a man, Sheikh Mohammed al-Maktoum, who is in effect both ruler and chief executive officer. 'If the country is a single business,' says Davis, 'then "representative government" is beside the point: after all, General Electric and Exxon are not democracies and no one – except for raving socialists – expects either to be so.'

What is left out is an idea of commonalty which, if it were permitted, would make unbearable the conflicts arising from having different rules for different people. The omission is political, legal, and spatial. There is little that could be called a public space in Dubai, a place in principle open to all people. When the city's migrant workers were driven beyond endurance into mass protest, they had to make spaces of demonstration out of zones intended for other purposes, such as the multi-lane Sheikh Zayed road or the construction site of the Burj Dubai, later the Burj Khalifa.

There are two versions of the city, the visible and the nearly invisible. The visible is the one that gets most of the press – the palm islands, the tallest building, the giant malls, the sail-like hotel, the delirious skyline, and so on and so forth – even though some of it is not actually there, but only projected. It sells, and it distracts. After all the excitement about the Palm-visible-from-space, it only seeped out, years later, that millions embezzled from the failed Bank of Afghanistan were laundered into properties on its fronds. The nearly invisible city is a patchwork of enclosed zones, designed to promote business, privilege some people, and keep others in their place.

In place of commonalty Dubai offers look. Through its visionary icons the city presents a powerful and consistent brand to the world that distracts from its segregated structure. The form is unified, the content is divided. You are urged to see one, and not the other. Other senses would reveal more – the scent of hotel pillows, the smell of work camps, the cool of pools, the mechanical balm of air conditioning, the thick heat of construction sites – but they would be hard to communicate via promotional videos, even if anyone wanted to.

In other words the famous architectural spectacle of Dubai, its empire of vision, and its invisibly divided structure, are financially driven. This is less a matter of construction budgets – if it costs a few extra million to achieve the desired sleights of hand, it is money well spent – than of finding the forms that best suit the operation of business, in the way Dubai likes to do it. Form follows finance.

In Britain, in the first decade of the twenty-first century, a rare combination was achieved of profligacy and meanness. Both government and businesses were willing to spend very large sums on building, but reluctant to invest in the forethought and detail – good design, in short – that might have helped these sums to be spent well.

The pattern was set at the start, by the New Millennium Experience, an event that aimed to celebrate the turn of the millennium, in ways that were never precisely defined, with a series of themed pavilions under the giant circular tent known as the Millennium Dome. Uncertain whether its aim was education or entertainment, it fell awkwardly between the two, and it achieved neither critical nor popular success. Its visitor numbers fell well short of its targets, and the best part of a billion pounds was tipped into an event that nobody wanted or asked for, which served no edifying purpose, and was almost entirely lacking in positive qualities.

Tony Blair's Labour government also conceived a plan to rebuild or renovate all the nation's secondary schools. The Prime Minister, when first seeking office, had declared that his priorities were 'education, education and education', and an immense construction programme looked like a good way of fulfilling his promises. Or at least, in a classic case of confusion between the symbolic and instrumental properties of buildings, being seen to fulfil them. There was not conclusive evidence that construction at this scale was the most cost-effective way of improving education.

Many of the schools were to be delivered under something called the Private Finance Initiative, a manifestation of the once-socialist Labour Party's faith in the effectiveness and wisdom of the private sector. Under PFI large companies would bid for contracts not only to build schools, but also to maintain them, clean them, and supply everything from toilet paper to software for a period of thirty years. Many schools would be bundled up into single-contract packages.

The theory was that the government could transfer risk and responsibility to the private sector, with the added advantage that a huge capital programme would not immediately appear on the public accounts: because payment would be over thirty years, future taxpayers would be paying for projects whose political benefit – ribbon-cutting at new buildings, the announcement of impressive targets met – could be harvested quickly.

One drawback was that quality would suffer. It is widely accepted, including by the government's own agencies, that good design comes when clients, users, and architects can work closely together, yet the machinery of PFI meant that teachers and governors had limited contact with the people designing their buildings. As schools were delivered in packages, responding to the specific circumstances of any one school became more difficult. And, no matter how much the enormous legal documents of PFI tried to describe quality, contractors in search of profit would inevitably seek to drive buildings down to the lowest level they could get away with. Some miserable school buildings – where, for example, small windows meant that electric lights had to be kept on all day – were designed and constructed.

Worse, it is unlikely that PFI really did save money. Contractors had to raise the finance on the money markets, at higher rates of interest than the government would have paid if it borrowed the money directly. The bidding process was cumbersome and expensive: it could cost contractors £3 million to bid for a package of schools. They would expect to win one in three, meaning that they would want to recover £9 million from each successful bid just to cover their bidding costs. It remains to be seen how successfully contractors will milk their contracts over the years to extract extra payments for unforeseen expenses. However, in a contest between their lawyers and the government's, the ones paid by private business are likely to be more astute.

In 2010 the new Coalition government took office, and the new Education Secretary, Michael Gove, started denouncing his predecessors' wastefulness. He also said, repeatedly, that architects were 'creaming off' exorbitant fees from the schools building programme, and crowed that he would not be 'getting any award-winning architects' to design them. He distorted facts, for the simple reason that, if the facts were not distorted, they would disprove his point.

If there was 'creaming off', it was being done by lawyers, and by financial institutions and their advisers. Possibly also by contractors, many of whom were found guilty, in 2008, of collusion and price-fixing: ripping off their clients, in other words. This was on projects other than schools, but it seems unlikely that price-fixing

never happened in school building. Architects, by contrast, usually undertook school design for minimal profit or at a loss; such work would often be the least lucrative in their office. They were also the first and sometimes only people to point out the flaws in PFI. More importantly, when good architects, against the odds, had been able to shape schools, teachers were very clear about the benefits of consideration given, for example, to lighting, acoustics, the movement of people, and the avoidance of places where bullying could occur. 'It's about enabling people to feel good,' said one head teacher. 'Good design produces a relaxed community. If we say education is important we can demonstrate that by putting children in decent environments.' Yet Gove persisted with his campaign, in order that standardized, minimally designed schools could be built, and even more power given to possibly colluding contractors.

Politicians framed the debate in terms of cost, but it was really about value, and values. They were willing to believe, without evidence, that big business and big finance would best deliver places of education, because they were ideologically inclined to think this. They were equally nervous about thinking that something as soft and intangible as good design was worth investment. They were positively afraid of the well-made, perhaps because of the vicious headlines that are directed at anything seen as superfluous. More than that, politicians seemed wary of the uncertainties associated with a question like design: the possibility you might be wrong and look foolish, the anxiety of aspiring to something that might not be achieved. Better to stick to the seemingly hard facts of targets and delivery.

They lacked faith that public bodies and public authorities would be capable of articulating desirable environments for learning, and of hiring design professionals to achieve them. They would rather spend £1,000 on an hour of a lawyer's time than on twelve hours of an architect's, or on buying slightly better chairs or lockers or door handles or floor finish. They would rather believe a contractor claiming, without hard evidence, that standardization is efficient, than listen to a head teacher telling them that design helps education.

It was an expression of the extreme faith in the wisdom of the markets, now notorious, of recent years. Politicians were concerned, above all, to look purposeful, tough and business-like, even if they were not. The result, lasting many decades, is a series of places of learning that look like units from a business park. As the German-born architectural historian Nikolaus Pevsner once said, the British will spare no expense to look cheap.

Tony Blair's government, in its early days, professed the importance of architecture. An architect, Lord Rogers (formerly Richard Rogers), had the ear of ministers to an extent matched by few of his profession in the past, and the greatness of British architects – the 'best in the world', it was often said – was proclaimed. It was part of a more general celebration of British creativity, in design, in music, in art, that went under the heading of 'Cool Britannia'.

Rogers was appointed head of an 'Urban Task Force', who in 1999 published a report, *Towards an Urban Renaissance*, which reached conclusions similar to those of Rogers' earlier book, *Cities for a Small Planet*. Something called the 'Compact City' was urged, in which high densities of population would lead not to squalor, but a critical mass of humanity whose proximity would generate 'vibrancy'. If people live close together, it was argued, and close to their work, they walk more, use more public transport and drive less. There would be enough of them to sustain local shops, restaurants, and schools, and to pay enough taxes to support well-kept streets and public places. Crime would be reduced, as there would be more 'eyes on the street' – more people passing by whose mere presence would make wrongdoers feel uncomfortable. Compact cities would be more sustainable, and use less land, than suburban sprawl.

There is much to be said for these arguments and, as Rogers and his allies pointed out, high-density cities like Paris, New York, and Barcelona manage to be highly desirable. The London Borough of Kensington and Chelsea is the most densely populated local authority in Britain (assuming you do not dilute the figures by including the rural second homes of many of its residents), and also one of the most expensive.

Sheer numbers, however, were not the whole story. 'Regeneration has to be design-led', said Rogers, so that 'towns and cities can once again become attractive places in which to live, work and socialise'. Architects would have to shape 'high-quality public spaces' between the high-density apartment blocks of the compact city. Vibrant public life needed a vessel, in which it could take place, and architects would play an essential role in making it. Again, the models were Paris and Barcelona, where care and resources are lavished on the streets and squares. The Task Force recognized that the British planning system had atrophied, and lacked the skills to shape future cities with wisdom and foresight. Strong leadership and 'meaningful and accessible' democratic processes were needed. 'Centres of Excellence' were recommended, entities which would help breed a new elite of town planners, employed by cities and local councils.

Many of Rogers' ideas were adopted, and over the following decade many 'urban regeneration' projects were carried out in ex-industrial cities across Britain, using approximations of his principles. A government body, the Commission for Architecture and the Built Environment, was set up, to help raise the quality of design: among its roles was 'design review', which meant commenting on the architectural merits, or otherwise, of significant proposed projects. CABE's views would carry weight when it was being decided whether planning permission should be granted.

Property developers were only too happy with the idea of high density, as it enabled them to put more flats and offices on their land. And as Blair's government liked business, including property developers, they were happy too. Unfortunately, however, the hoped-for apparatus of skilled planners, strong leadership, and democratic engagement envisaged by Rogers never came to pass. This would have meant spending public money, and would also have implied a return to old Labour values, such as investing power and resources in local government, that were now vanquished. It would have smelt too much of the manila and leather of old-fashioned town halls. Now delivery of almost everything was to be in the efficient hands of the private sector. The idea of 'Centres of Excellence' faded away.

'Good design', in the sense of anticipating future events and planning accordingly, or of balancing competing demands, or of organizing parts into a greater whole, was therefore impossible. There was no one to do it. A weaker notion of good design, or 'quality architecture', was deployed instead, a phrase whose emptiness could in the end permit almost anything. Under this notion an individual building project was deemed to be good if enough architects and other experts, speaking through bodies such as CABE's Design Review Committee, considered it to be so. Often 'quality architecture' equated with 'designed by an architect with a high reputation'. It was not 'design-led regeneration', as called for by the Task Force, but development with design attached.

Meanwhile, the New Millennium Experience, under the Rogers-designed Dome, took place. When Blair's government took office in 1997 one of the first decisions facing it was whether to proceed with this project, which had been conceived under the previous administration. Rogers lobbied furiously for it, even though it did not really conform to the principles of the Compact City: as then conceived it was a short-lived, unsustainable, out-of-town entertainment centre, housed in an inward-looking structure. The sickly miasma of displays it would eventually house could not be called good design. Certainly the resources spent on the Dome, deployed elsewhere, could have contributed more to the goals of vibrancy and quality public realm.

Rogers, however, acted according to the dictum of the nineteenth-century American architect H. H. Richardson, that the first principle of architecture is to get the job. He argued, charmed, and cajoled. The Deputy Prime Minister, John Prescott, said, 'If we can't make this work, we're not much of a government.' And so the Experience and the Dome proceeded, to ultimate disaster. (Some redemption was found in 2007, when the Dome re-opened as the O_2, a huge and profitable music venue cum phone-company advert. But the eventual achievement of a commercial project, which might be expected to succeed without special favours, is hardly a justification for the public investment that went into it.)

The Dome established certain principles, or rather patterns of behaviour. The political power of the gesture, for example, the irresistible attraction of something that appears purposeful and considered, at a very large scale, but is not. The Dome also proved the power of schmoozing, and of the deity Delivery. As it had to be completed by an immovable date, its achievement on time became its own justification.

Because it was supposedly creative and visionary, and an architect was associated with it, it gave a bad name to design, which would prove useful later in the Labour years, when design was pushed further into the margins. Above all, the Dome showed a willingness to spend huge amounts of money on almost anything except what might be useful, or thoughtful, or good.

Rogers' access to Blair diminished, in part perhaps because the

Dome he had helped sell to the Prime Minister turned out to be an embarrassment, but he found another patron in Ken Livingstone, the Mayor of London. Livingstone appointed Rogers as his chief adviser on architecture and urbanism, and installed close associates of the architect in influential positions. The Mayor, once seen as a left-wing extremist, had a big idea for his city: seeing an endless boom in financial services, he would do everything he could to encourage it, while taking a tithe from its profits to spend on 'affordable' housing, i.e. homes with subsidized costs for those increasing numbers of people who could not buy them at market rates, because of the property inflation caused in large part by the boom in financial services.

Livingstone flew down to Cannes every year to an event called MIPIM, a trade fair for property, in which developers and agents dealt in the futures of cities, represented by vast models and slick videos, while the growing wealth and influence of Russia could be measured, year by year, by the increasingly large yachts moored in the bay, and the increasing length of leg on show by girls presiding over sales displays. At Cannes he made a speech: London's property men should make as much money as they could, as long as he could have some of it.

Livingstone's policy meant bigger buildings, more densely occupying their land, so that more masters of the universe could work more financial magic, and make more money for their businesses, for the people who built their buildings, and for the Mayor's programmes. It meant stacking up more flats, so that more could be designated affordable. It also meant skyscrapers. Although high density can be achieved without towers, and they are expensive and slow to build, proposals to erect them were declarations of intent, and assertions of power by both Mayor and developers. It was repeatedly asserted that London's status as a 'world city' would be endangered by a failure to build high, and the fact that conservationists – who opposed the impact of skyscrapers on historic views – had first to be crushed, was all to the good. Politicians, developers, and architects all like towers, as it makes them look purposeful, and imprints their actions for ever on the skyline.

So there was synergy between Livingstone's big idea, the interests of developers and financial institutions, and Rogers' theory of the 'compact city'. All agreed that there should be more built stuff, containing more people, than had been there before. The only difficult part was achieving the 'good design' and the 'high-quality public realm' part of the package. There was some planning – there was a document called the London Plan – but there were not the means or will to imagine a coherent future form of the city. It was not possible to match the architecturally-led transformation of Barcelona, a model much cited by Rogers. The Mayor, under Rogers' influence, announced that he would create one hundred new public spaces, in emulation of the Catalan city's investment in such things: only five were completed before he left office. In the Gold Rush city of London, where the wisdom of the markets was considered paramount, it was all too likely that the business-friendly bits of the compact city would flourish better than the tricky public-spirited parts. And two old lefties, Livingstone and Rogers, went along with it.

It is possible to plan skyscrapers. Manhattan, using the New York City 1916 Zoning Resolution, which stipulates set-backs in order to stop towers blocking too much daylight, does it well. London half-plans them – there is a detailed, longstanding set of rules that stops towers blocking specific views of key monuments, especially of St Paul's Cathedral, some from as far away as Richmond Park, ten miles distant. Outside these strategic views, as they are called, little is defined. It becomes a matter of negotiation and discussion, of developers trying their luck, and the city's boroughs backing or blocking them, which decisions may then be appealed, subjected to a quasi-legal inquiry, and ultimately determined by the relevant government minister.

In the absence of well-defined rules, opinion counts for much. The judgement of CABE's Design Review panel carried weight, and at planning inquiries expert witnesses – often other architects – pronounced a particular proposal good or bad. Again, 'good design' meant something like 'considered to be good by panels that include other architects', and 'designed by an architect generally considered to be good'. Some architects on the Design Review panel were themselves designers of contentious tall-building proposals. They decorously declared their interest and left the room while their peers pronounced their work to be quality architecture, and at other times returned to the panel to praise the work of others. At public inquiries leading architects waxed eloquent about the genius of the project under consideration; when their turn came to be scrutinized, other architects did the same for them. A small number of people deemed experts in design, often performing several roles at once, exerted disproportionate influence, and the architects they liked prospered.

Developers started hiring architects who they thought would do well under this system. Rogers, adviser to the mayor and energetic expert witness, also ran a practice that was asked to design six or more skyscrapers in London in the noughties, as well as contentious developments at One Hyde Park and the former Chelsea Barracks. 'World class' architects like Rogers' former partner Renzo Piano, who designed the 1,000-foot tower called the Shard – were brought in. After a while, however, it became clear that architecture that was not really world class could also work its way through the system, if enough persistence was applied. The Strata tower in Elephant and Castle, London, where randomized vertical lines point to three tokenistic turbines at the top, is a case in point. The 600-foot Vauxhall Tower in South London is by a practice, Broadway Malyan,

not usually considered 'world class' (one of their works, next to the tower site, was twice voted worst building in the world in the *Architects' Journal*'s polls of fellow architects) and might be thought a confused jumble of contradictory motifs, with an ill-formed and inhospitable open space at its foot. It might be thought an intrusion into an officially recognized 'important view' from Westminster Bridge: certainly the official inspector in a public inquiry into the proposal thought so, and recommended refusal. He was overruled by the personal decision of the relevant minister, John Prescott. Ken Livingstone was also an enthusiastic backer of the Vauxhall Tower; CABE said it had a 'well worked out, clear and attractive plan'.

There was logic to this generous widening of the definition of 'world class'. Although a Renzo Piano tower might be in some senses better than a Broadway Malyan one – it might be more confident, more consistent, somehow better judged – it would not be a fundamentally different object. Beneath the better-or-worse external treatment it would be the same big thing. Indeed Piano's Shard was designed in collaboration with Broadway Malyan: it is partly their work.

Developers became mini-mayors, deciding the shape of whole neighbourhoods, with homes, shops, public spaces, and even schools as well as offices. They also spent ever-increasing amounts on hiring planning consultants, people skilled in manoeuvring proposals through the many committees and panels that determined the fate of a planning application. In another universe these consultants could have been employed by public authorities to exercise foresight, paid for by a portion of the lavish sums actually spent on the unproductive work of massaging and manipulating the system. But that would be too sane. Instead every building project became a haggle, a hustle, a speculation, a gambit, a punt. The process was not about being efficient, or avoiding waste, or being economical, or achieving the highest quality, but about allowing enough leverage that a developer could eventually work into a profitable planning consent.

Most architects will tell you, often with a pious catch in their voice, that a building is only as good as its brief. If, for example, a brief calls for a quantity of development on a given plot, such that whatever is built will inevitably overwhelm its neighbours, there is a limit to what the fanciest architect can do to mitigate it. If an architect is asked to design an individual building, in the absence of any consideration of the cumulative effect of this and other buildings, you are likely to get a series of disconnected gestures. In noughties London, good architects were given bad briefs, and asked to make them look respectable. Architecture was the lubricant for the penetration of the skyline.

Then Rogers' practice, Rogers Stirk Harbour + Partners, was invited to design what would be called 'the world's most glamorous address'. Their clients were the charming young brothers Nick and Christian Candy, who, named with Dickensian aptness, fed their era's palate with a sugar-rush of glamour, wealth, success, and style. Starting by turning a profit on a flat in Earls Court, they achieved startling feats of development, hired big-name architects, and got themselves talked up in flattering magazine profiles.

The project was to build One Hyde Park, the replacement of a big ugly 1960s building with something twice as big but hopefully less ugly. The new building would contain eighty-six apartments, which in due course would be celebrated, in persistent but unverifiable news stories, for their astonishing expense: £15 million for three bedrooms, £140 million for a 3,000-square-metre triplex penthouse, reportedly the most expensive apartment ever.

Built, it would be sold as having the best of everything: 'acclaimed art' by James Turrell, Rolex and McLaren shops at ground level, architecture by Rogers. Residents there need never touch the same ground nor breathe the same air as other Londoners. They can be driven deep inside the complex, and they can be magnificently fed with the help of an underground tunnel connecting to the neighbouring Mandarin Oriental Hotel, enabling its room service to get to the apartments. There is a twenty-one-metre swimming pool, spa, cinema, and golf simulator. If for some reason they fear that others may wish to harm them, a superlative security system including iris-recognition scanners and bullet-proof glass will put their mind at rest. Also security staff trained by the Special Air Service, the British special forces regiment which established its global brand in 1980, by ending terrorists' occupation of the Iranian Embassy in Prince's Gate, just up the road from the site of One Hyde Park.

The project was controversial. There were objections to its impact on Hyde Park. Mayor Livingstone, rallying to the side of his architectural adviser, and to the general cause of making his city wealth-friendly, pronounced that it was vital to London's 'role as a world city' that the blocks rise above the park's tree line. A compromise was however agreed: the proposed blocks were lowered a bit, without losing vital floor area, and London – by some miracle – remained as much a world city as it ever was.

That Rogers was the architect was undoubtedly valuable in the difficult planning discussions, in which many millions of pounds of potential profit were at stake. He fitted the description of 'quality architect', and his design duly won the approval of CABE. His closeness to the Mayor, and the Mayor's pro-development policies, can, one imagines, only have been helpful, or at very least have been thought to be helpful by his clients.

But this was an architect who, in 1997, wrote, 'a new type of citadel has emerged. At the touch of a button, access is blocked, bullet-proof screens are activated, bomb-proof shutters roll down.' Such citadels were 'segregating rich from poor and stripping citizenship of its very meaning'. He also wrote that 'unless cities work

constantly to prevent social, racial, physical and economic divisions, their communities will fall apart and the city will not work.'

Here he was designing what could fairly be called a citadel, whose publicity machine trumpeted the very security measures that Rogers had deplored, and which was not exactly integrating rich and poor. His practice's architectural role was limited to giving the best possible external treatment to the building, and to plan it for the benefit of the flats inside, and the overall impact on its surroundings. The planning was done effectively. The external treatment was a rendition of the firm's established style, which is to articulate and express such things as concrete frame, glazing, sunshades, and lifts, which are made in factories to high degrees of precision. It is a display of mechanical craftsmanship, delivered with some crispness and elegance, but also tending to create a harsh and assertive overall effect. In theory the style can be tuned to suit a given location: at One Hyde Park the white concrete and copper louvres are said to echo the stone and reddish brick of surrounding buildings, and its irregular skyline to have some relation to surrounding turrets and domes.

Once this style had something to do with socialist housing projects, and then public cultural buildings like the Pompidou. Here it satisfies no one. It looks too austere for the billionaires who might live there, and for the taste of its well-heeled neighbours, while failing to achieve the civic mission that Rogers set architecture, and which its style might once have suggested. It was rumoured that the Qatari government, who became the building's main backers, were unhappy with its lack of glitz. Meanwhile residents near the nearby Chelsea Barracks, which were to be redeveloped by another Candys/Rogers/Qatar collaboration, were terrified by the sight of One Hyde Park rising from the ground, and redoubled their ultimately successful efforts to block the plans there.

But what, finally, about the 'high-quality public spaces'? One

Hyde Park relocates a road that now gives begrudging access to the park, with narrow pavements and gates that can close it off. It has a covering, required for complex planning reasons, which gives the road the feeling of belonging to the development. There are also strange glass enclosures facing Knightsbridge containing miniature landscapes, sandwiched between the McLaren and Rolex shops and the Abu Dhabi Islamic Bank. Here the public is allowed to enter and sit, like mannequins in a shop window or fish in a tank, and goggle at the passers-by. Here, with this bathos, ends the Urban Renaissance.

In the end, a luxury development in Knightsbridge is what it is. Unless the super-rich are improbably legislated out of existence, they will want places like this, and it is arguably better that they are in the middle of a city than in gated suburbs. In a city, some part of their wealth can also be extracted and spent on public benefits. At One Hyde Park the politicians got their tithe to spend on affordable housing in the slightly less posh district of Pimlico.

Nor can architects like Rogers be blamed for taking the job. In a world where cities include projects such as this, it would be futile and quixotic of an architect to renounce commissions to design them. The issue is rather the gap between the idealism of his public statements and the realpolitik with which he operates. It would be more ethical, more productive and ultimately less embarrassing to acknowledge that architects work in a world of negotiation, within which they should fight for the best that they can.

One Hyde Park's flaws are not that it exists, but that the planning system allowed it to be bloated, and poorly defended such things as the quality of public access to the park. Also that its quasi-socialist style is at odds with its luxury content. It might have been better to express wealth frankly, while settling less aggressively into the surrounding fabric. There are plenty of buildings in Knightsbridge that do this.

Like the City's towers, One Hyde Park is a diagram of a particular relation of wealth to government, in a time and place where the highly speculative use of capital was given unusual respect, where it was considered a social and cultural force, as much as a simple matter of business. It was not a relation the left-leaning Rogers would have wished for, and I doubt if he or his employees went into architecture to deliver above-average detailing on a flawed and anti-social concept. But he seems to have decided quite early that in order to realize his vision of cities, it would be necessary to engage with politics and business, do deals and make compromises. In this the way was eased by the power of look, by the ability of architecture to appear one thing and be another, and as early as the Pompidou Centre apparently radical architecture served the interests of a conservative president. With the Pompidou the end justified the means – something extraordinary and city-changing was achieved, even if it was not quite as advertised.

At One Hyde Park the public sphere did not get such a good deal. It is likely that, being architects, Rogers and his practice would have been excited by the thrill of making the thing, the large and glittering object, to an extent that stopped them noticing quite what was happening. Architects are often quite easily satisfied that radical-looking structures are in reality radical. Look, in London as in Dubai, is helpful to financial speculation, as a sales tool and as a distraction.

It would be an over-simplification to say that all the developers of noughties London were cynical. Some at least wanted to improve their city and make decent buildings. There are easier ways to get very rich than property – gambling with other people's pensions, for example – and some people go into development because they actually like building things, and want to do a good job. But planners and politicians, entranced by the splendid frenzy of a boom, favoured dazzling architectural wrappings over forethought and overview.

And me? I fell for it, too. I tried to capture a fleck of foam from the financial wave, and turn it into extraordinary architecture. I helped to commission an icon – for all that it was more than an icon and that there was meaning to its striking forms – on a scrap of land too awkward for commercial development. We attempted the Everest of masterpiece-building without the right equipment, and the icon played its part in the game whereby spectacular architecture distracted from more fundamental questions of planning and development. If it had been built, in its first version, it might have been so astonishing a thing as to justify its own existence, and transcend the conditions of its making. As it was not, an opportunity was lost: the lighter, more adaptable, easier building first imagined could have been a quiet manifesto for a kind of thinking, whereby designs are well matched to their situation, which was not then so much in fashion.

7: The rapacity of 'hope'

'World trade means world peace,' said the architect. Therefore a centre of trade should 'become a representation of man's belief in humanity, his need for individual dignity, his beliefs in the cooperation of men, and through cooperation, his ability to find greatness.' This centre would, hoped the architect, be a place where the peoples of the world could gather, meet, and understand each other. They might stage performances from their homelands in the plaza he had designed. Above them, despite the architect's fear of heights, would be towers of abstract beauty, the tallest in the world, inspired by Japanese principles of harmony.

He was American-born, of Japanese ancestry, and was raised in a poor part of Seattle, where houses built on a steep slope were liable to slip and slide. He worked in the grim conditions of an Alaskan salmon-cannery to pay his way through college and vowed to achieve a better life for himself. He was not interned in the Second World War, as many Japanese-Americans were, but he came under the suspicion of the military for the unfortunate coincidence that he chose to get married two days before the attack on Pearl Harbor. 'I know from personal experience', he wrote, 'how prejudice and bigotry can affect one's total thought process . . . If all human beings were given the opportunity to achieve their highest degree of capability without suppression, our world would be a much better place.'

Later, a young Egyptian studied architecture. He noticed the way modern, American-style towers destroyed the fabric of traditional Arab cities. He studied the intricate tissue of the souk in Aleppo – so different from the rigid, bounded, uniform skyscraper – which allows huge numbers of overlapping territories and transactions to co-exist. We don't know for certain, as his work is now banned from public view, but it seems that he saw the souk as the opposite of the corporate monoculture he hated. He did more than study. He led a group of terrorists who, obeying orders from a higher authority, hijacked two passenger planes, and flew them, one each, into the towers that the Japanese-American had designed as beacons of peace. Nearly three thousand people were killed and a decade, at least, of warfare ensued.

That the twin towers of the World Trade Center failed to fulfil Minoru Yamasaki's hopes is an understatement. Somehow the architect failed to see his work the way some others saw it. Where he saw abstract beauty and world harmony, they saw overscaled citadels of imperial arrogance. Where he saw inclusion, they saw exclusion, where he saw a welcome to the world, they saw two hostile fingers. It was not only murderous extremists like Mohammed Atta who saw the twin towers this way. Even as it was being built in the 1960s, the World Trade Center was execrated for its aggression towards the pattern of streets in downtown Manhattan, which it blocked and interrupted, and for its blunt intrusion on the city's pinnacled skyline. Nor was it the only project of Yamasaki's that suffered misunderstanding. His Pruitt-Igoe housing in St Louis, intended to improve the lives of poor families there, became so battered with crime and vandalism that it was, in 1972, blown up by controlled explosions. The critic Charles Jencks declared this moment the death of modernism, although its failure was more to do with housing policy and management than architecture. Yamasaki acquired an unfortunate record: not one but two of his works happened to fall victim to destruction by deliberate explosion.

Another architect, Daniel Libeskind, once told Oprah Winfrey that 'I love architecture, because as an architect you have to be an optimist. You always have to believe that there is a better future.' Architects have to believe, in the face of all the discouragements and vicissitudes of the processes of building, that their construction will arrive in the end, and that it will be worth having. They also have to persuade their clients, and planners and politicians, that it is worth investing millions in their ideas, because they will make the world in some way better. Where writers and artists, especially in the twentieth century, could travel deep into nihilism and despair, architects could not. They could not ask clients to invest in darkness, in alienation, to get tower cranes and concrete mixers to erect representations of the profound dislocation of the modern world.

Architects might be gloomy in private. In 1909 the young Le Corbusier sent his parents an un-festive, indeed lunatic, Christmas card that declared

La misère de vivre faite homme . . .

The card was decorated with a drawing of a condor on a mountain top, beadily surveying the landscape, like an avian, predatory version of Caspar David Friedrich's painting *Wanderer above the Sea of Fog*. The condor can be taken to be Corbusier, who seemed to like identifying himself as a bird: his name, adopted by the architect for himself as more impressive than his original name of Charles-Eduoard Jeanneret, echoes the French for 'crow'. The inscription continued:

. . . et le dédain de la misère de vivre incarnée en l'ame du
GRAND CONDOR. ('The misery of living made man . . . and the
disdain for the misery of living incarnate in the soul of the
Grand Condor.')

Yet in public he would later promote utopias, whose very disconnection with the complexities and difficulties of life would end up creating something like the alienation of which he and other architects could not speak.

Simply to build is hopeful, to labour now in the belief that in the future it will prove to have been worth it. Sometimes the hoped-for reward is in the afterlife: in standard histories of architecture, it is often the case that more than half the buildings shown are churches or temples, and those things usually taken to be signs of 'high' architecture – symmetry, repetition, geometry, axiality; porticoes, pediments, domes, colonnades – tend to have their origin in sacred buildings. Even when religion has been discarded, architecture finds it hard to lose its messianic tone. Thus Le Corbusier, in more upbeat mood:

Space! This response to the aspirations of being, this release
offered to the respiration of the lungs and the beating of the
heart, this effusion of vision from afar, from on high, so vast,
infinite, limitless.

Even the weariest, stalest plan for inflicting, in the name of regeneration, shopping malls and luxury-lifestyle living on a regional town, feels obliged to use the word 'visionary'. The word 'regeneration' itself carries half-religious hints of rebirth and renewal.

There is a difference between the hopefulness of religious and of secular buildings. Religious buildings offer hope in the hereafter; they only represent a better world. Secular buildings, at least those that have chosen to retain the redemptive imagery of religion,

promise to bring that better world into being, in the very place where they are built.

They promise to be instruments as well as symbols and, because of the special power of buildings to convince people that something is being done, they are taken as evidence that a problem is being fixed, or a tragedy assuaged. To this power can be ascribed the recurring idea of the model village, or the ideal home. Examples include Saltaire, in Yorkshire, where in the 1850s the industrialist Sir Titus Salt started building homes for his workers around his textile mills, or Bournville, the town built on the edge of Birmingham by the Cadbury's chocolate company, from the 1890s. In both the aim was partly true philanthropy, to provide better, bigger, cleaner homes than normal in Victorian industrial cities, and partly good business, as the model villages secured a happy and obedient work-force. Both were also morally and physically reforming: Salt and the Quaker Cadburys banned pubs, while paying for places of sport and wholesome recreation and, in Salt's case, churches and chapels.

The usual elements of a model village are a benign but con-trolling landowner, physical and spiritual improvement, and an expression of these ambitions in visible form. They have clear boundaries, and are planned according to principles of regular geometric order, as Saltaire is, or quasi-natural informality, like Bournville. Their styles are architecturally consistent – plain stone at Saltaire, picturesque arts-and-crafts at Bournville. They have to be pictures of a better future, as well as the means to achieving it. There is no fundamental reason why reforming architecture must take place in a specially designated enclave, obeying special rules and a consistent style, yet this completeness, this fusing of ideals into a single graspable entity, has a special appeal to the people who sponsor it.

•

It is because of the power of buildings to represent hope that I find myself, one spring morning, talking to Debra Dupar, who is pregnant with her fifth child, as she sits with her friends outside her house. A few years previously this spot was lethal, as Hurricane Katrina pushed volumes of water up the Industrial Canal, which links the Mississippi to the nearby Lake Pontchartrain. The pressure broke the levee that was supposed to hold the water back, poorly built by the US Army Corps of Engineers following Hurricane Betsy in 1965. Its replacement, a horizontal ribbon of pale concrete, can be seen over Debra's shoulder. Her seventy-year-old neighbour Gloria owed her life to a tree, in which she spent nine and a half hours. Young Shanat Green, a few doors along, was not so lucky. Her grandfather hoisted her onto the roof of their house, turned to help his other grandchild, and found when he turned back to Shanat that she had disappeared. A small handmade memorial commemorates her, 2002–2005, and her grandmother Joyce, 1931–2005. A nearby trailer, a tableau of wreaths and writing, proclaims: 'We want our country to love us as much as we love our country. The strength of our country belongs to us all. Mr Bush rebuild New Orleans The Lower 9th Ward Cross the Canal Tennessee Street NOT IRAQ.' Then a later text: 'Obama, A New Era of Responsibility'.

Debra, Gloria, and the Greens all lived in the Lower Ninth Ward of New Orleans, the place worst hit by the hurricane, with over a thousand of the more than eighteen hundred deaths; more died later of suicide and stress-related disease. Before the hurricane the Lower Ninth had a population of 14,000, almost all black. Five years later, it was the place where devastation remained most visible. The touristic parts of New Orleans, the French Quarter and the Garden District, were built on higher ground and damaged less, and traces of the disaster were cleaned up. The Lower Ninth was a flat heath, gridded by streets serving wooden houses that were there only in the concrete ghosts of their foundation slabs, and short flights of brick steps that had risen to their porches, left like the shoes of dead men.

In the most devastated parts the distinctive features now were sinewy evergreen oaks, known as 'live oaks', and redundant telegraph poles. Elsewhere there were degrees of destruction – some houses were shattered wrecks, some were partially damaged and still bearing the symbols left by rescuers when the floodwaters were high, which indicated the numbers of people and pets, and how many were dead or alive, in each house. In some places residents were slowly patching up their houses, with the help of drips of federal compensation money.

Behind and around Debra Dupar, however, were new buildings, specced-up versions of the city's traditional timber houses, with bright colours or added swoops indicating the involvement of an architect. Construction work was going on here and there. A film crew was making a documentary for Spike Lee, and fashionably dressed white tourists turned up, scanned the scene with camcorders, and left. Ten or more tour buses visited every day.

The activity was due to Brad Pitt, who, before Katrina, was already known both for his social conscience and his interest in architecture. He had got to know Frank Gehry, Rem Koolhaas, and Zaha Hadid, and spent time in Gehry's office collaborating on projects. The disaster was a chance to put his passions to good effect, and he launched an organization called Make It Right, with the aim of building at least a hundred and fifty homes. More than that, the project would, he said, 'turn tragedy into victory', and 'offer a more humane building standard . . . We would create homes that were sustainable and build with clean building materials for a just quality of life . . . we would build for safety and storm resiliency. We'd create new jobs in the process and we wouldn't stop until we could achieve all of this affordably.' Pitt started living, at least some of the

time, in New Orleans, and he didn't shirk the tortuous meetings that go with community development projects.

'We'd call upon some of our great architectural minds to innovate these solutions,' he said, and create 'a template that could be replicated at the macro level. We would engage and rely on the community to define the function of their neighbourhood and adhere to their guidance.' For Pitt 'the most sickening thought is that this all could have been avoided', that professionals such as engineers, who were supposed to protect the people of the Lower Ninth, had betrayed them. Pitt's mission was to 'take what was wrong and make it right'.

He assembled a team of twenty-seven architects, led by the Berlin and Los Angeles practice GRAFT, with coordination by a local firm, Williams Architects. Most were a notch or two below the level of celebrity of Gehry, Koolhaas, and Hadid, but Morphosis, winners of the Pritzker Prize, were there, as were the well-known MVRDV, a group of grown-up *enfants terribles* from the Netherlands, and the Japanese Shigeru Ban, who had created emergency cardboard structures after the 1995 Kobe earthquake. There were Elemental, who had come up with the idea of 'half a good house' for squatters in Iquique, Chile, and the British architect David Adjaye. There were also firms from Louisiana and nearby states. All worked for no more than their air fares: they donated their time to the project.

The architects produced twenty-eight prototype designs, following certain guidelines. They had to have porches to shelter from sun and rain, in the manner of traditional New Orleans houses, and they had to be at least five feet off the ground. Residents could choose the prototype they preferred and have it modified. Many chose to raise the houses as high as possible, to protect against future floods and to make space to keep a car. The houses were for people who had owned homes before the flood – the Lower Ninth had high rates of home ownership – and now had little left but the plots. If they could not afford the full cost of building anew, they could take out 'forgivable loans', to be repaid only if they sold their houses.

The project was a particular challenge for the architects, as there is little necessary connection between conceiving unusual, stylish, witty, attention-grabbing designs that make architects famous, and tackling the hard, urgent needs of rebuilding housing after a disaster. These architects had to find humility, just as Pitt's celebrity had to adjust to the practical.

In the event, there was not a perfect union of flair and function. That the houses are much better than anything seen in the Lower Ninth before is due more to the specifications that all share than to the individual brilliance of each of the twenty-seven architects. Debra Dupar, having lived for four years in a trailer a hundred and fifty miles away, is happy with her home, but you don't feel that the curving swoop that its architects added is essential to this happiness.

One of the builders working for Make It Right said it was a struggle to get architects 'to realize they're not designing a five million dollar mansion'. At the same time the demands of the project stopped the architects strutting their usual stuff, and the buildings tend to be less dazzling and more muted than works by the same practices elsewhere. At worst the architects over-elaborated, as if they were nervous that people would forget they were there. At best they engendered variety, some interesting ways of arranging spaces, and good PR. They gave the place a presence and character that standardized design would not have brought.

Other, less glamorous, agencies built faster and more cheaply than Make It Right. More than thirteen hundred 'simple, decent and affordable' homes were built by the charity Habitat for Humanity, in four hurricane-affected states, compared to the fifty completed by Make It Right in 2011. Another organization, Global Green, is building sustainable houses in another part of the Lower Ninth, and advises individual owners on rebuilding their homes. Such agencies give the impression that they are grateful for the attention and fundraising power that Pitt has brought, but would rather it had been used to reinforce their efforts than create something different.

There is also the question whether the most useful action was to rebuild in the Lower Ninth at all, an area below sea level, where no one is completely confident that the new, better levees would be enough to withstand something worse than Katrina. New Orleans has shrunk from 625,000 people in 1960 to 455,000 in 2005 to 344,000 in 2010. 'It looks like a lot of that place could be bulldozed,' said the Republican Speaker of the House of Representatives, from Illinois, and you don't have to share his crudeness to see a case for consolidating new homes in under-inhabited, but safer parts of the city.

The Lower Ninth was not any neighbourhood, but a place of history and sentiment for New Orleans' black community, celebrated in film and song. Success could not get the R & B pianist Fats Domino to leave the district; only flood could do that. Sentiment was a compelling reason why the Lower Ninth was not abandoned, a more basic one being that homeowners' titles remained there, and no means existed to transfer them elsewhere. But, looking at Make It Right's brave houses standing amid the expanses of scrubby grass and empty plots, it is hard to imagine that the vibrant, busy place of fond memory will return.

As acts of Hollywood compassion go, Pitt's is more thoughtful and committed, and less superficial and self-promoting than most. It's also hard to know, given the complexities of New Orleans politics, which can stop almost anything happening at all, whether something more purely practical and rational would have succeeded. Perhaps a bit of theatre was needed. For Pitt's was still compassion that needed a stage – the charged land of the worst-hit, most resonant part of the city – and costume, in the stylistic touches of the architects. It made a hope show, a hope parade. As in model villages, hope could not only lead to an action; it had to have a form.

To question hope is not popular, but it also has a dark side. Or rather, it can be used as a cover or a distraction. By diverting attention to an ideal future, hope – or the forms of hope – can be used to deflect attention from a complex present. It can be used as an excuse for erasing the living, the there, the awkward, in the name of a perfection which turns out to be unreachable. But which erasure conveniently removes resistance, and creates a blank space for exploitation by power and money.

When, in 1962, Minoru Yamasaki saw the budget for the World Trade Center, it was so vast that he thought that a zero had been added by mistake. It was not a mistake: the plan was indeed to spend the then-boggling sum of $280,000,000, which later rose to $900,000,000. This could be done because the towers were to be built by the mighty Port Authority of New York and New Jersey, a public bureaucracy grown fat on revenues from airports, seaports, bus stations, bridges, and tunnels. The things that the architect saw as symbols of world peace were, to the Port Authority, totems and guarantors of their power on the island of Manhattan. By putting their wealth into the towers, they were investing it in something that could never be taken away.

The Port Authority had the power to buy properties and clear sites, which is what they did to the district of warehouses and electronics shops called Radio Row. Shops, homes, streets, and businesses were expunged to make the plaza, from which rose the towers. The Authority could also, within their territory, re-arrange New York's zoning laws. Elsewhere in the city these laws, intro-

duced to limit overshadowing of one building by another, give towers their distinctive stepped form, narrowing from broad base to pinnacle. Yamasaki's towers would rise sheer and vast, plumb vertical, from pavement to parapet.

Their violence to both ground and sky made them unpopular. New Yorkers and urban theorists lamented the lost vitality of Radio Row, even as the district's businesses fought their removal in the courts, and objected to the way that thoroughfares like Greenwich Street, which once ran across the site, were blocked off in mid-run. Due to a slope on the site the horizontal plaza was in places thirty feet above street level, presenting a barrier to the city. In his pursuit of generalized harmony, Yamasaki crushed immediate humanity. The towers, he said, had 'the proper scale relationship so necessary to man . . . They are intended to give him a soaring feeling, imparting pride and a sense of nobility in his environment', but others saw their endless rhythm of narrow, scale-less verticals as impervious and sterile. Near the base these lines flared slightly into Gothic or Islamic arch-shapes but such softenings of the pattern did not mollify the critics, who saw them as empty gestures, as 'pure schmaltz'. As for their presence on the skyline, they were seen as crude, alien, and over-scaled in relation to the delicate, tapering, intricate forms of the Chrysler or Woolworth buildings. They were 'giant cigarette cartons', 'monuments to boredom', 'tombstones'.

That they were aloof, and rigid, and blank, was typical of Yamasaki. Pruitt Igoe was also impervious and inexpressive, and his Rainier Tower in Seattle is an opaque vertical oblong perched on a giant stalk, as if to be absolutely sure that there could be no intimacy with the street. He sought fixity – perhaps in reaction to the unstable ground beneath his childhood home – and the feeling that, once there, his buildings could never be changed or destroyed.

But they began to exert fascination, then even gather affection. The high-wire artist Philippe Petit walked and danced on a line strung between the towers, the sort of feat with which daredevils had previously honoured Niagara or the Grand Canyon – they had become geology. The German artist Josef Beuys saw them as patron saints of capitalism, and renamed them after the early Christian martyrs Cosmas and Damian. Younger New Yorkers, who could not remember Radio Row, or the older skyline, accepted them as part of the grand scenography of the city. A certain minimalist beauty could be observed in the way they caught the changing light on their different sides, and could be seen in their serenity from unexpected viewpoints in the tumultuous city. They became part of the furniture of snowglobes sold to tourists, equal to the Statue of Liberty and the Brooklyn Bridge.

Then they fell, and the skyline looked shorn, and older. A man said by those who had met him to be impenetrable and aloof, Mohammed Atta, led an assault on buildings of which the same was said, and two rigid machine-age tubes, the planes, were used to destroy two others. Gone, it turned out they were loved. There followed a frenzy of suggestions for their replacement, as people struggled to make sense of the event, and connect it to the obvious facts that some very large buildings had gone, and that something would need to go in their place. Thousands of people felt compelled to put their ideas out, on websites, on drawings stuck to fences around the site, in 4,000 unsolicited proposals sent to the Lower Manhattan Development Corporation, the newly formed body that was supposed to guide reconstruction. There was a plan for 2,792 bronze angels, one for each victim, to line the huge hole where the towers had been. There were crystal domes, buildings shaped like stars and stripes, or a giant nine and a giant eleven. Many mused on mystical numerology:

> . . . have you ever wondered why 911 was chosen for the emergency number, just as 'Mayday' is a distress call? May Day, or

May 1st, is the high Sabbath of Beltaine and witchcraft. We also know that September 11th is the 254th day of the year, and that 2 + 5 + 4 = 11. This leaves 111 days left in the year, which are side-by-side 11s. The words 'New York City' have eleven 11 letters. The word 'Afghanistan' has 11 letters . . .

There were proposals that the void should become a park, where the wound would be healed by nature. Others were defiant, and wanted to stick it back to the terrorists. One, popular with the workers who were clearing the site, was that towers like Yamasaki's should be built, only there would be five of them, in a row. Four would be short and the middle one would be tall, so that it looked like a fist giving the finger to Osama bin Laden. It was circulated by emails and printed on T-shirts and boxer shorts and, more than the proposals that aimed to heal, it caught the mood of rage and revenge widespread after the attacks. Most popular with the general public was the simplest idea, that the towers should be rebuilt as they had been, preferably with an extra storey added.

Most of these ideas came from amateurs – a woodworker, a nun, a doctor – and many were visited by the idea that they, above all others, had the answer. Nurse Wagtskjold from Minnesota got her congressman to bombard both Mayor Bloomberg of New York and President Bush with her proposal, which involved a dome, a gold eagle, a fountain, and a statue of a firefighter in bronze. 'A feeling of certitude', a furniture designer from Oregon wrote to Bloomberg, 'compelled me to take my vision this far. It is a sense of confidence that comes from knowing in my heart and soul that the vision I have is quite possibly the best solution out there.'

Architects did much the same. Four months after the attacks, fifty-eight of them showed their ideas at the Max Protetch Gallery, in an exhibition mounted with arguably indecent haste. 'Too soon and too ghoulish,' said one who did not take part. The entries

showed some evidence of professional training, and sometimes came with more sophisticated texts than the amateurs'. They would be more ironic and less innocent – they might adopt an interesting position, such as that military and urban space were now one, or that the site was just real estate with no need to memorialize – but they showed similar urges. They wanted to respond to shock and grief by putting themselves in the centre of the void left behind, and to do this with a singular idea, where a very large building project would become a single message: 'pre-exploded towers', 'ponds of memory', staircases to the sky, great egotistical writhings of whatever signature shapes – worm-like tubes, fractured shards – an architect had chosen as his or her own. These were not fundamentally different from the domes and angels of the amateurs.

There can be glamour in horror, and narcissism in healing. A catastrophe like 9/11 is thought to bring people together, and inspire selflessness, collaboration and the sharing of bereavement. In many cases, as with the volunteers who worked to clear the site, it did, but it also prompted a carnival of bitch-slapping and back-stabbing, of name-calling, pretention, manipulation, and posturing, as individuals competed to be the one who could uniquely represent the great tragedy. The idea of dignity, in honour of the dead, was mislaid. Most involved in these arguments were directly and deeply affected by 9/11 – they knew people who died, or watched the towers fall at close quarters, or both – but some, not all, made the collective grief personal. For them the most urgent thing was that their individual inner loss should be assuaged and recognized, and that everyone else should know about it. On the stage cleared by the attacks, they all wanted to be Hamlet. Hence the peddlers of attention-seeking projects, and their belief that theirs was the best, the only possible.

Mayors and governors sought votes by making proclamations about what should be done, and timed decisions on the site to suit electoral cycles. Mayor Rudolph Giuliani, as he left office in December 2001, called for a 'soaring, beautiful memorial . . . I really believe we shouldn't be thinking about this site as a site for commercial development'. Governor George Pataki of New York State would declare that 'where the towers stood was hallowed ground'. The Lower Manhattan Development Corporation said its aim was 'to rebuild our City – not as it was, but better than before'. Heated by emotion, legitimate differences became vitriolic conflicts. People who lived near the site resisted the idea that their neighbourhood might become nothing but a memorial, for which one of the residents' leaders was told she would 'burn in hell'. And architects fought like bantam cocks.

The first official proposal for rebuilding the site, unveiled in July 2002, was by the worthy firm of Beyer Blinder Belle, much praised for their recent restoration of Grand Central Station. They produced six alternative masterplans, which showed how a certain amount of offices and other commercial uses, plus public space and room for a memorial, could be arranged on the site. They were following the brief set them by the Lower Manhattan Development Authority and the Port Authority of New York and New Jersey, and made no pretence that their studies would, on their own, be enough to honour 9/11. Their plans were quite sensible, as far as they went, and many of their ideas would eventually reappear in the layout of what is now being built, but they were represented by drab images of whitish blocks arranged without passion. Beyer Blinder Belle were flayed and pummelled by press and public for their seemingly cloth-eared failure to acknowledge that this was more than another office development. The *New York Times'* critic called the architects 'Bland, Bland and Bland', another critic called the plans 'six cookie-cutter losers', and they did not long survive the onslaught.

There followed an 'Innovative Design Study', in which seven design groups out of 406 entries were chosen to produce ideas. The intention was that the beauty and significance lacking in Beyer Blinder Belle's plans would be conjured by an international line-up of exciting and, as the title suggested, 'innovative' architects. Although the fact that each team was paid only $40,000, when costs such as model-making and staff time would run to the hundreds of thousands, and other consultants were paid more for work on other aspects of the site that were in theory less significant, suggests that innovation and meaning were not thought so important after all.

The study was meant to be a bit of blue-sky thinking, out of which might emerge a cloud of good ideas, from which the best ones might be selected to inform and enrich whatever might happen next. It was not supposed to be a contest, and there were not supposed to be winners. 'This is not a competition', said the particulars. But the form of the process looked very like a competition, and if seven groups of ambitious architects were to be put into a metaphorical arena, egged on by media hungry for a result, with the greatest architectural commission in the world in prospect, it was always going to be highly unlikely that the architects or anyone else would treat it as a winnerless show-and-tell session. The architects pitched for press support, and spread black propaganda about their rivals.

Two finalists were chosen and asked to take their ideas further: a consortium called THINK, and Daniel Libeskind and his practice. Both were officially called 'beautiful, compelling, meaningful'. Libeskind, and Rafael Vinoly and Fred Schwartz of THINK, appeared on *The Oprah Winfrey Show*, to talk about how (in Oprah's words) they would 'create inspiration where attackers meant to create nothingness'. Libeskind and his team spread the idea that THINK's proposal, in which the two towers were to be rebuilt as open frameworks, with smaller elements placed within them, looked like 'skeletons'. Enemies of Libeskind called his work 'a pit', 'a Disneyland of death',

'astonishingly tasteless', and 'kitsch'. Then a committee met, to choose a winner in this process that was not a competition, and chose THINK.

But, as Libeskind would later say, 'in our corner, we did have Edward D. Hayes . . . a legend in the city, one of those human connectors who knows everyone from the governor on down'. Hayes was the model for a memorable character in *The Bonfire of the Vanities*, the defence lawyer Tommy Killian, and the novel's dedicatee. He was also friend and lawyer to Libeskind, and a friend and former classmate of Governor Pataki's. Hayes pointed out each to the other the similarities of their immigrant origins, crystallized by the fact that each had a treasured photograph of themselves, as children, posed in front of a haystack. At the crucial moment Hayes reminded Pataki of the virtues of the Libeskind scheme. 'This project will define your legacy,' he told the Governor, 'as much as anything you've done. You gotta do whatever you think is right, whatever you think is best.' The day after the committee chose THINK, Pataki overruled them, and chose Libeskind. The latter's plan, he proclaimed, 'was born out of tragedy but forged in democracy'.

Daniel Libeskind was born in Poland in 1946, the son of survivors of the Holocaust. His family moved to Israel and then New York, where the teenage Daniel arrived, like immigrants of yore, by ship. He built his architectural reputation in academic circles, with designs that were conceptual and deliberately unbuildable, indeed with drawings that could not conventionally be called 'designs' at all. His first building was the Jewish Museum in Berlin, which attempted to represent the way that Jewish life had been enmeshed with that of the city, and the violence which ripped them apart. The museum's official opening, attended by Libeskind and his wife Nina, was on September 10th 2001.

His personal and professional history meant that Libeskind could talk convincingly of disaster, loss, and renewal. 'Part of my culture, part of my background is that you have to turn these evil things into something – into hope,' he told Oprah. And this was the theme of his plan for Ground Zero, which he called Memory Foundations, and presented with a garnish of artistic-looking calligraphy. He 'meditated for many days', he said in his presentation of the project, on a

seemingly impossible dichotomy. To acknowledge the terrible deaths which occurred on this site, while looking to the future with hope, seemed like two moments which could not be joined. I sought to find a solution which would bring these seemingly contradictory viewpoints into an unexpected unity.

And so he proposed to expose for ever the concrete slurry walls which held back the Hudson River so the towers could be built, and were most of what remained of them. The walls enclosed a huge space going down to the bedrock, that Libeskind proposed should be left open as a 'quiet, meditative and spiritual space' of memorial. It was this that critics called 'the pit'. For Libeskind these remnants

withstood the unimaginable trauma of the destruction and stand as eloquent as the Constitution itself asserting the durability of Democracy and the value of individual life.

There would be a museum 'of the event, of memory and hope'. There would be a 'Park of Heroes' and a 'Wedge of Light'. The latter would be an open space where

each year on September 11th between the hours of 8:46 a.m., when the first airplane hit, and 10:28 a.m., when the second tower collapsed, the sun will shine without shadow, in perpetual tribute to altruism and courage.

On the ground and up the walls of buildings were slashing, oblique lines, denoting both anguish and dynamic new life. Above, a spiral composition of office towers, intended to echo the torch on the Statue of Liberty, would ascend to the pinnacle of the tallest tower. Later named the Freedom Tower by Governor Pataki, this would be the tallest building in the world, as the Twin Towers had been when completed, at the height – chosen to honour the date of the Declaration of Independence – of 1,776 feet. The top of the tower would contain

> the 'Gardens of the World'. Why gardens? Because gardens are a constant affirmation of life. A skyscraper rises above its predecessors, reasserting the pre-eminence of freedom and beauty, restoring the spiritual peak to the city, creating an icon that speaks of our vitality in the face of danger and our optimism in the aftermath of tragedy.
>
> Life victorious.

But there was a problem. Libeskind had been chosen by Governor Pataki and commissioned by the Lower Manhattan Development Corporation. There was another player, the private developer Larry Silverstein, who had bought a lease on the site in the summer of 2001, with a view to refurbishing the towers. A clause in the lease, blind to the imminent events, obliged him to put back every one of the 10,000,000 square feet of offices, and 550,000 square feet of retail, that the towers had contained in the unlikely event of their destruction. Before the towers fell Silverstein had chosen his own architects for the refurbishment, the multinational Skidmore Owings and Merrill, which had dominated American architecture since the Second World War. They were still his architects two years later.

As the writer Philip Nobel has pointed out, Silverstein's lease was more enduring than the steel of the Twin Towers, and more influential than any vision, aspiration, masterplan, or proclamation. It decided, without reference to the significance of the catastrophe of which the lawyers who drafted it knew nothing, the fact that would determine the nature of the rebuilding more than any other, that it would contain a very large amount of office space. Which, if part of the site was to be left open for a memorial and public space, meant that very large towers would have to be built. It seemed there was no possibility of discussion whether such a colossal lump of rentable floor space was urbanistically desirable. Or even commercially so: Lower Manhattan was a declining location for the banks and financial businesses who would be the hoped-for tenants. It made no difference that powerful people, up to and including the President of the United States, were concerned with the site. The lease was inviolable. No Portia could undo it.

And if the site was to contain very large office blocks, there was a logic for hiring architects experienced in such things. According to one of his lieutenants, Larry Silverstein said to Daniel Libeskind, 'Congratulations, this is a phenomenal plan. But – no disrespect – I'd like my architects to design the individual buildings.' So David Childs of SOM was put into partnership with Libeskind. They were an odd couple, Childs being tall and calm in manner, with an owlish look that might be that of a Latin teacher, were it not that the quality of his conventional grey suits told you otherwise, and that he has the polite ruthlessness necessary to succeed in his business. Libeskind is short and frenetic, black-clad, tie-less, his hair bristling upwards as if with excess of energy, and given to outré style decisions, such as some cowboy boots that became famous in his moment of greatest celebrity. The pairing could not last, and after an unseemly wrestle, Childs became the architect of the Freedom Tower. Silverstein chose three other architects for the three other towers, Foster and Partners and Rogers Stirk Harbour + Partners from London, and the Japanese Fumihiko Maki.

Libeskind's dynamic vortex was straightened out, and any resemblance to the Statue of Liberty's torch became tenuous, not least because it might be many years, if ever, before the ensemble is completed. The eminent architects of the towers – 'significant' was the Silverstein Corporation's word – were in no mind to subordinate their designs so that they would form part of the unified composition envisaged in Memory Foundations. Instead each tower is singular, symmetrical, assertive, and indifferent to its neighbours. Each is branded as the work of its particular architect, through the use of their signature tics and traits. Foster's is crystalline, Rogers' has the big Xs of its cross-bracing on the outside, in a toned-down version of the practice's fondness for turning buildings inside out. Maki's tower is minimalist-cool. The Freedom Tower is blandly corporate, although Childs says the form is inspired by the obelisk of the George Washington Monument in Washington DC, in recognition of the tower's symbolic importance. It will also rise to 1,776 feet, with the help of a spike on the top, a desiccated remnant of Libeskind's ideas. Despite the fact that the tower is the most significant work of his career, Childs is scornful of the magic number of its height: '1776 feet, whatever that's worth,' he says. 'Nobody's going to count the feet.'

For all the angels, crystal domes, eagles, and magic numbers, and for all Libeskind's eloquence and the speeches of governors and mayors, the most conspicuous outcome of the years of battle and debate would be, as had always been ordained by the adamantine lease, an array of huge glass sentinels full of commercial office space. Except that they weren't exactly commercial. No sane developer would build so much space speculatively in this location, in a market which, after 2008, was challenging. They would also be expensive to build, because of their height, and because they would require extensive security provision to allay the reasonable fears of future office workers, who might otherwise flinch when they saw

a plane fly by. At a cost of $3.8 billion, according to the *Wall Street Journal*, the Freedom Tower is by far the most expensive office building in the history of the United States. According to Childs it is also, commercially speaking, in the wrong place: it would be better if it was as close as possible to public transport and to Wall Street, and it is in a spot where the ground conditions make it more difficult to build. It is there because Libeskind's plan said it should be there and, because this is ground charged with emotion, it was felt important to show some residual (and extremely expensive) respect to Memory Foundations.

Because the towers of business are not truly businesslike, they require public financial support. The Rogers and Maki towers are underwritten by the Port Authority, thereby cushioning Silverstein's risk. As for the Freedom Tower, Silverstein deemed it too chancy to build it at all, which required the Port Authority to take over completely, pay the construction cost with public funds, and hope rather than expect that the investment would be returned one day. Shortfalls, it turned out, would be covered in part by raising tolls on the Authority's bridges and tunnels. When the publishers Condé Nast booked a third of the floor space, it was at less than half the rate needed for the building to break even. 'In other words,' as the *New York Times* said, 'a company that publishes high-end magazines aimed at rich people will be getting an enormous government subsidy for the foreseeable future.' Humble users of the bridges and tunnels would pick up the tab.

So the four sentinels will be state-sponsored office towers. It might be thought that an office tower is something that should create its own commercial viability, but it was felt necessary to sponsor these ones, because it was felt necessary to build something, and to build something big. Those early T-shirts, with their fists of towers giving the finger to terrorists, stated an emotion that never went away. 'Don't forget 9/11. Delay means defeat', said the placards at demonstrations of construction workers when things were stalling.

Only really large skyscrapers would give the right message of defiance, even if it would take more than a decade to complete them, by which time Osama bin Laden would be dead, and it might not be completely clear precisely which audience of bad guys would be the object of the address, and whether they would be paying attention, unless to plot a new attack. The towers would be office blocks, but they would also be symbols, even if their symbolic role would fade a little: the Freedom Tower was renamed One World Trade Center, to lighten the weight of significance on future tenants.

For all the thousands of ideas and years of debate, fundamental questions were not vigorously pursued. Why, for example, try to build the tallest building in the world, an attempt that would be effortlessly outpaced by Dubai's Burj Khalifa, whose height of 2,717 feet is about 1,776 plus fifty per cent? Great height increases the risk of attack, and is likely to make the effects of an attack more devastating, which means expensive measures against structural collapse and flying glass, and for emergency escape.

At the base of the tower the contradictions of the project concentrated in a cladding material. Because of the site, and its provocative height, One World Trade Center is likely to be a target. What could be better for terrorists of the future than to knock everything down again? Or at least cause some damage. So the bottom 180 feet, which in most office towers would contain money-earning floor space, will contain nothing but lift shafts wrapped by a stupendously high atrium, wrapped in thick concrete with small openings. The thinking is to minimize the danger to life if, say, a truck bomb went off outside. But if revealed to the exterior, the concrete wall would not be the best possible image of the Freedom after which the tower was formerly named, especially as the tower will in honour of its symbolic role be open to the public, who will ride up to the inevitably spectacular views from the top. It has to be welcoming and fortified at once. It was therefore proposed to wrap the concrete in a special kind of crystalline glass, which would dissemble its massiveness and shatter harmlessly in an explosion, like a car windscreen. The glass was to be made by a Chinese manufacturer who then proved unable to deliver it as hoped, and the architects had to come up with an alternative, even as the tower's structure rose high above its problematic base.

The skyscrapers will not be the only new buildings in the place once called Radio Row, then the World Trade Center, then Ground Zero, and now the World Trade Center again. There will be a train station, serving several underground lines that intersect at this point, and roofed by a spectacular spiky structure, with moving parts, by Santiago Calatrava, a Valencia-born, Zurich-based architect who specializes in putting spectacular spiky structures over transport facilities. The station had to discharge some sort of symbolic duty too, which is why Calatrava was chosen and presumably why the station's budget has been allowed to rise towards a perfectly astonishing $4 billion. The roof, which sits between the second and third highest towers, is supposed to resemble a dove released from a child's hands, though a more obvious if less meaningful comparison would be with a porcupine.

The site will include 550,000 square feet of shopping, and it is hoped one day to build a performing arts centre by Frank Gehry, between the Tower formerly known as Freedom and Foster's yet-to-be-started crystalline shaft. But apart from the towers the most significant element is an eight-acre plaza containing 415 trees and two square holes, each an acre in size. The two squares occupy the footprint of the fallen towers, and in both a colossal quantity of water cascades perpetually down each of their 400-foot-long sides, gathers on a plane 30 feet below, and then falls another 30 feet into smaller squares in the centre. The names of the dead of 9/11, at

Ground Zero, the Pentagon, and on Flight 93, together with those killed in the 1993 bombing of the World Trade Center, are cut out of bronze panels that ring the two squares. Together the fountains and plaza form the official 9/11 Memorial, designed by Michael Arad and Peter Walker, conceived as place both of remembering and of the continuation of life: 'You walk through trees,' says Walker, 'and suddenly these waterfalls open up underneath you. Then you turn around and you're in a forest, which is a symbol of life.' Beneath the plaza is a museum with 100,000 square feet of exhibition space, where the victims will be remembered with photographs, personal belongings, and remembrances by their families, and there will be relics of the site such as crushed pieces of fire truck, twisted metal, and a steel fragment of the old towers that miraculously looks like a Christian cross.

With Libeskind's emoting angles gone, towers, museum, plaza, and station are arranged on a conventional grid of rectangular plots. It is a normal commercial/civic composition of glass and greenery, not unlike the Beyer Blinder Belle plans that were so roundly condemned, except that everything is extraordinarily big, and expensive, and slow to achieve. The second highest tower, Foster's, will if built exceed the Empire State. The total length of waterfall is a third of a mile. The museum has as much exhibition space as Tate Modern in London, excluding its Turbine Hall. Everything on the site seems driven by the fear that, whatever might be done to commemorate 9/11, it will not be big enough. At the same time there is a lack of communication or coherence among the constituent parts. The Memorial gives no sense that there is a museum underneath it. The skyscrapers, each speaking the personal language of its famous architect, make a Babel of towers. Calatrava's station refers only to itself.

In 2004 Philip Nobel wrote that 'only ten months after the attack all the limits that would define the plans were in place. The only politically acceptable solution was already apparent in the summer of 2002. The site would be rebuilt as a crowded, mixed-use, shopping-intensive corporate development surrounding a large but compromised memorial.' As the structures started emerging from the ground five years later, it could be seen that he was right.

It could have been better. Without the tyranny of the lease, there could have been less office space and more places to live, making a more varied district, and one more like the surrounding blocks. The site could have been planned to integrate more with these surroundings, rather than perpetuate the feeling, created by Yamasaki's buildings, that this is a zone apart. Without the lease, and without the obsession with height, there might not have been the parade of pointlessly vast towers, and the security they require. There could have been a railway station that did not try to make itself the most conspicuous object of all, as if a transport facility should grieve and aspire more than anything else. There could still have been plenty of opportunities for making money, but there could have been richer, subtler, happier relationships of the parts to one another.

The gross absurdity of a private developer's office towers being sponsored at colossal public cost could have been avoided, and the expensive duty to memorialize could have been removed from the skyscrapers and the station. The priority would then have been to create as good a piece of Manhattan, for living and working, as possible. The commemorating could all be done by the museum, and the Memorial. This could well have involved water, and trees, and names, and the footprints of the Twin Towers, but might possibly have allowed more intimacy, rather than the ceaseless shock and awe of insanely large quantities of falling water.

Or, as so many wanted, they could simply have put back Yamasaki's towers, with due measures to stop them falling as easily again. It would at least have been more eloquent, less garbled.

•

The fifty-year history of the World Trade Center is a chronicle of the uses and misuses of hope, and the ways in which they can mobilize many tons of building materials, tens of thousands of construction workers, and billions of dollars. From the beginning, there has been a superstructure of hope, an infrastructure of business and power, and a confused intersection between the two. Yamasaki's idealism acted as a cloak for the Port Authority's financial ambitions without, as it turned out, fooling anyone. Hope – of healing, of renewal, of rebuilding better than before – was after 9/11 the driving force, or seemingly so. But the big decisions were made by money: weirdly but not unusually, by private money lavishly augmented by public money. In this dance, or game, Libeskind represented hope, Childs money. Libeskind was allowed his *Oprah* spot, his headlines, his stirring speeches, the magazine profiles on his interesting life. But Childs was there all along, and he got to do the tower.

The game was made easier by the way Libeskind imagined buildings could carry meanings. They could do so through magic numbers, like 1776, or shapes like the spiral and the slashing lines, or episodes like the exposure of the slurry wall. These things are rhetorical devices: they assume a group of buildings are something like a speech. They can also be attached and detached with relative ease, meaning that others could play the same game as Libeskind. Childs could say his tower was like the George Washington Monument and Calatrava could say his roof was like a dove, and no one could say that these images were any less valid than the notion that Libeskind's spiral of towers would look like Lady Liberty's torch. The Tower Formerly Known as Freedom could keep its meaningful number of feet, and all concerned could pretend that thereby an essential aspiration was being protected.

It might seem that Libeskind was the good guy, being on the side of hope, with Childs on the dark side, that of money. In fact both might be credited with a genuine desire to do right by the site, and each was complicit in the outcome. Libeskind's rhetoric and fantasy cleared the space for the exploitation of the SOM scheme. Both left out the difficult middle, which is not a space where everything merges into a dull compromise, but where differences are manifest and creative. The critical decisions at the World Trade Center, the ones which determine what the place will really be like, include such questions as

— how do the parts connect to each other?
— for example, how is the transition made from memorial to office lobby, or museum to shopping mall?
— how do they connect to the surrounding streets and blocks?
— what will it actually be like to be in a street, or a lobby, or an underground space: will it feel like a piece of New York, or a development that might be anywhere?
— why glass, or steel, or stone, or concrete, or any material?
— what is the scale of the place: why is everything big and, as it is big, what is the relationship of a human being to the whole?

These questions were not wholly ignored. The landscape architect Peter Walker considered some of them in his design of the tree-filled plaza that contains the memorial cascades. Beyer Blinder Belle, Daniel Libeskind, and David Childs all proposed that the Manhattan grid pattern of streets, interrupted by Yamasaki, be reinstated, as would any architect following the contemporary consensus on city planning, which is all in favour of stitching together and 'permeability'. But this is broad-brush stuff. In all the myriad visions of Ground Zero, there was almost nothing that bothered to show what a street, at ground level, with people living their lives, might look like. There was a vagueness left to be filled with the generic unexamined substance of corporateness: glass, stainless steel, and stone, plus high levels of maintenance, management, control, and surveillance.

The difficult middle was overlooked because it was difficult. Politicians don't make speeches or newspapers write editorials about materials, scale, or connections between spaces. It was also overlooked because it might have got in the way of the biggest, also under-discussed, decisions. For example, had attention been fully focused on the way the height of the towers multiplied the costs and effects of security measures, this might have raised the question why the office towers needed to be so high, which would have challenged the need for so much office space. Or, had it been fully debated whether the site might become more like other parts of Manhattan, that is, a place to live as well as work, with small as well as large scales, with degrees of intimacy and grandeur, and with some degree of surprise or openness in what kind of shops there might be, and what might happen in the streets – had this question been fully pursued, it might also have exposed the logic, or lack of it, behind the 10,000,000 square feet. Few sites have been so much debated, by so many people, yet somehow fundamental decisions, the ones that will make the place what it will be, passed through with relatively little challenge.

When the towers fell, strange things happened to language. Victims became 'Heroes' and the word 'Freedom' acquired a special, adjectival usage, where it became a near-synonym of 'American'. A 'War on Terror' was declared, even though wars are usually against countries and peoples, rather than abstract nouns. An 'Axis of Evil' was discovered, linking countries that hated each other – Iran and Iraq – in supposed alliance. The phrase 'Ground Zero', originally applied to the far more numerous victims of American attacks on Hiroshima and Nagasaki, was appropriated and reversed, to describe American victimhood. However terrible the events of 9/11, they should not supplant those of August 1945.

Others have observed how the draining of meaning from words assisted political actions with a flawed rationale, such as the invasion of Iraq. This language of freedom and heroes was also applied to the rebuilding effort, and if the architectural effects were considerably less drastic than the military, there was still a disconnection with reality. This allowed grand gestures of dubious logic, and faulty engagement with conditions as they were on the ground.

In Yamasaki's towers of peace, in the memorial ideas of Nurse Wagtskjold from Minnesota and the furniture designer from Oregon, and in Libeskind's magic spiral and Calatrava's *soi disant* dove, the same thing happens. There is the universal, or at least the very big, and there is me. There is harmony/abstraction/the cosmos, and there is the individual creator whose unique life history and genius makes him or her the best possible person to realize these ideals. Between these poles a very great deal is overlooked: encounters, conflicts, resolutions, uncertainties, surprises, events, life.

The omitted could be summarized as friction. This – the never-resolved overlapping, intersection, confrontation, and collaboration of interests and desires – is the stuff of cities, their reason for being and the source of their material and spiritual wealth. It is a mechanical, biological, social, cultural, economic, and erotic truth that you can't live without friction. There is hope in friction.

Rhetorical hope denies it. Yamasaki's towers, Nurse Wagtskjold's dome and David Child's obelisk are all smooth-surfaced things that ideally make no contact with their surroundings. Because visions and fantasies are pursued in the name of hope, they are given an easy ride. But the operations of power also like to avoid friction, or rather conceal and displace it: Yamasaki's abstraction of hope helped the Port Authority to crush Radio Row, which was a place of friction. By clearing the difficult middle for a better future, these projects also open it up to what, with apologies to Barack Obama, might be called the rapacity of 'hope'.

8: Eternity is overrated

Which is not to argue for hopelessness. Rather, for an appreciation of the present, in both time and place, and of what it could become, for a faith in facts over fantasy, which includes facts that are ambiguous, strange, and mobile, and for a willingness to engage with complexities and obstacles.

An example might be another public work in Manhattan, achieved in the same years as the struggle to shape the new World Trade Center, but with less expense, fewer speeches, and more effect. This is the High Line, on the lower West Side, the making of an elevated linear park along the black steel viaduct of a freight railway, built in the 1930s and redundant since 1980.

It is a work of friction, generated from the encounter of industry and pleasure, but also peaceful. Not long ago public spaces in New York had an edge of confrontation, potential or actual, or, worse, violence. It was contested between different individuals and different identities. The High Line feels more like a beach. People stroll, sunbathe, paddle, take photographs of each other, and are largely thoughtful and polite in making way on the narrow paths. But they don't just drift: they are alert and conscious of themselves and others. They look, are seen and know that they are seen. People dress casually, but there is a touch of the catwalk about the old viaduct.

Such things might happen on the ground, in a pedestrianized street, but part of what makes the High Line interesting is its perspective. You get views once intended only for freight wagons, of backs of buildings and familiar landmarks seen from unfamiliar angles, of evening shadows which, elsewhere on the island, and at ground level, get blocked by buildings. Offices on the third or fourth floor, generally the least interesting level in New York, being neither street nor sky, acquire new status. Back becomes front, and ground level is multiplied. Because you are raised, you are taken out of the city, as if into some apprentice paradise, but you are also thrust back into it. The familiar interplay of blocks and streets is made more striking witnessed twenty or thirty feet off the ground.

The power of the High Line also comes from the making of a thing of hard industry into a playground. The planting of the park looks casual, loose, soft, with gatherings of plants of the kind that grew spontaneously when the tracks were abandoned. There are not trees or mown grass, but a series of micro-environments such as wetland, moss, or meadows, ordered according to 'agritecture', a neologistic hybrid of architecture and agriculture. In places water laps or eddies over the paving, seeping or bubbling up seemingly by accident, rather than performing within the bounded stage of a formal fountain. Relics of rails and sleepers are half-buried in the planting and paving. You don't forget what this thing was, but you also know that it is something different.

Paving, formed of long blocks of pebbledashed concrete, is simple and consistent along the High Line's 1.45 miles. It forms a staggered pattern, which widens and narrows like a stream, and can be interrupted and resumed as plants encroach and retreat. In places it rises out of the ground to support benches. The consistency of the paving turns attention elsewhere, to the city, the plants, and the other people, to the Hudson River that runs in rough parallel, to the oblong geology of the big blocks that line and sometimes straddle the viaduct, or into the glass-walled bedrooms of the Standard Hotel where, following complaints that guests were displaying their naked and coupling selves to the park, the following ambiguous notice is issued:

> please be aware of the transparency of our guest room windows and that activity in your room, when the curtains are open, may be visible from outside. We appreciate your consideration of the patrons of the High Line public park and surrounding neighborhood below.

The High Line is made possible by more things than design. It could only happen because of ingenious trade-offs of the rights for developing above it, and adequate provision for the upkeep of its delicate waterworks, and seemingly casual planting. It also owes its existence to Peter Obletz, a dance company manager, property consultant, and train enthusiast, who was fond of wearing a blue velvet smoking jacket and saddle shoes as he hosted elaborate dinner parties in a 68-ton antique Pullman dining carriage, which he kept on tracks near the High Line. He exploited a quirk in the law to buy the line for ten dollars in 1984, and then fought all-consuming legal battles against property interests who saw their chances of profit from the site disappear. He was ultimately unsuccessful, and died aged fifty in 1996, but he managed both to delay demolition and inspire others to campaign for the structure's rescue and conversion to public use.

It was championed by Amanda Burden, the director of the New York City Department of City Planning, who, as magazine profiles have pointed out, is an unusual combination of socialite and municipal bureaucrat. The daughter of an heir to the Standard Oil fortune, and a member of something called the International Best Dressed List, she also wrote a post-graduate thesis on the unglamorous subject of solid-waste management. For her the High Line would be 'a magical garden in the sky . . . I knew this incredible piece of urban infrastructure could become the defining feature of a new

neighborhood.' In a New York way, this social project was also a society project: celebrities and actors were enlisted to the cause, benefactors were charmed, financial alchemy was performed, and politicians won over. The landscape architect James Corner, the garden designer Piet Oudolf and the architects Diller Scofidio + Renfro were hired, and the park was made.

There are limits to the greatness of the High Line. Its relaxedness is achieved only with the help of sixteen prohibitions (smoking, alcohol outside designated areas, gatherings of more than twenty people, except by permit), announced at its entrances. It can be seen as an occupation of the public realm by the knowing, clever, design style of boutique hotels like the Standard. It is moot whether the Standard is an adjunct of the park, or the park is an extension of the hotel's foyer. Its success relies on the high land values of Manhattan, and the High Line package includes shops selling High Line branded perfumes and souvenirs. Then again, it is a space that was never public before, and is free to enter.

The High Line is a work of different kinds of time. There is the historic time of the old railway, its rise, abandonment, and re-use, its part in the industrial history of New York. There are the lifecycles of the plants and their seasonal changes. There are changes in light and weather over months and during a day, and as day turns into night. There are the activities of people, deliberately decelerated by the design, to make it a slower place than the nearby jogging and cycling routes along the Hudson River. There is the development of the High Line itself, built in stages, and the changes to its surroundings as the success of the park prompts new buildings and restaurants.

Most of these things exist without architecture, but built spaces can either suppress them or heighten them. The developers who fought Peter Obletz wanted to obliterate the old structure and replace it with generic offices and flats. Air conditioning would have tamed climate. The life that is now in the materials, in the differences between the old concrete and the new stone, would have been smoothed into ubiquitous glass. All accidents of view and perspective would have been normalized, and the simple pleasure of a park, now enjoyed by two million visitors a year, would not have been there.

Of course, all buildings exist in time. The word 'building' suggests an action that is ongoing, rather than a finished thing. We don't talk about 'builts'. The question is whether time is used to emancipate architecture, or if architecture is used to suppress time.

The High Line's openness to time is rare. More often architecture, especially at its grander end, aspires to immortality. For a building to be called 'timeless' is a compliment. Indeed, the ability of buildings to exceed human life spans, and so connect different generations, is a particular power of architecture. The fixed, the lasting, and the beyond-the-present are parts of an architect's repertoire.

It is possible, however, that eternity is overrated, and that excessive value is given to architecture that borrows the gravity of a tomb or a temple. There is a preference, both in history books and among the most highly praised contemporary buildings, for the complete, unchanging, stand-alone monument. This is most obvious when a building adopts the masonry and columns of an ancient temple, and only slightly less so with certain modernist masterpieces that aim for perfection of form. But there are also buildings that claim dynamism and motion, but end up being static and hostile to change.

As buildings tend to outlive their makers, and as we tend to live in cities surrounded by buildings made mostly by the dead, architecture has always been intimate with the mortal and immortal. We don't want to die, and one of the attractions of building, to architects and clients, is to leave something for eternity: all architects, said the American Philip Johnson, want to be immortal, and he made a good fist of it himself by living to be ninety-eight.

The first named architect invented the world's most enduring form for the commemoration of death. Imhotep, in the twenty-seventh century BC, hit on the idea of stacking up in diminishing sizes the table-like mounds, mastaba, that had been the traditional form of funerary monument until then. This formed the first pyramid, the step pyramid in Saqqara, which was the burial place of his client Pharaoh Zoser. Later versions of the idea would refine the prototype, replacing the stepping with a straight-lined triangular profile. Imhotep was rewarded for his innovative design by becoming a god – a notch above the knighthoods and peerages that are now conferred on eminent British architects – and thus immortal.

In 1879, in Brno, Moravia, the eight-year-old Adolf Loos was bereft by the death of his father Adolf Loos Senior, stonemason and sculptor of gravestones, monuments and architectural decorations, leaving him with happy memories of playing in the workshop, and a dread mother from whom he would eventually flee. As an adult Loos wrote

> only a very small part of architecture belongs to art: the tomb and the monument. Everything else that fulfils a function is to be excluded from the domain of art.

Then, later in the same essay,

> when we come across a mound in the wood, six feet long and three feet wide, raised to a pyramidal form by means of a spade, we become serious, and something in us says: somebody lies buried here. *This is architecture.*

For his own cenotaph, by his definition one of his most important works of architecture, he left a casual scribble of a plain

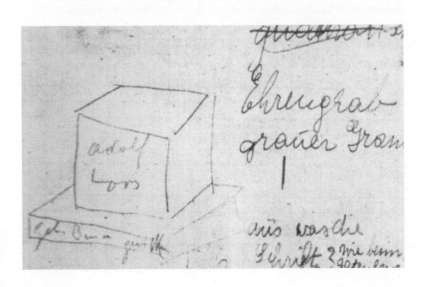

stone cube, sitting on a low plinth, with his name written across one face.

Between Imhotep and Loos span five millennia in which the thing called Western architecture was formed. Its most prominent and famous landmarks were sometimes tombs and memorials, and often temples or churches, also concerned with business of the immortal. The belief would arise that the architecture of eternity is the highest form to which all buildings should aspire. Even the spaces of the living – houses, parliaments, sometimes shops – would be given the forms of objects of the dead.

Imhotep's pyramid and Loos' cube compress into their shapes properties of the architecture of the eternal, which have also been imitated by structures of the everyday. Simple though they are, they have attributes prized by architects down to the present. They are stone, permanent, solid, where the material you see on the outside is the material that causes the structure to stand. They are ideally unchanging. They are detached, self-sufficient, fixed; objects that you can contemplate from any direction. They are unified, geometric, and complete. They are forms.

The architecture of the eternal tends to be symmetrical. The symmetry of buildings is often said to be based on that of human faces and bodies, which it is, but living people are almost always skewed by action and expression. You rarely see perfect symmetry in a human figure except when in prayer or prepared for burial, or in a human face except in a death mask. A tomb is often also geometric, a cylinder or a pyramid. It will probably set itself apart, in an enclosure defined by a wall, and placed so that it can be viewed unencumbered from all sides.

The architecture of death aims for completion. It is made of stuff that endures, and its designers usually seek a balance of parts to each other and to the whole, and for precise and finished detail: architectural perfection can be achieved more easily in structures

PARTHENON.

ARCHITECTURE

III

PURE CREATION OF THE MIND

subject to limited functional demands, and whose residents cause little trouble. Load-bearing columns and beams, or masonry walls, are usual, where structure and surface are one. Finality and resolution are sought, despite the many beliefs that death is the beginning of a new and greater life than the one we know. Usually, funerary architecture wants to freeze time.

Similar properties can be found in classical temples, in particular in the Parthenon, often seen as the ultimate exemplar not only of its type, but of all buildings. According to one writer it is 'the most perfect example ever achieved of architecture finding its fulfilment in bodily beauty', to another, 'the most unrivalled triumph of architecture and sculpture that the world ever saw'. Le Corbusier called it 'a decisive moment for architecture . . . the pinnacle of [the] pure creation of the mind . . . a work of perfection, of high spirituality'.

It has symmetry, geometry, frontal or axial composition, mass, permanence, masonry construction, load-bearing columns and beams, the making of a thing or place apart, the marking of boundaries and thresholds, repetition, consistency, control, completeness. It is, at least in the state that it appears now, a free-standing, self-sufficient, form. It is the type of what we now think of as classical architecture, as realized in recent centuries in houses, law courts, art galleries, parliaments, churches, and banks.

A seeming opposite of the tomb is the idea of the crystal, which has fascinated architects for at least a century. It is about light, not dark, and it is celestial, not heavy. Architects use it as a symbol of hope for the future, not of memories of the past, yet it has more in common with old pyramids and temples than you might expect.

In 1919 the Berlin architect Bruno Taut published *Alpine Architecture*, a series of visionary drawings he made between autumn 1917 and summer 1918. On the cover he inscribed

> aedificare necesse est . . . vivere non est necesse
> to build is necessary, to live not necessary

which extreme motto might be the secret belief of quite a few architects, but is rarely admitted. His drawings, some in washes of lurid pink and orange, showed a new world that could follow the horrors of the First World War, in which cities would be abandoned and people could once again live amid nature. Taut declared:

> GREAT IS NATURE,
> eternally beautiful, eternally creative, in the atom as in the
> gigantic mountain . . .
> LET US CREATE IN HER AND WITH HER, AND LET US
> EMBELLISH HER!

The Swiss Alps would be the starting point and spiritual centre of this new order, where crystal structures would be built among the mountains. The Wetterhorn, 3,703 metres high, would be improved by a glass sphere on its summit; other mountains would receive crowns of glass arches, or terraces where crowds could gather to witness aeronautic displays by planes and dirigibles, and shows of light and water jets. Glass petals, arranged like layers of lips, would surround the long oval of a lake, such that aeronauts could look down on a great blossom. Surrounding terrain would be dentilated with clusters of spikes, across which light from huge projectors would play.

Most important was the Crystal House, a cathedral-like structure to be built entirely of coloured glass, in the zone where snow never melts. Here no one would be permitted to talk, and there would be nothing resembling religious ceremonies. There would only be silence, or sometimes 'delicate orchestra and organ music', the magnificent architecture, and views of the much more magnificent landscape.

Taut's plans did not stop with the Alps. He imagined lighting up the Andes and Micronesia, and creating 'Star Buildings' – cathedrals in space. He conceded it would not be easy – 'the cost is enormous and what sacrifices!' – but his desire was to mobilize the resources which the war had applied to destruction, and turn them to peace and beauty. He appealed to the 'People of Europe' to

> take away quarrels, conflict, and war . . . carry along the masses in a vast enterprise which fulfils everyone, from the least to the greatest. An enterprise which demands courage, energy, and immense sacrifices in terms of courage, power and blood from billions.

Thomas Mann, in *The Magic Mountain*, would portray the Swiss Alps as a microcosm of an enervated continent about to be purged by war. Taut saw them as a place where a Europe destroyed by both ennui and fighting could find renewal. He wanted to make them the centre of a world above nationality, conflict, and politics, but also above bourgeois property. He blamed the war on 'pure boredom', and in 1917 he wrote to his wife that

> boredom is the mother of all evils. Are we not plunged into boredom today? With what does the whole world concern itself? Eating, drinking, knives, forks, trains, bridges etc. What results from all that?

Taut was not alone in his belief in the messianic powers of glass. In 1914 the poet and novelist Paul Scheerbart had claimed that glass architecture would 'raise our culture to a higher level'. In 1918 an architect ally of Taut's, Adolf Behne, argued that glass construction would be uncomfortable, which aspect 'is not its least advantage, for first of all the European must be wrenched out of cosiness'. When glass buildings became commonplace later in the century there were frequent complaints about their tendency to

Tal
als
Beute

Wände sind
die Abhänge
hinauf
aufgestellt,
aus farbigem
Glase in
festen Rah-
men ~
Das durch-
schauende
Licht er-
zeugt viel-
fach wech-
selnde Effekte,
sowohl für
die im Tal
und zwischen
ihnen Ge-
henden wie
für die
Luftschiffer.
Der Blick
aus der
Luft
wird die
Architektur
sehr um
wandeln
und
neue
die
Architekten

freeze and overheat. It is rarely realized that, for some architects at least, these faults were intended.

If glass architecture was beyond politics, nationhood, and petty concerns, it was also beyond time. Once the great effort of construction was complete, it would for ever stand frozen amid the snow. By going to the mountains Taut sought a place where he would not have to engage with a place such as a city, which is tangled with history and memory. He would make a completely fresh start, an abolition of the world-as-found, which, given the state of this world in 1917, is understandable.

Even if it is concerned with the future rather than the past, the crystal turns out to be similar to the tomb. They are both objects set apart, outside time, unchanging, finished, impervious to the present. Taut's crystal world also has little space for the individual, apart from the hyper-individual, himself, who designed it. His drawings show no people, except for occasional ant-like dots. His fantastic structures give no indication of scale in relation to humans; only in relation to mountains.

Taut's Alpine architecture could be dismissed as visual ravings brought on by the stress of war, or as early contributions to the art of science fiction, if it were not that Taut was a serious figure, and his influence great, down to the present day. Despite his utopian fantasies he designed working-class housing projects in Berlin that are humane, practical, and delightful. He also helped to make glass architecture the ubiquitous form of building that it is today.

The Farnsworth House of 1946–51, in Plano, Illinois, fuses temple and crystal, and is one of the most admired and influential buildings of the twentieth century. Like a temple, it is a raised pavilion where a portico prefaces an interior. It is axial and symmetrical, except that it is approached by an off-centre flight of steps, and has an off-centre

bathroom core inside. Its structure is naked, and trabeated – that is, composed like a classical temple of pillars and beams – even if it is in slender white-painted steel, rather than marble. And if its steel and glass are modern, its travertine paving gives an aura of antiquity. Or, rather, the house aspires to be outside time, to exist in a sublime realm where the materials of Roman monuments and of Chicagoan industry are as one. 'Temporal fact', as a writer on the Farnsworth put it, is 'elevated to the level of ageless truth.'

Like a crystal it is prismatic. It seeks a sheer, seamless surface of glass, transparent, reflective, and refracting. Its architect, Mies van der Rohe, who was working in Berlin at the same time as Taut, had in the 1920s imagined faceted glass skyscrapers that translated the dreams of *Alpine Architecture* back into structures that might conceivably be built. By the time of the Farnsworth House he had restricted himself to right angles and straight lines, but the fascination with the flawless glass object remained.

Like a memorial, a temple, and a crystal, it is a form – a free-standing object untouched, except where it lightly touches the ground, by anything else. It is ideally timeless and changeless, designed not to weather but to be cleaned and repainted as necessary to return it to its pristine state. Mies aimed expensively for perfection. He had the welds in the steel ground down, and joints in the stone paving made exceptionally fine. He achieved a quality prized by architects, 'resolution', which means that each part has been considered, and made to fit into the conception of the whole. As Mies put it:

> by structure we have a philosophical idea. The structure is the whole from top to bottom, to the last detail – with the same ideas. That is what we call structure.

His obsessiveness made the house beautiful, but like a tomb it is happier if its resident doesn't make her presence felt. Faithful to the contempt for comfort shown by Taut and his allies, Mies designed a house that would overheat, steam up in the cold, and – as he fought against spoiling it with mosquito nets – become infested with insects. After bitterly and litigiously falling out with Mies, Edith Farnsworth complained of the 'alienation' she felt from her own house. It was later owned by the British property developer and Mies enthusiast Peter Palumbo, for whom it was a collectible artwork as much as a holiday home. Now it is uninhabited and can be visited by arranged tour.

It would be wrong to call the Farnsworth House a thing of pure immobility. Part of its effect lies in the combination of its symmetrical perfection with the asymmetric L-shaped journey up the steps and into the pavilion, with landscape shifting around you. The glass, with its transparency and reflections, plays its part in this abstract dance of culture and nature, going beyond its role of being pristine and crystal-like. This version of time means the building is not as dull as a tomb, but it is still highly selective, and controlled, and excludes a great deal of what a house might be.

If Mies seems extreme, in making buildings of use into monuments, he is only following the examples of others. In the sixteenth century, Andrea Palladio started applying the forms of classical temple fronts, with pediments and columns, to the villas and ennobled farmhouses that he designed for the landed gentry of the Veneto. The pedimented portico is now so commonplace, as a shorthand gesture for aspiration, that we hardly notice it, still less realize that it was once the radical appropriation of the forms of the immortal to the places of the living.

The over-valuation of monuments can be found in Nikolaus Pevsner's *Outline of European Architecture*, for decades the standard introduction to the subject, in which the majority of buildings shown are cathedrals and churches, and where individual works of any kind are preferred to urban spaces made of groups of buildings. Tourists show similar bias when they chalk off monuments as a way of visiting and understanding a city. The dilution of the word monument is also revealing: originally applied specifically to sepulchres and memorials, it now covers all buildings with a degree of endurance and significance.

The idea that great architecture has to be timeless is common, and the potential longevity of buildings, with their ability to carry memories and connect different periods of time, is important. But the cult of the timeless overlooks the mobile and the transient, and distorts our idea of what architecture is. Eighteenth-century London, for example, is now represented by its enduring squares and terraces, and by some elegant villas and churches, but the lost pleasure gardens at Vauxhall were equally vital to the city as a social, festive, and erotic locus, and were attractive precisely because they were insubstantial.

The lonely perfection now ascribed to the Parthenon ignores several things: that its marble was not naked, but painted; that it was not designed as a solitary object, but as part of an ensemble, which defined a series of external spaces; that ceremonies and rituals might have taken place around it, for which it might have been dressed and enhanced with theatrical effects. When Le Corbusier presented it as an example of 'the masterly, correct and magnificent play of forms in light', he neglected that it was about darkness as well as sunlight. Conjectural reconstructions of the interior show an alternative version of the building, with a gigantic gold and ivory statue of Athena, gleaming in the shadowy central chamber.

The eternity of the Parthenon is questionable. It has changed physically, from decorated, roofed building to bare ruin. It has at different times been partly rebuilt, then taken apart and reassembled again. Some of its stones are, due to restoration, not original.

It has changed them as the body exchanges cells. It has had different uses, including temple, church, mosque, explosives store, quarry, and tourist destination. It has looked like different things to different people – to Lord Elgin as a treasure trove, to Lord Byron as a prompt to poetic tears, to modern Greeks as a national icon and stimulant of tourist revenue. It is still in some ways the same building as it was in the fifth century BC, and some parts and qualities that were there then are still there, but the resemblance is like an old man's to the boy he was. The British architect Cedric Price said that all buildings are temporary, but some are more temporary than others, and even the Parthenon proves him right.

It is not original to point out Mies van der Rohe's monumentality. His contemporaries knew it, and there are opposing versions of modern architecture that celebrate fluidity and flexibility, and the liberating power of technology. One such version was developed by the American engineer, architect, inventor, ecologist, poet, seer, and autodidact Buckminster Fuller; nine years younger than Mies, his declared task was to pursue

> the search for the principles governing the universe and help advance the evolution of humanity in accordance with them . . . finding ways of doing more with less to the end that all people everywhere can have more and more.

He is famous for the geodesic dome, which had been invented by others – Bruno Taut had built an early prototype in 1914 – but was refined and promoted by Fuller. This is a structure formed of a lattice of triangles curved into some portion of a sphere. The lattice can be made of steel, or aluminium, or bamboo, or cardboard tubes, and the spaces between can be filled with glass, plastic, aluminium or plywood. It can be built quickly, and it is astonishingly light in

relation to its strength. Fuller hoped that hundreds of thousands of geodesic domes would populate America, quickly making cheap but beautiful homes:

> Let architects sing of aesthetics
> [he wrote, and on occasion sang]
> That bring rich clients in hordes to their knees;
> Just give me a home, in a great circle dome
> Where stresses and strains are at ease . . .

> Roam home to a dome
> Where Georgian and Gothic once stood
> Now chemical bonds alone guard our blondes
> And even the plumbing looks good.

In 1968 he imagined a single geodesic dome covering Manhattan from 22nd Street to 64th Street, and across the width of the island, creating beneath its weatherproof, smog-proof shelter, and with extraordinary efficiency of materials, a benign environment where individual buildings would no longer have to wrap themselves against the elements. The Crystal Palace of 1851 inspired in John Ruskin a nightmare of its multiplying a thousandfold to cover London; for Fuller the nightmare was a dream. The geodesic dome, of whatever size, would bring freedom: below its man-made sky people could do whatever they wanted. The technical know-how of the military-industrial complex could deliver a hippie heaven.

Fuller is sometimes presented as a practical American man, in contrast with the over-cultured Mies, who was born in Aachen and lived and worked in Berlin before moving to Chicago. He saw it this way himself, saying of Bauhaus architects like Mies that they were only interested in changing the outward appearance of the components of a building, and not the technology behind them:

> they only looked at the problems of modifications of the sur-

face of end products, which end products were inherently sub functions of a technically obsolete world.

Philip Johnson, Mies' backer and collaborator, confirmed this view:

Let Bucky Fuller put together the . . . dwellings of the people, so long as we architects can design their tombs and monuments.

Yet, although there is technical brilliance to Fuller's most famous work, and its engineering principles have been influential, it has not changed the world as Fuller hoped. Geodesic domes were built for World's Fairs in New York (1964), Montreal (1967), and Vancouver (1986), looking progressively less convincing as the harbingers of the future they were supposed to be. They respectively became an aviary, a museum of the St Lawrence River, and a 'world of science' that is featuring at the time of writing a show on 'Extreme Dinosaurs' – all diverting places, perhaps, but hardly vital ones. Disney built a geodesic sphere at their EPCOT theme park. The US military experimented with geodesic structures light enough to be carried by helicopter, and built others to shelter radar arrays to detect incoming nuclear missiles. Fuller built one as a home for himself and his wife, which is now protected by inclusion on the National Register of Historic Places. It is in Carbondale, in the same state, Illinois, as the Farnsworth House. No less than Mies's temple, Fuller's dome has become a monument.

As often happens with futuristic inventions, the dome found its natural habitat in theme parks and world's fairs, and failed to transform the way people live and house themselves. The geodesic dome's weakness is that it is, like the Farnsworth House and Taut's Alpine architecture, a fixed form, consistent, perfect, but also rigid and indifferent to the contingent, specific, and temporal.

The geodesic dome ignores such things as the shape of building plots – not usually round – and the fact that it is easier to arrange houses into a street, or furniture and partitions into interiors, if they are roughly rectangular. It has trouble with things like chimneys, windows, and ventilation pipes, and its many joints make it prone to leaking. If it allows freedoms within its shelter, the structure itself is hard to adapt or extend. Fuller's concept invests too much magic in the hardware, in the structure, in the thing that he, as an architect, controls.

Despite the claims for the liberating effects of geodesic domes, they are implements of power. Their indifference to complexity suppresses the personal histories and desires of whoever might live in or near them, and the status they give to the architect's form-making raises his authority. The Manhattan dome would have required an entity of immense power, wealth, and organization to command the agreement of all the people who lived, worked, and had interests underneath it. Our experience of huge roofed-in places – shopping malls, for example – is usually that they are created by large corporations and, while sometimes serving our pleasure and use, manipulate us for their profit. Within their embrace the rules are set by the owners.

There is another line of descent from *Alpine Architecture* to the corporate architecture of the present day. Taut's idea of the crystal monument was adapted by Mies van der Rohe in his skyscraper designs of the 1920s, and by other modernist architects, and, though Taut's extravagant shapes were initially rejected in favour of austere oblongs, the notion of the perfect glass object remained. The glass box, derived from designs by Mies and others, became the generic form of post-war office buildings. Apart from an interlude called postmodernism, when people got bored with it, it still is, but now the technology exists to achieve Taut's shapes as well. A block of offices, or of flats, can still be plain and rectangular, or it can be jagged and faceted, or swooping and curved.

So the skyline of Dubai is a weird parody of Alpine architecture.

It is Taut's vision without the mountains, without the socialism and brotherly love, and, except on the famous indoor ski-slope, the snow. Meanwhile architects from Reykjavik to Sydney proclaim their buildings 'crystalline', a word which nicely combines the authority of nature, some notion of value and beauty – it might make you think of diamonds, or fancy goblets – and the freedom for the architects to make something any shape they want, so long as it is shiny and has sharp edges.

I once worked alongside an architect who told me a story about his childhood. His parents gave him a patch of the family garden, where he could nurture and grow things. The future architect was interested in this project, and took it seriously, and set about doing what he thought best for its beauty and well-being. He smoothed and tidied the soil. He eradicated any speck or sign of impurity, and all uninvited foreign bodies. He banned earthworms. And so in time he produced a rectangle of perfect sterility, a mini-Gobi which nonetheless was orderly, and of which he was master. And in later life he rose efficiently through the firm where we worked, delivering buildings with exemplary professionalism, to the point where he is now a director of the enterprise, whereas I did not.

Gardening is a companion of building, sometimes seen as an opposite – soft against hard, female against male: definitely different, but from which building might learn. A garden has a less direct relationship to practical function, except when it grows produce, and to the constraints of construction. Its function is more elusive, if still real: to serve contemplation or pleasure, as in Mme de T—'s garden in *Point de Lendemain*; sometimes parties, games, or ceremonies. Its constraints, rather than the statics of placing beam on column, are the conditions of soil, climate, light, and water, the preferences and characteristics of different plants.

It is more obviously enmeshed in time than a building, with the cycle of the seasons and of day and night, with the times when plants flourish and die, with the growth of trees over years. A garden is never finished, but is always being made and re-made through maintenance and tending. In restoring a garden, it is never possible to take it back to some 'original' state where it perfectly accords with its designers' intentions. This state would not have been when it was new, when all the trees were saplings, nor at any other precise point. Rather the nature of a garden emerges over time.

A garden's endurance does not rely on its physical strength, but on continued care and, sometimes, the warding-off of threats such as plans to build over it. It has to mean enough to somebody – a private owner, a city government, a preservation society – to look after it. It is not like a pyramid, which can be left for centuries. It is also experienced over time: it cannot be captured in a single view (again, unlike a pyramid) but needs to be walked around, used and inhabited, in different weathers, seasons and lights. It is never the same garden twice.

The Katsura imperial villa and gardens in Kyoto were created over a few decades of the seventeenth century. They have had a particular fascination for both Western and Japanese architects since Bruno Taut, fourteen years after the publication of *Alpine Architecture*, visited it, and published his rapturous responses. By now Taut, who had advocated the abolition of nationality, was stateless. His attempts to build a career in Soviet Russia had failed and, being both socialist and Jewish, he could not return to Germany, which had fallen under Nazi rule. He eventually settled in Istanbul where, one month before his death in 1938, he designed the catafalque of Mustafa Kemal Atatürk.

Like his Swiss utopia, Katsura was for Taut an image of a harmonious cosmos, of the world as it ought to be, yet it was different from his earlier fantasies. Apart from having no glass or crystal whatsoever, Katsura is 'a good society of free individuals'; it 'reflects human relationships and ties in an extremely refined form'. It was such relationships and such freedom that were hard to find among the few ant-like specks drawn in his crystal cathedrals and monuments.

Katsura was created as a suburban retreat, for Imperial Prince Toshihito, and continued by his successor, Toshitada. Toshihito lived in a time when the power of the imperial court was restricted, even as the shoguns, who were effectively in charge, wanted to exploit the authority of the imperial title. He was something of an honoured prisoner, and puppet. The Prince was fond of literature from happier periods, and the Japanese modernist architect Kenzo Tange has speculated that Katsura was inspired by his reading, for example a description in the eleventh-century *Tale of Genji* of music and rustling pines on a moonlit night. The Prince was 'a person intoxicated by the poignancy of things', suggested Tange, who also saw in the villa and garden 'a marvellous balance between stillness and movement, between the aristocratic and the common, between perfection of form and sheer invention'.

It was a place of contemplation and solace which, nonetheless, could not wholly escape courtly rituals and ceremonies. Its main building is made of a series of three connecting structures, called the Old Shoin, the Middle Shoin, and the New Goten, Shoin meaning 'audience hall' and Goten meaning 'palace'. They were built over time with gathering grandeur, the last to honour a visit by the Emperor. Katsura's other structures are tea pavilions, spread over a garden formed around a central irregular lake, together with a tomb, entry gates, and bridges. Garden and structures together were designed to be experienced as a route on foot and by boat, marked with stone lanterns, with pauses at chosen spots to appreciate a particular view or sensation.

At Katsura, building and nature interpenetrate. The *shoin*,

large-roofed timber-framed structures, are well-defined pavilions largely standing separate from the landscape, but layers of verandas and screens cause the inside and outside to overlap. There are direct connections between inside and out, for example between the main room of the Old Shoin and the Moon-Viewing Platform, an oblong of bamboo, without balustrade or ornament, placed to catch views of the satellite and its reflection in the lake. As Taut said, when the paper-covered sliding doors are opened,

> the 'picture' of the garden like a part of the house bursts in on you all at once with an overwhelming effect. The presence of the garden dominates the interior so much that all the surfaces of the walls appear designed to reflect it, and the reflection is especially vivid in the opaque gold and silver of the sliding partitions.

With the tea houses and gates, gardening and building become more intimate. They use materials which are close to their natural form, such as mud, thatch, and rough stone, or irregular branches or cork oak trunks still bearing their bark. The ground is allowed to run into the interiors, which are not fully enclosed. Fragments of view are captured between columns and in window openings, and forest light is filtered through lattice screens. The tea houses are placed to answer significant elements in the garden – a bridge, an island, a path, a tree – and internal landscapes are made out of such things as the clay hearths and sinks for making tea, which compose themselves with the rocks and trees beyond.

The garden is a work of the found and the contrived. Natural elements – such as the slopes of the site, the path of the moon or an unusually magnificent tree – are exploited and enhanced. Fireflies are encouraged by lanterns to fly over a particular stretch of water. Stones are chosen for their inherent properties of shape and texture, and then arranged with an eye to their juxtapositions.

Some, pointy and vertical, are grouped to look like a mountain range. Black pebbles are gathered and then tipped, seemingly carelessly, into the water, to form a promontory. Moss is encouraged to grow, on a slope or on a thatched roof.

There is interpenetration, but not blurring. There is an acute awareness of the difference between in and out, and light and shadow, and the gradations from one to the other are played out with subtle sequences of surfaces and thresholds: rush matting, to timber edging, to stone step, to earth floor, to pebbles, to moss, to water. There is an awareness of the properties of materials, and a playful pleasure in exaggerating their differences. Paving can be made of rough rocks or square-cut slabs. A stone can be a loose pebble or a single monolith, five metres long, that forms a bridge. Trees might be clipped or sprawling; they might naturally flourish on this spot or require wrapping from the cold in the winter. A naturally vermiculated stone is placed near vigorously grained wood, to bring out the likenesses in their writhing patterns. In a small area of shelving next to the imperial dais, eighteen different types of timber are used. And, lest anyone fall into the misconception that Japanese architecture is all about natural simplicity, there are outbreaks of gold, silver, and lacquer, and figurative painting, and there is deliberate grotesquerie in some of the rocks and planting, as in the clump of out-of-place pines.

You sense the acoustics of stone or timber, and their warmth and coolness, and a stone basin is placed below a waterfall so that it amplifies its crashing. There are scents, of mud, flowers, and pine, the tea ceremony's sensations of taste and touch, and there would have been music. The paving, irregular and unpredictable, obliges you to look down and take notice of where you are walking, and see your surroundings from different angles. The absence of balustrades on bridges and platforms makes you pay attention to what your body is doing.

Bruno Taut saw an elevated functionalism in Katsura. This is in the detail: the facts that wooden columns need to stand on stones to keep them out of puddles, or that roofs of thatch, tile, or shingle need different degrees of slope to be effective, become part of the richness of the place. So too porous screens for ventilation, or the copings like little roofs that stop mud walls from disintegrating in the rain. The shoe stone, a monolith where guests remove their shoes before entering the Shoin, has a slight camber to stop rainwater gathering. The design savours the difference between, for example, something heatproof for making tea, a nearby rush mat for sitting on, and a wooden shelf for drying utensils.

It is also in the whole. Taut said:

> Every part of the complex, from whichever side you view it, is remarkably elastic in fulfilling the purpose that they, like the whole, are meant to serve, whether of ordinary everyday utility or official purposes or even in the expression of an elevated philosophical spirituality. And the wonderful thing is that all three of these purposes are so closely united that one cannot perceive the confines between one and the other.

In other words a moon-viewing platform, a shoe stone, a tea stand, a shelf, a kitchen, an imperial dais, a lawn for ball games, and some stepping stones descending into a stream so that people can wash their hands are all part of the totality.

Time is an essential ingredient. The villa and garden are inhabited through movement through them, both in the structured routes of tea ceremonies and whatever casual wanderings might have taken place at different times of day and year. Sliding screens change relationships between rooms, and between inside and outside. Time is in the grain of the wood, which records a tree's life, in the geological time of the stones and in the cycles of the moon, the days and the seasons, in the flow of the water and the growth of trees, flowers, or moss on roofs. When blossom or leaves fall, they combine with the pebbles and paving stones to pattern the ground. Time is in the ageing and different lifespans of the building materials, of mud, paper, thatch, wood, and stone. There is a consciousness of the making of things, such as the contrast between worked and un-worked stone, the jointing of wood, or the placing of pebbles or paviours, which draws attention to the time of building.

At Katsura, gardening and building come close. Although it is clear which is which, neither makes sense without the other. More than that, their properties overlap. Many of the buildings' materials – mud, thatch, paper, bamboo – are fragile and impermanent. They require tending, maintenance, and renewal, like plants in a garden, whereas the garden is partly made of durable and hard-to-move rocks. The idea common in Western architecture, that a building is hard and permanent, and a garden soft and transient, is absent.

Instead Katsura has a different kind of strength. The Roman architect and writer Vitruvius said that the essentials of architecture were 'commodity, firmness and delight', an observation at once so obvious and so dull that it is hard to know what to do or say next. The Swiss architect Jacques Herzog, however, has pointed out that the trinity becomes more interesting if its parts are interrelated. The commodity of a building, its ability to serve us well, might make it delightful. If a building charms no one, and has no commodity, it will also lack firmness – in that people will want to destroy it – as the various concrete tower blocks that have been blown up testify. Conversely, if a building inspires delight, but is made of fragile stuff, it will have strength. Katsura, and indeed all the gardens, temples, and palaces of Kyoto show this. Without maintenance they would disappear, but they inspire people to look after them and so endure.

A contrast can be made with the Twin Towers of the World Trade Center, which, according to their architect Minoru Yamasaki, were inspired by principles of harmony to be found at Katsura and other historic sites in Kyoto. In the Second World War, the latter escaped the infernos that destroyed other Japanese cities, and the atomic bomb that was eventually dropped on Nagasaki, as the US Secretary of War Henry L. Stimson had spent his honeymoon in Kyoto, and insisted that places so beautiful should be spared. The Twin Towers, whose carapaces were designed to resist ageing and damage, somehow attracted the aggression that would destroy them less than three decades after they were built. The princes who built Katsura were not nicer, or more reasonable and democratic, than the Port Authority of New York and New Jersey, but their architectural expressions had very different effects. Mud and paper proved stronger than steel.

The Parthenon complex is pervasive in Western architecture. It is the cult of the fixed, complete object, to which nothing can be added or taken away, inspired by the ancient temple to the virgin goddess Athena. Or, rather, by an imagined version of the temple that ignores several aspects of the real thing, preferring tomblike qualities such as formal perfection and structural nakedness to colour, dressing and context.

The aim is to go beyond life and time, into eternity. In so doing the architects assume power, to themselves and to their clients, as the status of things in their control – form, structure, detail – is heightened, while the contributions of others are diminished: the memories and desires of the places and people among whom the magic object might appear, for example, or chance, or the effects of use and users, or ageing, or other buildings. Identities are suppressed or ignored, other than the building's.

The forms of the architecture of power – repetition, symmetry, permanence, apartness, completeness, solidity – are those of tombs. By borrowing from the funerary, architects give gravity to their office blocks and houses; they make themselves guardians of the immortal. The Parthenon complex touches even those who seem to reject it, like Buckminster Fuller. For all his talk of his buildings being means not ends, they can't help being monuments.

Eternity is overrated, but this is not to say that timelessness is unimportant. Despite their apparent indifference to the everyday, Mies van der Rohe's buildings are potent and impressive, changing the rhythm and register of life around them. The Parthenon, with its modern illusion of being outside time, is as moving as it is possible for a single uninhabited object to be. And, as all architecture is a work of power, it is fatuous to wish away the use of the forms of immortality to assert that power. The point is that the timeless, or rather the very long-lived, is one register among many, whereas the Parthenon complex prefers only one form of time.

The strength of Katsura and the High Line lies in their use of different levels of time. The High Line combines industrial archaeology with the rhythms of plant growth and human use. Katsura is made of both blossom and stones. In both cases their subtleness and multiplicity is made easier to achieve by the fact that they are works of landscaping and planting, as well as building. It is still possible, however, to achieve sensitivity to the temporal without a growing thing in sight. Architecture and gardening do not have to be opposites, but different aspects of the business of making space.

The ninth-century mosque in Kairouan, Tunisia, is an example. This has a simple enough plan, with a large arcaded courtyard preceding a many-columned prayer hall, within which carpets can be laid and worshippers can choose their places. It uses Roman columns brought from the ruins of Carthage, a hundred miles away, variegated in size and shape and so without the regular order

they would have had in their original setting. Kairouan is in an arid region, and the mosque doubles as a water collector and reservoir. Rain runs from the roofs into the courtyard, and then through into a single hole in the middle, fringed with scalloped marble to filter dust, into cisterns below. After it has rained the building slowly dries, with a cloud of damp shrinking towards the central hole, into which it disappears. Without trying too hard, and in part accidentally, the mosque gracefully accommodates the historic time of the Roman fragments, the human time of the worshippers, and the meteorological time of the rain.

Then there is the 21st Century Museum of Contemporary Art in Kanazawa, Japan, by Kazuyo Sejima and Ryue Nishizawa of the practice SANAA. Here, the museum being a flat disc in a park, the circle is employed, the form of eternity and mausoleums. It is also wrapped in glass: a tomb/crystal surely. But it is sufficiently low and wide that it is not seen from the outside as a monumental object, but as a continually curving surface animated by the reflections and transparencies of the glass. You don't stand back and see it from a distance, but move around it in search of its elusive entrance.

Inside it is arranged as a loose grid of square, oblong, and circular spaces, sometimes galleries, a cafe, offices, a lecture theatre, sometimes open courts. It is like an abstracted town, crisscrossed by street-like passages. There are varying degrees of openness, sometimes with views filtering through layers of glass to the outside, sometimes with wholly enclosing walls. Permanent installations, a pool, a wall of shaggy plants, a room by James Turrell, create landmarks – otherwise the galleries are open to changing exhibitions.

It is something that is discovered by walking through it. There are multiple routes, none given priority over the other, such that it is never the same on different visits. The museum is indeed more brittle and rigid than Katsura or the High Line, and the apparent

fixity of its precise circular boundary serves as a register of permanence, but it is subject to dissolution, as the view passes through its glass walls. Circles tend to give importance to a culminating centre but here the middle is diffuse. There is not one point that is more important than the others. There is a play of getting lost and finding yourself: the circle disorients, the grid plan re-orients, the ubiquitous white walls and glass make the spaces alike, the landmark installations make them distinct. It is a benign labyrinth.

And there was the Cineroleum, a temporary cinema formed out of an old petrol station in Clerkenwell, London, for fifteen screenings in 2010. It was built for a budget of £6,500, by a group of students which did not really have a name, using their own labour and abilities to ask for favours. A curtain of Tyvek, a silvery synthetic fabric usually used as a water barrier in house building, was hung from the sides of the petrol station's canopy, enclosing a bank of rough bleachers. At the end of each screening the curtains were lifted, so that the audience were suddenly looking onto the street, which became an ad-hoc additional show, and they became visible to passers-by. An amused self-consciousness descended, a sudden sense of spectators become spectacle.

The charm of this work came from its seizing of the opportunities of the temporary: the moment when the petrol station was available, the freedoms allowed by planners (who might not have allowed a permanent cinema) to short-lived structures, the invention mothered by the necessities of minimal time and money. With the coup of the rising curtains, and the visible signs of its making in the not-really-finished construction, architecture came close to performance. Indeed the films shown there, mostly classics of the '60s and '70s which will be preserved more or less for ever, are considerably more durable than the Cineroleum.

This is an architecture of spontaneity and movement. It occupied a place made for cars, and housed motion pictures. It made a

bubble in time in which, apart from the sheer pleasure of it, it was possible to glimpse a modified version of London, one more festive and dream-like than usual.

9: *Life, and the look of life*

If the High Line might be thought gentrified, and gentrifying, such doubts do not apply to the cultural and social centre that Lina Bo Bardi made in an industrial zone of São Paulo from 1977 to 1986, called SESC Pompéia. Its purpose was not simply to present art and shows to a passive audience. Things and events were to be made here, and it was to be a social place, of creation, enjoyment, sport and action. Its uses included a theatre for twelve hundred people, a swimming pool, basketball courts, workshops, a library, a photographic lab, bars and a restaurant, a solarium, and places for gymnastics, wrestling, and dancing. SESC (from 'Social Service for Commerce' in Portuguese) is an organization funded by businesses that aims to make everything from culture to dentistry accessible; SESC Pompéia is one of several of its centres.

Bo Bardi had undergone lean years. Military dictatorship had taken power in Brazil and her version of left-wing politics fell out of favour. SESC Pompéia was her first big project since the Art Museum, completed a decade earlier. The site was an old factory, which had made at different times metal drums and refrigerators, and the obvious thing would have been to knock it down, except that, on a second visit to the leaky half-ruin, she found it already inhabited by the sociability for which she was supposed to be creating the setting:

happy people, children, mothers, parents and OAPs, went from one shed to another. Kids ran, youngsters played football in rain falling through broken roofs, laughing as they kicked the ball through the water. Mothers barbecued and made sandwiches at the entrance to Rua Clécia; there was a puppet theatre near it, full of children. I thought: it has to continue like this, with so much happiness. I returned many times, Saturdays and Sundays, until I really got it – understood those happy things people were doing.

She set up her office on the site and collaborated with both the builders of the project and the people who would use it. She decided that the old factory, already so good at its new use, had to stay, and the main changes would be interior: furniture, the removal or building of partitions, surfaces, signs. She opened much of the space up, making what she called, using the English word, a 'landscape'. Where possible she built half-height walls to separate spaces, in order to keep the openness of the whole. It could also be compared to a village of different uses, formed around a hall or roofed-over village square for many or any activities, open to the adaptions and inventions of its users.

In imagining how SESC might develop, she made free, loose drawings populated with dots, squiggles, arrows, and scribbled notes, with splashes of colour, hairy hatching, and staccato lines. They represent thought, motion, action, space, and construction all at once. They show the discipline and technique of her training in Italy, but are also childlike. Trees, water, and symbols of motion are given equal weight with columns and walls.

These are not, like many architectural drawings, either instructions or tools for selling. They are means of communication and discussion with the builders and users, their directness intended to break down the professional barriers that technical drafting can create. Or else they are messages to herself, ways of making a thought physical and out in the world, such that she could see it, reabsorb it, and change it.

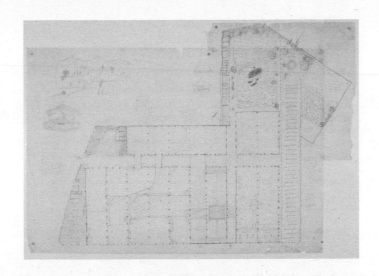

She threw out ideas; some seeded, some did not. She imagined a miniaturized version of the Rio São Francisco, the river that runs through several provinces of north-east Brazil. She tested different ways in which it would wind and gush through the complex, until it eventually found form in a sinuous pebble-bottomed pool, under the roof of the old factory, inside a large hall intended for multiple uses. She proposed to place sansevierias, a plant thought to avert the evil eye, along the access path to SESC. According to one note she wanted to make a 'big wall (142m) with writing, graffiti, paintings. History of Brazil.' She later wanted to make a long 'carpet' from Brazilian marbles and semi-precious stones.

A hearth was built next to the internal river. She set seashells and fragments of glass and marble into the concrete floor and built a long sunbathing deck, called 'the beach', over an external watercourse. She designed a logo for SESC, showing flowers issuing from its chimney-like water tower, to celebrate its change from industrial work to social play. She would also create exhibitions there, of *A Thousand Toys for Brazilian Kids*, or *Interval for Children*, which showed the country's insects. She proposed as an opening exhibition a celebration of all the country's football teams, from the best to the 'most mediocre'.

More than the art museum, SESC expresses Bo Bardi's passion for Brazil's land and cultures, from religious cults to football. In particular she was fascinated by the north-east, and the city of Salvador, where she had lived and worked, and designed earthier, smaller, and cheaper buildings than in São Paulo. She had mounted exhibitions there showing votive limbs and heads, and photographs of life on crowded riverboats, and had planned a museum of popular art that was terminated by the arrival of the dictatorship. At SESC these interests led to an exhibition called *Yokels, Hicks: Wattle and Daub*.

She came to think of São Paulo as 'a pile of bones', compared to the north-east, and 'the world champion city for self-destruction'. SESC can be seen as an attempt to nurture vitality in a corner of the metropolis, using less sophisticated parts of Brazil as an inspiration. Hence the 'Rio San Francisco', and the exhibitions of toys and 'yokels', spread about the village-like interior of the old factory.

Then, next to the village, she built a castle, made of three concrete towers. One is a stack of sports courts above a ground-floor swimming pool. The second contains changing rooms and bars to serve the courts, and rooms for wrestling, gymnastics, and dancing. These two towers are joined by a set of flying bridges, so that the usually mundane journey from changing room to court becomes aerial and dramatic. The third is the cylindrical water tower.

Each tower is blunt, primitive, and distinctive. The stack of courts is punctuated with windows in the shape of ragged holes that seem punched out by some caveman. The tower of changing rooms is an angular tree-trunk, from which the bridges grow like branches. The water tower is ringed with wobbly lines, sixty-eight in all, left by the daily pour of concrete. Such marks are a normal part of the construction process, and are sometimes smoothed over, sometimes left exposed, but they are rarely as rough as these.

The towers are as assertive as the adjustments of the old factory are subtle, and as enclosing as the latter is open. They form an emblem of SESC, and have a force that might be seen as a response to Brazil's tough politics: they stake their claim on the skyline as equal to the towers of business; they make it harder for a hostile regime to remove them. The complex has been called 'a Citadel of Liberty', a place defended but accessible.

Lina Bo Bardi spoke of

theatre going out into the squares and roads, invading the city, chairs and furniture that leave houses, and people, men,

women, children, a mass of people who inspired Le Corbusier in 1936 when he visited Brazil and wrote a famous letter to the minister Gustavo Capanema: 'Sir, do not commission *Theatres* with *stages* and *seats*, leave the Squares, Roads and Green Spaces free, just commission timber platforms open to the Public, and the Brazilian People will occupy them, "improvising" with their natural elegance and intelligence.'

At SESC she created an enclave of spaces, open and unprescriptive, where such improvisation could and does happen. Some are internal, some outdoors, but together they make something parklike, where specific purposes co-exist with the freedom to sit, read, meet, reflect, or otherwise do what you like. She did so through a combination of leaving alone and of decisive interventions, of subtle adjustments and the emphatic towers. As she put it

the architecture of the Pompéia factory recreation centre arose from the desire to create another reality. We just put a few little things there: a little bit of water, a hearth

although this understates the three towers, which are not 'little things'. The ultimate purpose was to

honour the people, allowing them the social integration to which they are fully entitled.

These are hopeful words, and her references to children and peasants might verge on the sentimental, if her sharp, determined face did not suggest that she was anything but. She was playful but also tough, and her hopes are more convincingly put into practice than the ones mouthed around, for example, Ground Zero. This hope is rooted and engaged, not superimposed. It exists through actions more than objects; objects, including buildings, are props, settings, tools, and intermediaries rather than ends in themselves.

SESC is mobile, with the fixed parts being there to serve the mobility. Bo Bardi made exhibitions, and designed for the stage as well as permanent buildings, and she made little distinction between the permanent and the temporary: they were all architecture. If the castle and the village make an odd couple, and if there are loose ends or things left incomplete, that is intended. SESC only makes sense through the use and expression of the people within it. If, as Bo Bardi said, she wanted to make SESC 'even uglier' than MASP, that is because its beauties should come from people rather than buildings.

SESC's version of hope involves time. In choosing to retain the factory rather than erase it, Bo Bardi kept alive the memories of the old building, and the rhythms of the 'happy people' she found there. There are the unknown times of the myths and folklore she invoked, and the time of construction, which for her was something to be lived and enjoyed, not to be endured in order to achieve a completion date. The towers, with the marks of the concrete pours, are registers of the daily events of their building. The bridges between them celebrate movement. She also proposed that the four sports courts should be named after the four seasons, with colour schemes to match, such that you might agree to meet on the 'spring' or 'autumn' court, rather number one or three.

And SESC is fulfilled over time, through the exhibitions and events that Bo Bardi and others mounted, and the things that people do there, down to and beyond the present.

Architects like to talk about 'life'. Some sketch diagrams with hearts drawing people into some magic place, or arrows symbolizing the flow of happy folk. They tell tales of simple citizens who have

expressed delight at the effects of their design. They do so with varying degrees of sincerity, but always conscious that they are prone to being accused of not actually caring about human life, being too concerned with the creation of their personal monuments. For it is a cliché that architects do not understand life. There are urban myths about males of the profession specifying urinals for female toilets, or being clueless about the layout of kitchens. The pretentious building that suffers pratfalls at the hands of reality is a comic archetype.

Architects also like to make forms in which life is expected to take place. In the 1970s there was a fashion for 'conversation pits', sunken, cushion-filled spaces where people could recline in the style of the day, and converse. At a larger scale there are 'atria' – which entered the repertoire at roughly the same time as conversation pits but have proved more enduring – as signs of community. Also plazas or piazzas (Hispanic or Italian – you can take your pick, so long as it sounds warm and lively).

Yet these forms do not always germinate life as promised. Conversation is something too subtle, mobile, and self-generating to be commanded into being by a pit, as is public life by a piazza. Nothing defeats itself more than the instruction 'now talk'. Architecture can be more or less conducive to sociability, but if it tries to prescribe it, it will fail. It is also sometimes doubtful if architects really want the happy buzz their shapes imply. As Stewart Brand observed, the 'massive atrium' in I. M. Pei's Media Lab at MIT, which might be expected to 'bring people together with open stairways, casual meeting areas, and a shared entrance', actually

> cuts people off from each other. There are three widely separated entrances (each huge and glassy), three elevators, few stairs, and from nowhere can you see other humans in the five-storey-high space. Where people might be visible,

they are carefully obscured by internal windows of smoked glass.

Such spaces seem made more for the architect to dwell, to be there in spirit even after the construction has been signed off and handed over.

There are now two dominating approaches to the question of building, at a large scale, to accommodate and encourage collective life. They are the big roof and the theme park, seeming opposites, actually in hidden alliance. They have a long lineage, at least as old as the Crystal Palace and the Great Exhibition of 1851 that it housed. There Joseph Paxton's glass and steel structure, a miraculous feat of efficient, speedy, and innovative construction, housed a display of artefacts and curiosities, encrusted with ornament and parodic versions of historical styles. Above were the clean lines of brilliant engineering, below a bazaar of stuff gushed out by the incontinent force of manufacturing. As a place to wander, and have your senses provoked by outrageous displays of kitsch, it was a prototype theme park.

The seventeen-year-old William Morris was revolted, as was John Ruskin. A later writer ranted that

> the aesthetic quality of the products was abominable . . . wrong from any point of view . . . rich in atrocities . . . so bulging, so overdone . . . the insensibility of the artist towards the beauty of pure shape, pure material, pure decorative pattern, is monstrous.

The Crystal Palace became an inspiration for modern architecture, thanks to its technical daring and its unconcern with conventional styles. Its influence hovered behind Bruno Taut's crystal cathedral and Buckminster Fuller's domes, and then onto the oversailing roofs designed by Norman Foster for the Great Court of the British Museum and Beijing Airport, or by Richard Rogers' unbuilt covering for the South Bank Centre in London, or his Millennium Dome. Such was the power of the Crystal Palace that projects could re-work its basic idea a century and a half later, and still be called 'innovative'.

The bric-a-brac of the Great Exhibition took the low road, but it did not disappear. The world's fairs and expos which followed the model of 1851 would continue to generate bold, forward-looking structures like the Eiffel Tower and the Halle des Machines at the 1889 Paris International Exhibition, the Dome of Discovery at the 1951 Festival of Britain, and Buckminster Fuller's sphere at Montreal in 1967. But there would also be replicas of Venice, Paris, Rome and a 'street in Cairo', complete with belly dancers, at the 1893 World's Columbian Exhibition in Chicago, an exultation of American wealth and power that introduced the Ferris Wheel, Shredded Wheat, and precursors of fluorescent lights and zips to the world. The event, while giving employment to a construction worker called Elias Disney, caused in the young Frank Lloyd Wright dismay similar to that experienced by William Morris in 1851. For Wright the retrograde revamping of European styles was the opposite of the distinctive national architecture that a confident young country should be producing.

Later Elias's son Walt would take the model of the Columbian Exhibition, and make it into never-ending pageants of programmed excitement, first at Disneyland in California, then Disney World in Florida, then at further iterations of the Magic Kingdom in Tokyo, Paris, and Hong Kong. He took from the 1893 model both its planning, with a great central avenue off which tributary routes would lead to various attractions, and its promiscuous appropriation of whatever architectural look – Bavarian castle, rustic cottage,

American main street – might most appeal to paying punters. It was an idea with precedents, as in Dreamland on Coney Island, which offered a synthetic Switzerland and Venice, and a Pompeii daily engulfed, until an all-too-genuine fire destroyed the whole complex in 1911. The idea had followers: by the 1990s the idea of theming, which in Disney's parks takes place within defined boundaries, would expand onto the street, in the form of the resort hotels of Las Vegas, where evocations of Egypt, Arthurian England, ancient Rome, Paris, and Caribbean pirate islands jostle on The Strip. Here theming was no longer parenthesized by the boundary of a park: it shaped the city, it was the city. And if Las Vegas is still a special case, being constructed around entertainment and escape, it would not be long before the idea of theming would wholly embrace the everyday, with the Disney-built town of Celebration in Florida and, later, places like the short-lived Holland Village in Shenyang, demolished after its billionaire developer was jailed for tax evasion. Here the monuments and canals of Amsterdam were replicated as a residential development in northern China.

The idea of the big roof is to create an all-embracing shelter beneath which, in theory, people can gather to do whatever they like. It aspires to the indifferent distance of the sky, while tempering some of the actual sky's less comfortable effects. The idea of the theme park is to engage people directly, to get under their skin so much that it programs their sensations and reactions in advance. Your level of fear on a ride is plotted, as is the moment when you will scream for the automatic camera. Your smiles, gasps, and hunger pangs will be stimulated and satisfied to plan, and approaching ennui will be warded off before you know it is there.

The architecture of big roofs is abstract and scaleless. That of theme parks is familiar, presenting you with castles and pieces of Venice that entered your consciousness at a point too early to remember, perhaps in a childhood picture book or on a biscuit tin.

Or rather it is hyper-familiar, presenting versions of the originals that are more like them than the things themselves, having neutralized those surprising qualities – a smell, a juxtaposition, something unexpected about their size – that are the most striking aspects of famous places experienced for the first time. Theme parks take your expectation, crystallize and purify it, and feed it back to you. Or they satisfy expectations you did not know you had, indeed did not have, but are planted in you.

These techniques, of creating a fictional reality in a desig-nated zone, can be found in places that are not precisely theme parks, but in new-built residential developments. They can be found in Poundbury, a make-believe version of traditional England created under the Prince of Wales's guidance in Dorset, that comes complete with village stores, a market hall, pubs and a more con-temporary 'Poundbury Wealth Management Office', all created in the last twenty years. Or, realized with American determina-tion, in Celebration, Florida, which was initiated by the Disney Corporation in the 1990s, in posthumous fulfilment of old Walt's dream to build a model town. Here, off a freeway exit beyond EPCOT and Disneyland, the aim is to restore old-fashioned neigh-bourliness with an old-fashioned architecture of porches and row houses: Celebration, goes the blurb, 'takes the best of what made small towns great in our past and adds a vision of the future'.

You are offered a version of the past – one in which you can buy a house, live, work, and raise kids – that never really existed. The prevailing style is colonial, with big porches and verandas, in which people naturally place rocking chairs, set in well-maintained land-scaping. There are New England-style churches, and art deco is selected as an appropriately nostalgic style for the office buildings. There is a Main Street, with inescapable music piped through speakers placed amid the shrubberies. There is something like a Town Hall, and an old-fashioned diner, and a town newspaper, the

Celebration News. There does not appear to be a gay quarter, or a red-light district. There is no ghetto, but then there does not need to be, as almost everyone is white. Even the sky is doctored: gazing up at the delightful fluffs of white, you see one which by some meteorological fluke looks like a smiley face. Except that it is not a fluke; a hidden hand has made it like that.

Big roofs have structure and form. They have what architects call 'integrity', whereby the stuff of which a building is made, the ways in which it stands up, and the thing you see are one and the same. Theme parks are about look and image. Whatever they are made of – is it plastic? plaster? plywood? paint? – is unclear and irrelevant. The overall shape is lost in a slurry of stimulation and simulation. In New York New York, a resort hotel and casino in Las Vegas, the skyscrapers, brownstones, hydrants, yellow taxis, delis, and graffiti of the east-coast city are mimicked, and there is a pocket, indoors, version of Central Park, but its gridded street plan is replaced by a wandering, amorphous, disorienting layout, which makes visitors into passive browsers, dependent on the bounty and care of the resort and relieved of the burden of making decisions about anything except what to buy. The only horizon is consumption.

You can draw, with a compass and without looking at it, the boundary of a Buckminster Fuller dome. A Foster airport is not much more difficult. The outline of Disneyworld is indistinct and, if seen, seemingly inconsequential. Whatever the reasons for it – and in theme parks everything has a reason, everything is calculated – they are obscure.

The big roof and the theme park are adopted by opposing cultures of taste. The big roof is artistically respectable, critically acclaimed, award winning, designed by architects (often famous ones), 'innovative', seemingly public-spirited. It is a relative of the crystal and the tomb, the perfected, singular, complete object. The theme park is consumerist, vulgar, exploitative, retrograde, and made by 'imagineers', to use Disney's coinage, and other faceless consultants. One is modernist, the other postmodern; one abstract, the other pop. One is more likely to be the work of governments pursuing internationalist or mildly left-wing politics; the other is made by entertainment corporations in pursuit of profit.

In architectural histories the schizophrenia of the Crystal Palace is seen as an unfortunate aberration or mistake, which would surely not be repeated too many times. Yet repeated it was, and is. One of the most enthusiastic takers of the geodesic dome was Disney, at EPCOT, while the domes at expos, for example the one in Vancouver with its 'Extreme Dinosaurs' exhibit, tended to end up containing themed attractions.

When Norman Foster designed Stansted Airport he made a big roof of elegance and clarity, only for its ground plane, much to his dismay, to coagulate with shopping. He then designed Chek Lap Kok Airport in Hong Kong, with an equally elegant but much bigger roof, under which a gaudy mess of selling and consuming also gathered. He was dismayed again, but later he designed Beijing's new airport, with a roof still elegant and yet bigger. Even before it opened, fake pagodas and bright totems were accumulating, inexorable as zombies, presumably in a way the architect did not like.

With every airport the format of the Crystal Palace – big roof above, theme park below – kept replicating itself. It did it again with the Millennium Dome in London, both in its original incarnation as a celebration of the millennium, and in its relaunch as the O_2 music venue. The superstructure was a big roof, a Teflon-coated skin supported on a steel net, hanging from twelve masts which made some allusion to the hours of the clock, but also referred to the optimistic modernist structures of the Festival of Britain. Tony Blair promised that beneath this structure would be a

celebration that is so bold, so beautiful, so inspiring that it embodies at once the spirit of confidence and adventure in Britain and the spirit of the future of the world.

It would be

exhilarating like Disney World, yet different. Educational and interactive, like the Science Museum, yet different. Emotional and uplifting like a West End musical – yet different.

In practice the contents turned out to be a similar sort of crowd-pleasing gunk – a giant human figure, gaudy gesticulations of bulbous and pointy objects, patronizing messages about humanity and the world – to that which had encrusted the lower limbs of the Crystal Palace, with the unfortunate detail that it did not please the crowds very much. The difference with Disney World turned out to be mainly that Disney is more professional, and more fun. Then, following the Millennium celebrations, a few years were spent agonizing about what to do with this structure, after which an oblong 20,000-seat concert arena was rammed into it, with gaps between the oblong and the dome filled with a Vegas-like internal city of retail and shopping. The yellow masts were now half-buried, or engulfed humiliatingly in faux art-deco styling.

At some point, after a hundred and sixty years of repetition, the contamination of big roofs with theme parks must be recognized less as a regrettable accident, more as a pathology. There has to be something which explains this compulsive attraction of apparent opposites. The linking factor might, conceivably, be a lack of interest in the singularity of life, or hostility to it. The big roof, while in theory honouring the masses it shelters, sees people as atoms, as dots in a flow, as generic beings whose specific desires are of no great interest, and can be left to look after themselves. Its beneficence is distant, and the experience it offers to viewers is disengaged awe: wow, that's big, you might say, now what? The theme park in theory satisfies those specific desires, and engages more directly with its customers, but it offers only satisfactions composed according to formulas, even if those formulas might nowadays be sophisticated.

Both require a cleansed and empty site, the tabula rasa that gives complete freedom of action. The big roof is futurist, the theme park nostalgic, but both exist in a confected time that offers a plastic version of past and future, which excludes the complexity of the present. Both obliterate lived memory – despite the apparent homage paid it by nostalgia – except that which is supplied by the designers or scriptwriters.

They enlist the rhetoric of the global. Prince Albert believed that his Great Exhibition would celebrate and assist 'the accomplishment of that great end to which indeed all history points, the realisation of the unity of mankind'. Among the attractions at Disneyland, a personal favourite of Walt's was *It's a Small World*, in which over three hundred audio-animatronic dolls, dressed in national costumes from all over the world, and supported by props such as the Leaning Tower of Pisa and St Basil's Cathedral, sing an approximation of Prince Albert's sentiments. With frequent repetitions of the phrase 'It's a small world after all', the dolls stress the hopes, tears, and so forth that all humanity shares.

Later replicated at other Magic Kingdoms, *It's a Small World* was originally created, with Walt Disney's close involvement, for the Pepsi-sponsored UNICEF pavilion at the 1964 New York World's Fair. The Disney staff composers Robert and Richard Sherman were hauled off their vital work on the forth-coming *Mary Poppins* to write the song.

Between Albert and Walt, and indeed down to the present, every expo and world's fair has adopted this talk of global harmony, even as such events are also used, from London 1851 to Chicago 1893, to the Shanghai Expo of 2010, as assertions of the host country's power. It's hard to argue with the basic sentiment – who would not want world peace? – but the Prince and the animator's worldspeak carries with it an obliteration of detail and difference. By saying that we are all the same, apart from picturesque variations in costume, they annul the specifics of time and place that constitute life. Which, as it happens, made it easier for the empire ruled by Albert's wife and the corporation founded by Walt to conduct their aggressive international business, and overrule awkward opposition.

Big roofs and theme parks enlist the imagery of The World, even as they aim to create self-sufficient worlds that obliterate all place beyond their boundaries. They have only internal horizons, and no awareness of anything outside their scenarios and scripts. Both types are controlled, and controlling, eventually finding perfect if fictional union in *The Truman Show*. In this movie a very big roof, which looks from inside like a sky, shields an idyllic town which, unbeknown to Truman Burbank, is actually the set of a reality TV show of which he is the hero, his life being controlled and manipulated by a producer of whom he knows nothing.

The Truman Show was filmed in the classically-styled model community of Seaside, Florida, a pioneer work of the 'new urbanist' school of town building that would also create Celebration. Both Seaside and Celebration are built fictions which, as you can actually live in them, are in some sense 'real'. Both relieve you of the burden of using your own imagination. In *The Truman Show* Seaside is made back into a fiction, believed to be real, by the fictional character. The big roof contains him and the town's theme-park-like verisimilitude controls him. Here Buckminster Fuller and Walt Disney hold hands, and smile down from their bright blue paradise, having jointly accomplished the annihilation of what it is to be human.

The achievement of Lina Bo Bardi, at SESC and the Art Museum, and of the architects of the High Line, is to find, enlarge, and enrich the space that is neither the big roof nor the theme park. They have the openness of one, the evocative detail of the other, and the totalitarian ambitions of neither. They offer freedom of movement but not frictionless atomic flows, and cues to memory and imagination, but not scripts. They neither abandon you in a technological void, nor program your thoughts and emotions. They are powerful places, but not overpowering.

The old factory of SESC is a big roof, as are the upper two floors of MASP, hovering above the plaza below, but they are not abstract or indifferent. One carries history, the other is inhabited by art, and the experience of art. The old viaduct of the High Line is, like a geodesic dome, a piece of engineering, a megastructure, but through time, redundancy, and adaptation it has also become habitable, by both body and imagination. At SESC memory and imagination are prompted by the fictional river, the castle-like towers, their cave-like windows, and the temporary exhibits of folk art. On the High Line this is done by the treatment of railway relics, and the wild-artificial planting.

The success of these works depends on their poise. They know when to assert and when to withdraw. They know when to be extreme – they are far from bland or average – as in the concrete towers or the straddling of the High Line with the Standard Hotel. They choose what to retain, embellish, or remove in the structures they adapt. They are decisive, but also incomplete, allowing users to finish them in their own way. There is no book of rules that can order how such openness is achieved – it relies on the awareness of architects and their clients, and the lucky confluence of events. The important thing is that such luck is not precluded at the outset by the hunt for magic crystals or perfect scripts, and that someone is able to recognize and cherish it when it appears.

SESC, MASP, and the High Line are impressive, and rare, for functioning at the scale of large modern cities. It is relatively easy to dream with a house in the woods or a church on a mountain, less so in a metropolis like São Paulo or New York. It is striking that the road that MASP faces, Avenida Paulista, is not much smaller than Sheikh Zayed Road in Dubai, yet there is nothing along the latter with the complexity or richness of public space that MASP offers.

They are, however, still small constructions in relation to the scale at which cities are now built. If, in China, a city like Shenzhen can grow from a few thousand people to ten or more million in thirty years, and if there will by 2025 be eight cities there with a population of more than ten million, it would seem that something bigger and more robust is required than Lina Bo Bardi's slow reworking of an old factory with care and handicraft. It is a question of speed as well as size: when a single developer might throw up a cluster of thirty-storey towers in one go, what chance is there of nuance, dream, detail, poise, openness, or anything at all apart from the sheer production of units? And if SESC and the High Line draw on the unexpected riches found on their respective sites, what might be done when the site is a big square of dust, with no obvious connection to any other time or place?

It is also a question of embodiment, as the progress of technology is also the history of the increasing redundancy of built fabric. In a large Victorian house there are separate spaces – a larder, a pantry, an ice house, a laundry – each with its own physical properties of temperature, airflow, dimension, and surface, to fulfil the tasks now carried out by 60x60x90cm white goods: fridge, dishwasher, freezer, washing machine.

If the Gothic cathedral is sometimes compared with modern airports and train stations, as a great space achieved with supreme engineering, a more accurate comparison would be with movies. In the Middle Ages the best way to create a compelling spectacle, rich in content, sensorily engaging, animated by light, was by architecture: to build an armature of stone which would carry stained

glass, sculpture, and painting, and would house music, performance, and ritual. Their arches, ribs, and buttresses were means to the end of enabling more light, and therefore more spectacle. Although impressive in themselves, and fascinating to future historians and tourists, these elements played much the same role as the circuitry on the back of a TV set.

Cathedrals and movies require similar mobilizations of talent and money. The credit list for a cathedral would include architects, painters, sculptors, masons, glassmakers, wood carvers, carpenters, mosaicists, gilders, silversmiths, leadworkers, musicians, choirs, and clergy. Credits for movies run from producers, directors, and actors through scriptwriters and cameramen to key grips. The budget for a big film is enough to pay for a substantial building. In 1997 the movie *Titanic* and the Guggenheim Museum Bilbao opened, one at a cost of $200 million, the other at $100m.

Film condenses spectacle and, with the miracle of projection, allows it to be shown without limit in blacked-out rooms. Early cinema designers felt the need to create grand, ornate, religiose auditoria; it was gradually discovered that, so enrapturing were movies themselves, they required only the dumbest of boxes packed in multiplexes with as little art as organizing parking spaces in a multi-storey, and with desultory decoration. Eventually films ended up on phones: a level of spectacle that once required a building hundreds of feet long and a hundred or so high now fits into a pocket.

If technology, whether of refrigeration or fascination, has reduced the need for buildings, and if architecture is relieved of much of its responsibility to entertain, it has to work in a different way from that which might have been taken for granted until the nineteenth century. It can and often does respond to this uncertainty of purpose by looking extraordinary, but this only gets so far, as at the level of sheer fun and excitement it is hard for a building to beat a

movie. Architecture can also respond by stressing those properties that other media lack, such as its three-dimensional material presence, its ability to endure, its constructed or crafted nature. This is the idea of minimalist design: by stripping away distractions, the attention is focused on the grain of wood or stone, or their cutting and jointing, or the fall of light, or proportion.

But for architecture to withdraw into its own craftedness also has limitations. As it has to exist in a culture in love with image, it risks insignificance if it ignores this circumstance. Or else it will be made into image whether it likes it or not: for all its aim to go beyond mere look, minimalism became a style beloved of magazines, something which, with enough white paint and pale wood, could be replicated by interior decorators the world over.

The reality, one not particularly easy to make into a rallying call or to put on a banner, is that good architecture runs with all these properties and possibilities. It works, or plays, with its characters as a thing made, as a thing inhabited, and as a thing seen. It exists in this working or playing, rather than settling in a place of repose where it is definitely one or another. If it insists too much on the visual, it becomes an icon and nothing else, a more or less interesting shape within which anything might happen; if too much on its crafting it can become a game for connoisseurs, not much connected with the life going on around it. As for inhabitation, both physically and with the imagination, this might be the main purpose of architecture, but it is not best served by considering it on its own.

Two of Europe's most celebrated architectural practices have tried to make some sense of the scale of the Chinese city, with monuments conceived for the 2008 Beijing Olympics. The practices are the Office of Metropolitan Architecture and Herzog & de Meuron, situated at opposite ends of the River Rhine, in Rotterdam and Basel, in small prosperous countries, one very flat and the other very mountainous. Their monuments are the stadium for the Games, and the headquarters for the Chinese state television company, CCTV.

There is an affinity between the two offices, based on a common ability to think conceptually about their projects, and then translate idea into provocative form. OMA is the more intellectual, HdM the more sensual, but with each practice thought and making intersect. Their works are highly recognizable, but by attitude and approach rather than by a signature style. In the twentieth century architects had rallied around the banner of the modern movement, which elevated certain materials and forms – steel, glass, and concrete; plain surfaces above decorated ones. The Rhine masters might favour plastic on one project, mud on another, mirror-glass on a third, straight lines or curves, right angles or acute ones, blankness or ornament. They could not be pinned down with a stylistic label.

The modern movement also demanded devoted allegiance to its principles, in imitation of political ideologies like (especially) Marxism. OMA and HdM prospered in an age of more fluid politics, when belief and ethics seemed more elusive and less fixed. Both offices were favoured by commissions from Prada as well as the People's Republic of China, with both fashion house and empire seeing something potent in their combination of sophistication and dazzle. Miuccia Prada is an international businesswoman who was once a member of the Communist Party; the PRC is an ostensibly communist state deeply in love with business. Each settled on the same architects to express their power, and their ambiguities.

In recent decades sports stadia have been considered as pieces of equipment, which have to fulfil practical considerations such as sightlines and crowd handling, and where the business of holding

up the roof is the main opportunity for expression. Straining masts and cables, great cantilevers and trusses, and the huge parabolic arch above Wembley Stadium in London all dramatize the practical question of keeping rain and sun off spectators. The Beijing stadium, designed by Herzog and de Meuron in collaboration with the artist Ai Wei Wei, was conceived as something both greater and smaller: it was to be an urban building, a significant new piece of the huge city of which it is part, but also a single object, like a bowl.

It was planned in advance to be 'a unique historical landmark', its spatial effect being 'novel and radical and yet simple and of an almost archaic immediacy'. The stated aim was to be as effective an icon of Beijing as the Eiffel Tower is of Paris. At the same time it was hoped to avoid making the kind of sterile object that sports stadia usually are when events are not being held in them.

Seen from the outside it is indeed a single bowl-like shape, gently swelling and dipping, and rounded at the edges. It has a bold pattern formed by the crisscrossing lattice, seemingly random, of steel members, which were rapidly compared to the twigs of a bird's nest, and earned the stadium its now ubiquitous nickname. Wrapping round, the crisscrossing structure forms both wall and roof. Except the wall is really a screen, allowing you to look through and walk through to the stuff of the stadium – the concourses, stairs, bars, and restaurants – within. It holds a zone within the circumference of the structure, open but sheltered, which the architects describe as an arcade, where the urban life of Beijing could carry on during and after the games, no matter when or whether sport was taking place inside. It was hoped that the activities – physical exercises, games, trading – that seem to spring up in most spare spaces in Chinese cities would do so here. As for the main business of the project, the arena within, this was smooth and white-grey, like the inside of an oyster shell. Here concentration was on the action, and 'the human crowd formed the architecture'.

The building plays perceptual games. It is plainly vast but, as a single bowl-like object, it looks as if it could be picked up and carried away. Its structure is naked and exposed, in the tradition of the Parthenon (the modern ruined version, not the ancient painted one) and of modern engineering, but the screen of slanting lines seems to deny their weight, making them seem drawn more than built, or into one-dimensional sgraffito etched onto a two-dimensional surface. Only when you get close do you feel their heft. Then, the surface having been defined, it goes missing. There are only the lines.

If the Bird's Nest stadium flips between different scales without settling on one, it also flirts with different metaphors – bowl or birds' nest – that come dangerously close to being patronizing emblems of Chinese-ness. But its near-kitsch is part of its effect, combined with its formal and structural audacity, and visual complexity. It is Parthenon *and* bauble, natural phenomenon *and* tourist tat. It teases. It is as memorable as the Eiffel Tower, and can be turned with equal ease into gifts and knick-knacks.

As an icon, the stadium was a success. Television loved it, and the Olympics are a televisual event. It said everything about the People's Republic of China that its rulers must have hoped for: powerful, bold, forward-looking, confident, smart, sophisticated. Its grandeur was not bombastic, like that of the stadium the Nazis built for the 1936 Berlin games. It was profligate in its use of steel and human life – the stadium for the London 2012 Olympics would use a quarter as much metal – and an undisclosed number of deaths resulted from Beijing's labour-intensive, not-very-safety-conscious construction process. Engineers pained by its lack of economy declared it 'an insult to birds.' But it was, and is, a fascinating thing to look at.

It is a landmark, arresting the view from unexpected points, both gleaming and fading into the smog-smudged air, a shape in the seemingly shapeless extent of Beijing's spread. In its life after the Olympics it has met varying degrees of success. It has held only a handful of events, unable to escape the curse that befalls most Olympic stadia: they are huge, heavy, expensive structures made to serve a brief and singular festival, which then struggle to find another purpose. The diverse public life, flowing in and out of the arcades, has not happened precisely as hoped: indeed, a perimeter fence has been installed that makes it impossible. It has, however, become a popular tourist attraction, with people paying to tour the mostly-empty building and photograph each other there. As a machine for being looked at – as a new Eiffel Tower – it is highly successful.

The stadium has had two lives, as an effective temporary structure for the games, and as a powerful sculptural object of uncertain purpose thereafter. With its intricacy and depth, with the sense of something happening beyond the screen of steel twigs, it has the look of life, but it is look as much as reality.

In competing for and winning the competition to build the China Central Television headquarters (CCTV), Rem Koolhaas, founder and leader of OMA, was making a statement about the shift of power in the world. It was the year, 2002, of the great debate about the rebuilding of Ground Zero, and it was expected that Koolhaas, as the world's most fascinating architect, and one idolized moreover by the then architecture critic of the *New York Times* (who in one study was found to mention Koolhaas in 37 per cent of his articles), would compete for the job of masterplanning the site. But the architect passed up the chance of the prospective greatest commission in the world in favour of what he saw as a greater one, an icon of a coming country rather than a memorial work in one possibly passing its peak. 'It was a matter of focus,' he said. As events played out at Ground Zero, it turned out to be a wise choice.

Koolhaas was criticized by the writer Ian Buruma for taking on a project central to the workings of a brutal dictatorship. TV stations rank with police headquarters and presidential palaces as instruments of tyranny, and when regimes are overthrown – as happened with the fall of Milošević in Belgrade – the TV station is often the focus of the revolutionary crowds' attack. They know the symbolic and actual power of information and misinformation.

As Buruma said,

> it is hard to imagine a cool European architect in the 1970s building a television station for General Pinochet without losing a great deal of street cred.

Herzog & de Meuron were inoculated from similar criticisms by their collaboration with Ai Wei Wei, who after beatings and imprisonment has become one of China's best-known dissidents. He said that the Beijing Olympics were 'an empty event' that did nothing for Chinese people, but if someone of his courage and principles was prepared to lend his talent to the regime's trophy structure, who else dared criticize?

As for Koolhaas, he and his allies had three responses. The first was that if presidents and prime ministers, and corporate CEOs, and the International Olympic Committee, abased themselves before the Chinese government, why should architects alone have to carry the conscience of Western democracy? The second was that by doing this work, OMA might engage with and strengthen more progressive elements of the modern Chinese ruling classes. Koolhaas has said:

> I was aware of negative developments there, of course. But on the whole there was also an incredible sense of change at that moment. There was a real desire to improve things, especially in Beijing.

The third was that, as the building was going to be built anyway, it would be better if it benefited from whatever intelligence a practice like OMA could bring to it. If it could embody alternative values to those of monolithic dictatorship, that would be a job worth doing. It is an argument that can lead to strange places: given that it is unlikely that his clients would allow a radical transformation of existing relationships of power, the architect's benign influence would be restricted to more peripheral aspects of design, which, if the argument of enlightened intervention is to be sustained, would require that certain kinds of detail, or form, are somehow more democratic than others. There is also a risk to this strategy: rather than liberalize the clients, the use of an architect like Koolhaas might only be to launder their image, to give the appearance rather than the actuality of progress.

OMA beat SOM in the CCTV competition, despite lobbying on the latter's behalf by President Bush, and Koolhaas presented his proposal as the opposite of the 'exhausted typology' of the American-style skyscraper. Rather than a single shaft served by a core of lifts, and heading to a dead end in the sky, he proposed a big loop, fifty-one storeys and 234 metres high. A square tube would rise (at an angle) from a plinth, turn horizontally at the top, crank sideways, and then descend again to the plinth. To put it another way, it would be a structure of two square legs joined at top and bottom, with a large hole in the middle. Special lifts, capable of travelling sideways as well as vertically, would connect the interior of the building. The theory was to engender intercommunication, and break down the barriers between departments that tend to occur when they are stacked up floor on floor.

Most skyscrapers, say OMA, 'accommodate merely routine activity, arranged according to predictable patterns. Formally, their expressions of verticality have proven to stunt the imagination: as verticality soars, creativity crashes.' CCTV will by contrast consolidate

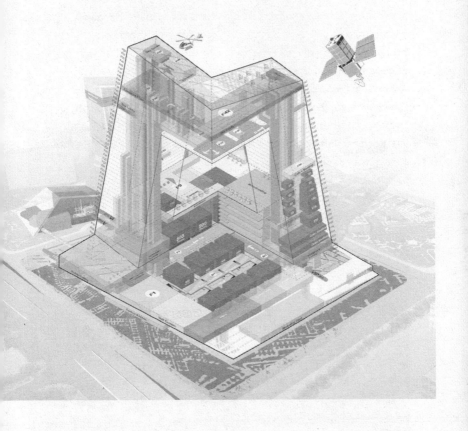

'all its operations in a continuous flow, allowing each worker to be permanently aware of her colleagues – a chain of interdependence that promotes solidarity rather than isolation, collaboration instead of opposition'. Its loop will facilitate 'an unprecedented degree of public access', with visitors permitted to take a path through the building, seeing both its activities and views of the city beyond.

It is as yet impossible to test the strength of OMA's theories about their building's workings, and will not be until it has been in use for some years. CCTV had originally been intended as a companion landmark to the stadium, to be ready in time for the 2008 games. This deadline was missed, and in 2009 a fire wrecked the planned Mandarin Oriental Hotel, in a tower next to the main building, and also designed by OMA; the cause was an illegal firework display, as part of the celebrations of the lunar New Year. Progress was delayed still further, and more than could be explained only by the fire.

On the face of it, however, it seems dubious to claim that, by turning the tube of the building into a loop rather than a simple vertical shaft, greater interaction will ensue. Reaching a distant department is not made easier by travelling around a circuit than by going up and down in a conventional lift. Ease of communication would be better achieved by wider floors that could be traversed on foot. It is possible that the public route through the building, stimulated by the novelty of a sideways-moving lift, will successfully activate it, but this seems vulnerable to the security policies which, more than the architecture, will decide its openness. Although the building started operating in 2012, there was no immediate sign that the promised openness of access would materialize. CCTV risks, until proved otherwise, becoming a large example of the conversation-pit syndrome, form that suggests community without completely achieving it.

Like the stadium, its aspirations to foster public life may not be wholly successful. Also like the stadium, it is an astonishing-looking thing on the skyline of Beijing. The city first appears as an indistinct, diffuse spread of low-rise buildings and towers that look disposable and generic despite wiggles of individual styling – a pagoda roof here, a point, swoop, or pyramid there – and the force and boldness of CCTV arrest attention as none of the other gesticulating buildings do. It has heft and mass, and three-dimensional quality that requires it to be experienced from different places, whereas most of the other architecture is about wrapping. CCTV asserts location: seen from distant freeways and suburbs, it tells you where you are; up close it defines its territory.

The Dutch-designed icon has other resemblances to the Swiss one. It has similar uncertainties or ambiguities of scale, with the register of floors suppressed in favour of an overall patterning. It expresses its structure, which is not one of columns and beams but an erratic-looking lattice of crisscrossing lines, which gather and knot in the places where the stresses are greatest.

There is nothing like a normal-sized door or window to help you read its size, just the extremely large opening within the loop which, if it is a portal or gateway, is a purely symbolic one. It is obviously big (1.5 million square feet), but it also has the appearance of something portable, like a desk ornament. Horizontal and vertical surfaces are given the same treatment, which reinforce this sense of its being a single object. Like the stadium it suggests metaphors without settling on one: it could be a Chinese character, and the Beijing public have compared it to boxer shorts, or a pornographic image of a kneeling woman's hind half. (Koolhaas had to deny publicly that this last was intentional.) It looks like something specific, but you cannot quite say what.

CCTV is more forbidding and less charming than the stadium, with its opaque surface and severe angular form, but it too aims for the look of life. Its huge portal shape is a gesture of welcome or inhabitation, and its surface of compressing and releasing lines imparts a kind of energy. A large piazza is formed at the bottom, which may or may not become a rich and dynamic public place.

If the stadium's biggest moment has passed, CCTV's has yet to come, but both address the vastness and speed of modern Chinese cities in similar ways. Each makes a bold gesture which achieves the Eiffel Tower's formula of being both replicable and inimitable. They are graphic and logo-like, but also massive and sculptural. Then, lest they be the one-liners you get in Dubai (it's a sail, it's a tulip, it's a pearl), they play their teasing games with image, and also offer intricacy and intrigue. If you look more, you see more.

It is a belief underlying this book that the importance of the look and shape of buildings is usually exaggerated. Architects expect magic to come from form, but form alone does not mean much if separated from light, scale, making, context, and time. A building could be angular or round, plain or decorated, symmetrical or picturesque, Gothic or modern, and none of these characteristics would on its own decide whether it was grotesque, beautiful, forbidding, welcoming, conducive to or destructive of the lives in and around it. A pagoda in a Chinese garden is different from one in Kew Gardens is different from one in a theme park, and one made of wood and tile is different from one made of concrete and forty storeys high: the essence is not in the pagoda's shape. What might be exquisite in a Florentine church might be less so transported to Larry Dean's mansion in Atlanta, Georgia. Nor, if a building is the shape of a pink heart, does it follow that it will be loveable. Form is rather one implement (or property, or effect) among several. It is not wholly unlike the forms of language, of sentences, words, and verse, in that it is significant, but not on its own. It requires interaction with, for example, sense, sensuality, and use. With life, that is, and architecture obsessed with form tends to deny life.

Herzog & de Meuron and OMA know this better than many contemporary architects, but the Beijing Olympic stadium and CCTV are most impressive at the level of look and shape. Their attempts at publicness are not worthless – whether or not they will be fully successful in the end, just in making the attempt they already go further than most Olympic stadia or totalitarian broadcasting centres. The looks they offer are also far from dumb – they manage to be suggestive, while also having a potent effect on a large extent of city. They are not just to be gawped at, but alter the perception of a large area. Somehow their formal strangeness is less gratuitous than that of Dubai's towers; they convey at least a kind of intelligence.

The Olympic Games employ the same worldspeak as great exhibitions, expos, and theme parks. They champion global harmony, the coming-together of nations, brotherhood and peace. They do so out of an innocent belief in such ideals but, by pursuing the universal at the expense of the specific, they lend themselves to the interests of power. Berlin in 1936 and Beijing in 2008 were used to exalt and cleanse the image of tyrannies. In almost all iterations of the games the vast construction required is used to scrub out areas of city considered awkward, and offer them up for redevelopment. In Beijing the construction boom before and during the Olympics erased large areas of *hutongs*, the traditional blocks of courtyard housing whose tissues of small streets sustained particular ways of living. Only relatively recently has the worth of *hutongs* been recognized, whereupon many of those remaining have been restored, gentrified, and repackaged as desirable and expensive places to live.

The stadium and CCTV have a paradoxical purpose, which is to reinstate some idea of difference, and friction, and distinctiveness, to projects – the Olympic Games and the redevelopment of Beijing – whose ideology tends to destroy such things. They attempt this making of difference through intent – the idea of the vivacious public arcade around the stadium; the 'loop' taking people around the multiple internal aspects of CCTV – with as yet unknown results. They attempt it through appearance with more conviction, as both structures have the look of complexity, which runs the risk that this look is illusory, that each has only made a style of difference to wrap a monolith.

These two buildings are stabs at dealing with the vastness of modern cities. They are sketches or first drafts of an architecture that operates at the levels of international media, of a very big metropolis, and of a specific locality.

10: Indispensable as bread

When Larry Dean commissioned his doomed palace in Atlanta, his motives may not have been fundamentally different from those of Amanda Burden, when she pushed forward the High Line, or the Asam brothers, or Minoru Yamasaki, or the princes who built Katsura. They were all trying to create an altered version of the world, or part of the world, that reflected their hopes about how things should be. Each of these people had their own aches to assuage, their own voids to fill, their own dreams and loves, but they shared a common impulse. They all put faith in the power of building to make real, or at least physical, their desires.

That they had varying degrees of success is due partly to luck. It is also due to the properties of the medium of architecture, and the ways in which each did or did not work with these properties. Larry Dean, for example, might be said to have over-invested in the power of form and appearance, and took too little account of the human realities around him. If the High Line seems happier, it is because its makers paid attention to the memories and possibilities they found on the site and to the lives that might take place there. Their interventions were not then imposed, but grew out of their discoveries, and left room for inhabitation and interpretation in the future.

For if buildings are obviously and literally built by their builders, by the contractors, architects, consultants, and clients who come together before they are there, they are also built by their users, in the way they inhabit them, and in the imaginations and experiences of people who experience them, from owners and tenants to passers-by. Most people are neither a Pharaoh Zozer nor a house-moving Newfoundland fisherman, but nonetheless want to make their own piece of the world. If we cannot do it by clearing land and commissioning contractors, we do it by inhabiting and shaping, physically and in the imagination, the spaces that we find. If we do not build with cranes and steel, we make places as John Berger said with 'words, jokes, opinions, gestures', the ways we dress and move.

Architecture is shaped by human emotions and desires, and then becomes the setting for further emotions and desires. It goes from the animate to the inanimate and back again. For this reason it is always incomplete, or rather is only completed by the lives in and around it. It is background. Which, given that Venice, or Manhattan, or the Alps can be background, does not mean that is has to be dull and retiring.

For all that they look fixed, buildings are in motion, through construction, inhabitation, ageing, renovation, and adaptation. They are temporary, some more temporary than others. If architecture is often treated as a separate discipline from the design of gardens, interiors, or stage sets, on the basis of its greater durability, the distinction is a false one. Rather the landscapes of Katsura or the High Line, with their use of things both found and growing, suggest how time can be part of the fabric of space.

Architecture does not act alone, but in combination with whatever is around it – other buildings, climate, landscape, culture, politics. If the Beijing Olympic stadium had to address the space made by electronic media, as well as its immediate physical context, that too is part of its surroundings. There is no such thing as an empty site. Architecture is not the design of buildings, but of the spaces inside and out which might be formed and changed, more or less gently or drastically, by the construction or adaptation of a building.

Buildings entail relationships of power, between their different users, such as between landowners and citizens, client and contractor, the dreams of the architect and the experiences of the users. They encounter friction, caused by the overlapping of interests and desires, that they can welcome or seek to obliterate. They can have properties that are more or less empowering, that allow freedoms and possibilities and enrich what is around them, or they can block, freeze, and impose. They can oppress with dullness and indifference, or with completeness or perfection, or fixedness or immobility, or reliance on visible form. So too can over-programmed buildings that seek to predict all future actions.

Architecture functions as both symbol and instrument. It can do one thing, and look as if it is doing something else. In this deceptiveness lies the potential for catastrophe, as when the physical substance of Dubai's towers concealed an absence of financial support, but the instability of architecture is also its grace. It allows the works of tyrants to be humane and beautiful. It enabled Sir John Soane's house and museum, which failed as a tool for the civilized raising of his family, to be something else, a habitable image of a world nourished by knowledge and art, which, at the least, was a beautiful consolation. It allows the Pompidou Centre, which does not precisely fulfil its revolutionary ideals, or its theory of flexibility, still to transform the experience of Paris, or the Asamkirche to be more than propaganda for reactionary eighteenth-century Catholicism.

Better, there can be a rapport of space and use, and form and content, which might be called an architectural form of poetry. Sheikh Mohammed and Lina Bo Bardi both sought something each called 'poetry', but their understandings of it are almost opposite. For him it seems to be a matter of buildings that swoop and soar, like the falcons in his verses; that display the forms of ecstasy to admiring but passive spectators. For her it was about bringing together in space aspects of humanity and nature, such that rhymes and assonances can be found between them: intrinsic to this is the active involvement of those who inhabit and experience her works. Two properties of poetry, in the literary sense, are openness to the world and the ability to make revealing connections through metaphor and rhyme. These properties are also in her architecture.

I am inside the Edifício Copan, thanks to the kindness of a friend who owns a flat there. This is a landmark in the brooding city of São Paulo, a thirty-eight-storey mass of concrete, containing homes sufficient for three thousand people, formed as if with a single sweep of a pencil into a nonchalant S-curve. It gives shape and energy to the huddle of blocks around it. Its facade vibrates with a rhythm of much-repeated horizontals, made by a *brise-soleil*, a structure of deep sunshades protecting a glass wall behind. At two points in the ascent up this curvaceous cliff the horizontals skip a beat, to allow wider bands in which communal facilities and gardens were planned. It is hard to avoid the cliché that Copan is like a samba, and if it does not literally sway so cool and swing so gentle, it looks as if it might.

Copan was designed in the 1950s by the legendary and long-lived architect Oscar Niemeyer, who died in 2012 at the age of 104, and was the creator among other things of the parliament, presidential palace, law courts, cathedral, and several ministries in the new capital of Brasilia. Niemeyer's buildings, with their freeform curves in dazzling white, are to architecture what 'The Girl from Ipanema' is to music, celebrations of Brazilian freedom, passion, and grace, fuelled by male desire. Women's bodies, Niemeyer has never tired of saying, are inspirations for his buildings. And, just as 'The Girl from Ipanema' became a staple background theme of elevators, hotel bars, and phone ringtones the world over, there is no shortage of swooping architectural musak derived from Niemeyer.

It was conceived and sold as a Brazilian Rockefeller Center, but Copan was delayed by the bursting of a construction bubble that had been inflated by the building of Brasilia. When it was finished in 1966, it was not wholly in accordance with its architect's wishes. The space intended for communal gardens, for example, was taken over by additional flats. The area around it, Centro, declined, and if the streets are not the terrifying war zones of which some had warned me, they were still a place where, in daylight, what sounded like gunfire could be heard. Copan has aged a little, its mosaic cladding peeling away in places, although now both it and the neighbourhood are beginning to come up in the world.

'It's that dumb ass Niemeyer,' said fat, dirty Márcio Flávio, reportedly one of the last great Brazilian playwrights, in the fictional *Stories from the Copan Building*. 'Like everything he did, it's good for taking pictures, but lousy to live in. The bathrooms in this section, for example, have no windows. If you fart you'll asphyxiate.' A little later an eighty-eight-year-old woman, embittered by her experiences of investing in the Copan during the crash, and infuriated by the playwright's failure to close the door of the rubbish chute, murders him with bleach and a silver-knobbed cane.

I have sympathy with Flávio's view, my own feeling about Niemeyer being that he *was* brilliant, but a bit of a tart, achieving spectacular effects of form at the expense of his interiors. Copan tends to bear this out, in that the *brise-soleil*, which contributes so much to the building's external stylishness, is an obstacle to views from the inside. (And, indeed, it is not 100 per cent efficient at shading the sun.) Then again, Niemeyer's design does something lovely at ground level, where a winding, sloping shopping arcade is

carved out, and lined with the cafes and manicurists essential to the well-being of the block. Large and singular though it is, Copan reconnects with its surroundings with the help of this arcade.

Around it is a grid of streets where classical formality just about coheres. Many buildings have parking garages and repair workshops punched into their lower levels, as a car-based city was retrofitted into older urban forms. Several grand-looking apartment blocks in Centro (which is no longer the centre of the city) are empty, because they cannot offer the security and parking space now essential for high-end property. Their huge, 400-square-metre apartments are unlit, and they lend a strange darkness to the avenues.

Hookers roam some of the streets, impressive of bust and fine of leg, only revealing by the tone of their voice that they are men. In the same district, in a battered modernist block, is the office of the Pritzker-winning architect Paulo Mendes da Rocha, a serene room transported from the past, computer-free, with paper, T-squares, triangles, pencils, and rows of brown filing boxes. The nearby Praça Roosevelt is full of cafe-theatres and bars. Off in one direction heads the broad Rua da Consolação, past an immense walled cemetery populated with Gothic and Egyptian family tombs, towards what are now more prosperous parts of town. In places concrete flyovers descend, as part of the attempt to handle the city's traffic, leaving uncertain spaces underneath them. One ramp stands uncompleted and unconnected, with pedestrians strolling over it with unaccustomed liberty.

São Paulo is landlocked, with only a modest, off-centre river. It is a strange place to put a city, still less one which now has a population of over eleven million, but the logic of a coffee boom around the turn of the nineteenth and twentieth centuries lifted it from its earlier existence as small colonial outpost. Now it is a business city, with sometimes scanty public places, and a pragmatic attitude to

throwing up blunt new blocks as and when required. It is faintly reminiscent of Los Angeles, in that it seems to spread for ever, and it depends on big roads, but it is denser – towers rise where there would be low-slung houses in LA. It is a place with little sense of a beyond. Seen from vertiginous spiral escape stairs at the back of the Copan, the horizon is made of buildings, a mass of blocks punctuated by luridly lit TV masts.

I am in São Paulo to see places described in this book, as well as meeting architects, seeing other places of interest, and taking in the sights and experiences of an interested visitor: the hilly district of artsy shops that is a little like San Francisco, the flea market in the Italian quarter, a samba stadium on the road from the airport, the smell of smoke and fat from big barbecue restaurants, the many helicopters which the rich use to avoid traffic jams and kidnapping, the rotting mansions of 1920s coffee barons now dwarfed by surrounding towers, the fancy restaurant centred on an enormous fig tree, and, at another, a miraculous guava soufflé.

In the old district of Luz, near to the handsome Pinacoteca and a park full of Laocoön-rooted trees, is a train station, built by the British in 1901. On one side is a ticket hall like a cultured Victorian salon, with high white Corinthian columns and an upright piano in the middle where gifted musicians, a girl and then an oldish man, sit down to play to passers-by. A beautiful Jamaican listens. A bridge crosses the sunken tracks to the other side, where amid wrecked buildings are scenes of misery: people with the contortions of drug addiction, prostitutes signalling their price with fingers behind their back, their prospective clients pleading and haggling, people just standing, with menace or vacancy. An armed policeman stands on the bridge, to keep the worlds of the pianists and of the addicts apart. Then he leaves, and one starts flowing into the other.

In another part of the city an architect discusses his subtle plan for improving the favela of Paraisopolis, not by erasing and starting over, in the traditional manner of slum clearance, but by adjusting what is already there. The business and economics editor of *Folha de São Paolo*, a man with a fanatical passion for architecture, conducts a midnight tour of the fine modernist apartment blocks of Hygienopolis, a district originally sold as its name suggests on the basis of its healthiness. Now, in 2011, the economy is doing well, and people are optimistic, inducing a curiously altered perspective to a visitor from troubled Europe, like the changed angle of the moon when seen in the southern hemisphere.

At SESC Pompéia ranks of old men play chess, in the same space as children watch a somewhat grating puppet show, near an installation by a prince of international contemporary art, Olafur Eliasson. In its tower of sports halls five-a-side football is played with the skill and touch for which Brazil is reputed, and from its concrete bridges can be seen a new shopping mall unremarkable except for the double spiral ramp of its multi-storey car park, with up and down intertwined such that there is a constant flow of opposite motions; it is a motorized version of an interlocking spiral for visitors to the Vatican museums in Rome. People sunbathe on SESC's 'beach' of wooden boards; standing figures, beneath a near-tropical sun almost directly above, cast minimal shadow. In the evening, as the audience arrives for a dance show, rain pelts down. The large downpipes and drains of the complex come to life, the former spouting water as from a poor person's Trevi into pebble-lined torrents. 'When it's raining on Oxford Street, the buildings are no more important than the rain', said David Greene. Here the rain and the architecture are inseparable.

In short, I am in a city. Its built fabric is formed by gambles, ideals, vanities, power plays, the directives of planners, transport engineering, plumbing, political and religious gestures, accidents, habitual methods of construction, adaptations, individual struggles

to make a home or a business, selling, advertising, the practical requirements of people and cars. This fabric, both inside and out, is used and abused in ways foreseen and unforeseen by its makers. Its effects are achieved through disposition, relationships, proportion, light and dark, materials, acoustics, scent, signs, art, decoration, mass, substance, degrees of permanence, surface, detail, workmanship.

It is subject to weather, pollution, vegetation, furnishing, maintenance, decay, taste, property prices, laws, freedoms and restrictions of access and use, sentiment, symbol, association, perception, traffic, density, customs, mood, activity, fear, clothes, food, technology, seismic conditions, artificial and natural light. The fabric will respond more or less readily to these influences, sometimes enhancing, sometimes suppressing or opposing them.

Within this fabric are exceptional works of architecture, whether a Gothic–baroque church where clouds of damp combine with its lavish paintwork to create surfaces of ripe mottledness, or Copan, or SESC. Such buildings might command attention, or move or provoke you. They might be landmarks or visitor destinations, singled out by postcards and guidebooks, or as film locations or the settings of novels. But they will never exist independently of the stuff around them, and the events and thoughts that occur inside them and out. One description of bad architecture is that it ignores this inescapable circumstance.

The most obvious facts about architecture are the most misleading ones – that it is solid, fixed, permanent, that it is about the creation of single and singular objects, that it is visual. These are at best half-truths.

To build requires determination, conviction, and finality. A building makes a proposition about the future, which will never exactly match what actually happens. It therefore has to combine its decisiveness with openness to events.

For these reasons architecture is slippery. It is prone to tricks of perception and inversions of value. For all the labour of architecture, its effects are unstable, its benefits elusive, its risks high. But plays of substance and appearance, and of masonry and life, are also part of its fascination.

'Enchantment', said the Italian architect Gio Ponti: 'a useless thing, but indispensable as bread.' By this he did not mean that we should all live in fairyland, and the Italian word he used – *incanto* – has nuances of charm and grace as well as magic. Rather he was describing the poetry of the everyday inhabitation of built space, which should not be considered only as a luxury for Medicis and oligarchs. '*Da nobis hodie*,' he continued, '*incantum quotidianum*': give us this day our daily enchantment.

Architecture is like fashion, cuisine, or love, the elaboration of something essential to existence. It embellishes shelter as the others do clothing, food, and reproduction, and if it is an embellishment, it is one that people rarely live without. Cities are full of buildings that are not perfectly functional, the products of dreams, strivings, and of budgets or plans that do not always match their official goals. Some of these works are hard to justify on their own, but if there were none of them it would no longer be worth living in such cities.

List of illustrations

Sir John Soane, 1812. © Sir John Soane's Museum / Richard
Bryant / Arcaid.co.uk

Below: rooftop restaurant, Madison Square Garden, New York.
© Bettmann / Corbis

137 Above left: Adolf Loos. Private collection, courtesy Neue
Galerie New York © 2012 Neue Galerie New York / Art
Resource / Scala, Florence
Above right: Josephine Baker. © Roger Viollet / Getty Images
Below: proposal for Josephine Baker House, Paris, by Adolf
Loos, 1928. Model. © Albertina, Vienna

141 Above: Müller House, Prague, by Adolf Loos, 1930. Exterior.
© Rowan Moore
Below: Müller House, Prague. *Zimmer der dame*. © Rowan
Moore

142 Above: marble pattern in an apartment, Plzeň, Czech Republic,
by Adolf Loos. © Rowan Moore
Below: fish tanks in the Müller House, Prague, by Adolf Loos.
© Rowan Moore

144 Above: Lina Loos' bedroom, by Adolf Loos, 1903. Private
Collection
Below: Müller House, Prague. View from the living room into
the dining room. © Rowan Moore

149 Tempio Malatestiano, Rimini, by Leon Battista Alberti, c. 1450.
© Alinari / The Bridgeman Art Library

152 Vitruvian man, by Cesare Cesariano, 1521. © The Stapleton
Collection / Bridgeman Art Library

153 Park of the Monsters, Bomarzo, by Pirro Ligorio, mid-sixteenth
century. © Rowan Moore

159 Lina Bo Bardi, on the construction site of the Museu de Arte
de São Paulo, mid-1960s. © Instituto Lina Bo e P.M. Bardi,
São Paulo, Brazil and AE (Agência Estado) / Lew Parella

161 The Museu de Arte de São Paulo, by Lina Bo Bardi, 1968, with
Trianon park beyond. © David R Frazier Photolibrary, Inc. /
Alamy

163 The Museu de Arte de São Paulo, concert in the piazza beneath elevated galleries. © Instituto Lina Bo e P.M. Bardi, São Paulo, Brazil and AE (Agência Estado) / Itamar Miranda

166 Painting and woman, in the Museu de Arte de São Paulo. © Instituto Lina Bo e P.M. Bardi, São Paulo, Brazil and AE (Agência Estado)

167 Gallery, the Museu de Arte de São Paulo. © Instituto Lina Bo e P.M. Bardi, São Paulo, Brazil and Paolo Gasparini

170 Bayterek Tower, Astana, Kazakhstan. © Rowan Moore

174 Above: Isaac Bell House, Newport, Rhode Island, by McKim Mead and White, 1881–3. © Rowan Moore
Below: dining room, Kingscote, Newport, Rhode Island, by McKim Mead and White, 1880–81. © 2012 Jonathan Wallen

175 Ogden Mills House, Staatsburg, New York, by McKim Mead and White, 1895–7. © 2012 Jonathan Wallen

182 An art nouveau interior: dining room by Eugène Vallin. © Hemis.fr / SuperStock

186 Building the Avenue de l'Opéra, Paris: last demolitions. 1876. © Bibliothèque Nationale de France / Bridgeman Art Library

187 Jamaa el Fna, Marrakesh. © Gavin Hellier / Robert Harding World Imagery / Corbis

193 Above: Le Baiser de l'Hôtel de Ville, by Robert Doisneau, 1950. © Robert Doisneau / Gamma-Rapho via Getty Images
Below: City Hall, London, by Foster and Partners, 2002. © Rowan Moore

198 Palestra del Duce, Foro Italico, Rome, by Luigi Moretti, 1936. Courtesy: Carte Moretti, Archivio centrale dello Stato, Roma

204 Above: Zaha Hadid. Courtesy: Zaha Hadid Architects. Photographer: Steve Double
Below: the Peak, Hong Kong, by Zaha Hadid, 1983. Courtesy: Zaha Hadid Architects.

Selected bibliography

The following are publications which were useful/invaluable in writing this book and/or will be helpful to readers wishing to find out more about the people, places and ideas described.

Chapter 1

Christopher M. Davidson. *Dubai, the Vulnerability of Success*. Hurst 2008.

Edited by Mitra Khoubrou, Ole Bouman, Rem Koolhaas – *Al Manakh*. Archis 2007.

Edited by Todd Reisz. *Al Manakh Continued*. Archis 2010.

Edited by Mike Davis and Daniel Bertrand Monk. *Evil Paradises: Dreamwolds of Neoliberalism*. The New Press 2007.

Edited by Shumon Basar, Antonia Carver and Markus Miessen. *With/Without: Spatial Products, Practices and Politics in the Middle East*. Bidoun and Moutamarat 2007.

Edited by Shumon Basar – *Cities From Zero*. Architectural Association 2007.

www.sheikhmohammed.co.ae

Edited by Marcelo Carvalho Ferraz. *Lina Bo Bardi*. Instituto Lina Bo e P.M.Bardi 2008.

Olivia de Oliveira. *Subtle Substances. The architecture of Lina Bo Bardi*. Romano Guerra/Gustavo Gili 2006.

Lina Bo Bardi and Marcelo Carvalho Ferraz. *Casa de Vidro*; The Glass House. Instituto Lina Bo e P.M.Bardi 1999.

Chapter 2

'In Georgia, a Megamansion is Finally Sold'. Katharine Q. Seelye. http://www.nytimes.com/2010/08/22/us/22house.html

http://deangardens.com

A New Description of Sir John Soane's Museum. Sir John Soane's Museum 1988.

John Summerson and others. *John Soane*. Academy Editions 1983.

John Summerson. 'Sir John Soane and the Furniture of Death', essay in *The Unromantic Castle*. Thames and Hudson 1990.

Louis Aragon. *Paris Peasant*, trans. Simon Watson Taylor. Picador 1980.

Francesco Careri. *Walkscapes: Walking as an aesthetic practice*. Gustavo Gili 2009.

Bruce Chatwin. *The Songlines*. Picador 1988.

Journeys: how travelling fruit, ideas and buildings rearrange our environment – Canadian Centre for Architecture/Actar 2010.

Robert Mellin. *Tilting: house launching, slide hauling, potato trenching, and other tales from a Newfoundland fishing village*. Princeton Architectural Press 2003.

John Berger. *And Our Faces, My Heart, Brief As Photos*. Bloomsbury 2005.

Jonathan Raban. *Soft City*. Picador 2008.

F. H. W. Sheppard (general editor) – *Survey of London*: volume 37: *Northern Kensington*. English Heritage 1973.

Nicholas Fox Weber. *Le Corbusier: a life*. Knopf 2008.

Chapter 3

Richard Rogers + Architects: from the house to the city. Fiell 2010.

Stewart Brand. *How Buildings Learn*. Viking 1994.

Stewart Brand. *How Buildings Learn* (revised 1997 UK edition).

Deborah Howard. *The Architectural History of Venice*. Yale University Press 2002.

Alexei Tarkhanov and Sergei Kavtaradze. *Architecture of the Stalin Era*. Rizzoli 1992.

Charles Jencks. *The Language of Post-Modern Architecture*. Academy 1977.

Karsten Harries. *Bavarian Rococo Church: Between Faith and Aestheticism*. Yale University Press 1983.

Walter Benjamin. *Illuminations: essays and reflections*. Pimlico 1999.

John Ruskin. *The Seven Lamps of Architecture*. Dover Architecture 1989.

John Ruskin. *The Stones of Venice*. Edited by J. G .Links. Da Capo Press 2003.

Chapter 4

Vivant Denon. *No Tomorrow*. New York Review Books 2009.

Jean-François de Bastide. *The Little House: an architectural seduction*. Princeton Architectural Press 1995.

Misty Keasler (photographer), with essays by Rod Slemmons and Natsuo Kimiro. *Love Hotels: the hidden fantasy rooms of Japan*. Chronicle Books 2006.

www.deansameshima.com

Dan Cruickshank. *The Secret History of Georgian London: how the wages of sin shaped the capital*. Random House 2009.

Steen Eiler Rasmussen. *London, the Unique City*. The MIT Press 1982.

Susannah Lessard. *The Architect of Desire: beauty and danger in the Stanford White family*. The Dial Press 1996.

Adolf Loos. 'Ladies' Fashion' in *Spoken into the Void: Collected Essays 1897–1900*. The MIT Press 1987.

Adolf Loos. 'Ornament and Crime' in *The architecture of Adolf Loos*. Arts Council 1985.

Adolf Loos – works in the Czech lands. City of Prague Museum and KANT Publishers 2009.

Claire Beck Loos. *Adolf Loos: a private portrait*. DoppelHouse Press 2011.

Hal Foster. *Prosthetic Gods*. The MIT Press 2004.

Anne Anlin Cheng. *Second Skin: Josephine Baker and the modern surface*. Oxford University Press 2011.

Leon Battista Alberti, trans. Joseph Rykwert, Neil Leach, Robert Tavernor. *On the Art of Building in Ten Books*. The MIT press 1988.

Leon Battista Alberti, trans. Renée Neu Watkins. *The Family in Renaissance Florence*. Waveland Press 1994.

Anthony Grafton. *Leon Battista Alberti*. Penguin 2001.

Edited by Beatriz Colomina. *Sexuality and Space*. Princeton Papers on Architecture 1992.

Le Corbusier. *Modulor 2*. Birkhauser 2000.

Aaron Betsky. *Building Sex: men, women, architecture and the construction of sexuality*. Morrow 1995.

Aaron Betsky. *Queer Space*. Morrow 1997.

Chapter 5

Museu de Arte de São Paulo; Sao Paulo Art Museum. Instituto Lina Bo e P. M. Bardi 1997.

Jonathan Aitken. *Nazarbayev and the Making of Modern Kazakhastan*. Continuum Trade Publishing 2009.

Deyan Sudjic. *Norman Foster: A Life in Architecture*. Weidenfeld and Nicolson 2010.

Deyan Sudjic. *The Edifice Complex: how the rich and powerful shape the world*. Penguin 2005.

Franz Schulze. *Mies van der Rohe: a critical biography*. The University
    of Chicago Press 1985.

Susannah Lessard (see chapter 4).

Samuel G. White. *The Houses of McKim Mead & White*. Thames and
    Hudson 1998.

Henry James. *The American Scene*. Penguin 1994.

Adolf Loos. 'The Poor Little Rich Man', in *Spoken Into the Void* (see
    chapter 4).

Louis Aragon (see chapter 2).

Edited by Bruno Reichlin and Letizia Tedeschi. *Luigi Moretti:
    razionalismo e trasgressivita tra barocco e informale*. Electa 2010.

Anna Minton. *Ground Control*. Penguin 2012.

Chapter 6

Aaron Betsky. *Zaha Hadid: the complete buildings and projects*. Thames
    and Hudson 1998.

Zaha Hadid Complete Works. Thames and Hudson 2004.

Brendan Gill. *Many Masks: a life of Frank Lloyd Wright*. Da Capo 1998.

Gijs van Hensbergen. *Gaudí: the biography*. Harper Collins 2001.

S. Frederick Starr. *Melnikov: Solo Architect in Mass Society*. Princeton
    University Press 1981.

Francesco Dal Co and Kurt W. Forster. *Frank O. Gehry: the complete
    works*. The Monacelli Press 1998.

Suketu Mehta. *Maximum City: Bombay lost and found*.
    Headline/Review 2004.

Alejandro Aravena: the forces in architecture. Toto 2011.

Mike Davis and Daniel Bertrand Monk (see Chapter 1).

Mike Davis. *Planet of Slums*. Verso 2007.

Richard Rogers, edited by Philip Gumuchdjian. *Cities for a Small Planet*.
    Faber and Faber 1997.

http://www.onehydepark.com

Chapter 7

Minoru Yamasaki. *A Life in Architecture*. Weatherhill 1979.

Charles Jencks. *Le Corbusier and the Tragic View of Architecture*.
Penguin 1987.

Edited by Kristin Feireiss (editor). *Architecture in Times of Need*.
Prestel 2009.

Philip Nobel. *Sixteen Acres: the rebuilding of the World Trade Center site*.
Granta 2005.

Paul Goldberger. *Up From Zero: politics, architecture and the rebuilding
of New York*. Random House 2005.

Daniel Libeskind. *Breaking Ground: adventures in life and architecture*.
John Murray 2004.

Michael Sorkin. *All Over the Map: writings on buildings and cities*.
Verso 2011.

www.renewnyc.com

Chapter 8

Joshua David and Robert Hammond. *High Line: the inside story of New
York's park in the sky*. Farrar Straus and Giroux 2011.

John Freeman Gill. 'The Charming Gadfly who saved the High Line'.
http://www.nytimes.com/2007/05/13/nyregion/thecity/13oble.htm

Diane Cardwell. 'Once at Cotillions, Now Reshaping the Cityscape'.
http://www.nytimes.com/2007/01/15/nyregion/15amanda.html

Adolf Loos. 'Architecture', essay in *The Architecture of Adolf Loos*.
Arts Council 1985.

James Stevens Curl. *Death and Architecture*. Sutton 2002.

Le Corbusier. *Towards an Architecture*, trans. John Goodman. Frances
Lincoln 2008.

Bruno Taut. *Alpine Architecture: a utopia*. Prestel 2004.

Franz Schulze (See chapter 5).

Phyllis Lambert. *Mies in America*. Harry N. Abrams 2001.

Kenneth Frampton. *Modern Architecture: a critical history*. Thames and Hudson 1980.

Nikolaus Pevsner. *An Outline of European Architecture*. Penguin 1968.

David Coke and Alan Borg. *Vauxhall Gardens: a history*. Yale University Press 2011.

Mary Beard. *The Parthenon*. Profile 2002.

R. Buckminster Fuller, James Meller. *Buckminster Fuller Reader*. Penguin 1972.

Martin Pawley. *Buckminster Fuller*. Trefoil 1990.

Virginia Ponciroli (editor). Katsura Imperial Villa. Electa 2005.

Kazuyo Sejima + Ryue Nishizawa SANAA. *21st Century Museum of Contemporary Art, Kanazawa*. Orpheus 2005.

www.cineroleum.co.uk/

Chapter 9

Citadela da Liberdade. SESC São Paulo/Instituto Lina Bo e P.M.Bardi 1999.

Stuart Brand (see chapter 3).

Nikolaus Pevsner. *Pioneers of Modern Design*. Penguin 1960.

Rem Koolhaas. *Delirious New York*. 010 1994.

Edited by Michael Sorkin. *Variations on a Theme Park: the New American City and the End of Public Space*. Farrar, Straus and Giroux 1992.

www.celebration.fl.us

Peter Katz. *The New Urbanism*. McGraw Hill 1994.

Dieter Hassenpflug. *The Urban Code of China*. Birkhauser 2010.

Harvard Project on the City. *Great Leap Forward*. Taschen 2001.

www.nytimes.com/2011/07/13/arts/design/koolhaass-cctv-building-fits-beijing-as-city-of-the-future.html

Hans Ulrich Obrist. *Ai Weiwei Speaks*. Penguin 2011.

Ian Buruma. 'Don't be fooled – China is not squeaky clean'.
www.guardian.co.uk/world/2002/jul/30/china.features11

Chapter 10

Oscar Niemeyer. *The Curves of Time: the Memoirs of Oscar Niemeyer*.
Phaidon 2000.
Edited by Paul Andreas and Ingeborg Flagge. *Oscar Niemeyer: a Legend of Modernsim*. Birkhauser 2003.
Regina Rheda. *First World Third Class, and Other Tales of the Global Mix*.
University of Texas 2005.
Gio Ponti. *In Praise of Architecture*. F. W. Dodge Corporation 1960.

Acknowledgements

*The following, some without even knowing it, have provided in dif-
ferent ways the inspiration, information, education, help, love and/or
DNA without which this book would have been impossible.*

Paul Baggaley, Kris Doyle, Stuart Wilson, Wilf Dickie and all at Picador.
David Bass. Noemi Blager. Instituto Lina Bo e PM Bardi. Embassy of
Brazil in London. Peter Carl. Clementine Cecil. Alessandra Cianchetta.
Alan Colam. Commission for Architecture and the Built Environment.
Jim Cogan. Crear, space to create, and Kate Lithgow. Jane Ferguson.
Zaha Hadid Architects. Andrew Higgott. Nigel Hugill. Tahiyya Jurdine.
Andrew Kidd. Denys Lasdun. Raul Juste Lores. Ann Moore. Charles
Moore. Charlotte Moore. Helena Moore. Richard Moore. Stella Moore.
Irena Murray. Gerrard O'Carroll. OMA. Jonathan Pegg. Fred Scott.
SESC. Sir John Soane's Museum. Jane Southern. Carolyn Steel. Deyan
Sudjic. The Architecture Foundation. Lizzie Treip. Dalibor Vesely. Esther
Zumsteg.

Index